THE HIDDEN PLACES OF
THE LAKE DISTRICT AND CUMBRIA

By Peter Long

Published by: Travel Publishing Ltd, 7a Apollo House,
Calleva Park, Aldermaston, Berks, RG7 8TN

ISBN13 9781904434672

© Travel Publishing Ltd

First published 1990, second edition 1993,
third edition 1996, fourth edition 1998,
fifth edition 2001, sixth edition 2003,
seventh edition 2005, eighth edition 2007

Printing by: Ashford Colour Press, Gosport

Maps by: © Maps in Minutes (2007) &
© Collins Bartholomew (2007)

Editor: Peter Long

Cover Design: Lines and Words, Aldermaston

Cover Photograph: Rhododendrons by Wastwater and
Great Gable, Cumbria © www.picturesofbritain.co.uk

Text Photographs: © www.picturesofbritain.co.uk
and © Bob Brooks, Weston super Mare
www.britainhistoricsites.co.uk

Foreword

This is the 8th edition of The Hidden Places of the Lake District & Cumbria taking you on a relaxed but informative tour of **Cumbria** and the "jewell in its crown", **The Lake District**. The guide has been been fully updated and in this respect we would like to thank the Tourist Information Centres in Cumbria for helping us update the editorial content. The guide is packed with information on the many interesting places to visit in one of England's most spectacular tourist destinations. In addition, you will find details of places of interest and advertisers of places to stay, eat and drink included under each village, town or city, which are cross referenced to more detailed information contained in a separate, easy-to-use section to the rear of the book. This section is also available as a free supplement from the local Tourist Information Offices.

The delightful county of **Cumbria** in which the Lakes reside is England's second largest county, but surprisingly has a relatively small population of only 490,000 people which is only slightly more numerous than the city of Leeds. The **Lake District** is most famous for its impressive mountain scenery but also encompasses green rolling hills, fast flowing rivers, deep lush forests and of course the enchanting and languid lakes. Below the fells, peaceful country lanes meander through beautiful little hamlets and tiny rural villages, many steeped in history. This wonderful scenery is of course celebrated by the "Lake Poets" - Wordswoth, Coleridge and Southey. Apart from the Lake District, Cumbria offers the visitor gentle moorland, craggy coastal headlands, scattered woodlands and a fascinating history and cultural heritage.

The Hidden Places of the Lake District & Cumbria contains a wealth of interesting information on the history, the countryside, the towns and villages and the more established places of interest. But it also promotes the more secluded and little known visitor attractions and places to stay, eat and drink many of which are easy to miss unless you know exactly where you are going.

We include hotels, bed & breakfasts, restaurants, pubs, bars, teashops and cafes as well as historic houses, museums, gardens and many other attractions throughout the Lake District and Cumbria, all of which are comprehensively indexed. Many places are accompanied by an attractive photograph and are easily located by using the map at the beginning of each chapter. We do not award merit marks or rankings but concentrate on describing the more interesting, unusual or unique features of each place with the aim of making the reader's stay in the local area an enjoyable and stimulating experience.

Whether you are travelling around the Lake District and Cumbria on business or for pleasure we do hope that you enjoy reading and using this book. We are always interested in what readers think of places covered (or not covered) in our guides so please do not hesitate to use the reader reaction form provided to give us your considered comments. We also welcome any general comments which will help us improve the guides themselves. Finally if you are planning to visit any other corner of the British Isles we would like to refer you to the list of other Hidden Places titles to be found to the rear of the book and to the Travel Publishing website.

Travel Publishing

Did you know that you can also search our website for details of thousands of places to see, stay, eat or drink throughout Britain and Ireland? Our site has become increasingly popular and now receives over **40,000** hits per day. Try it!

website: www.travelpublishing.co.uk

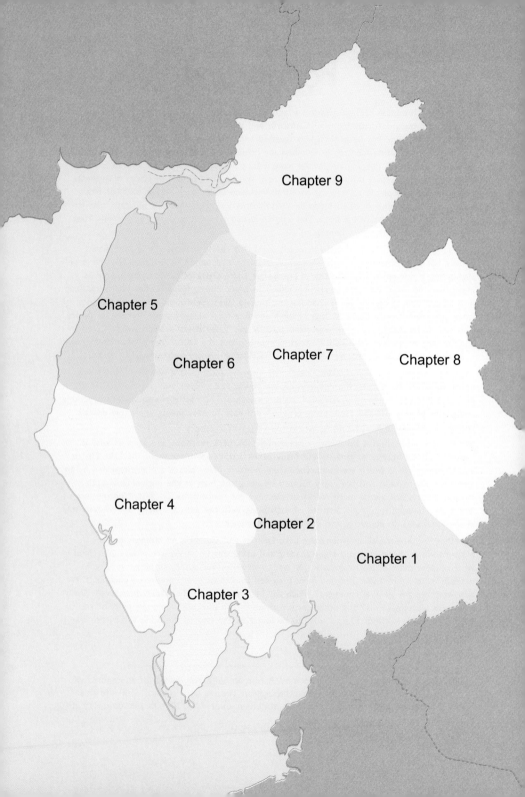

Contents

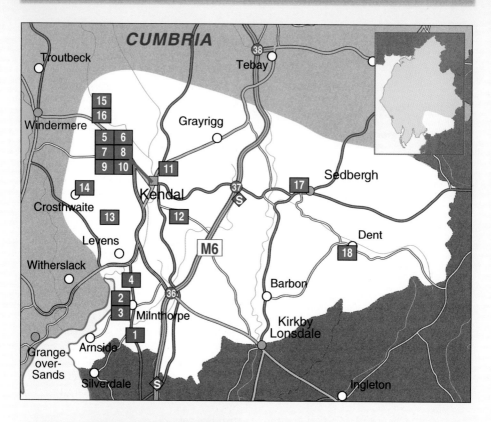

Gateway to the Lakes

An irresistible combination of enchanting lakes, picturesque villages and some of the most dramatic scenery in England draws millions of visitors from all over the world to the Lake District. The region boasts England's highest mountain – Scafell Pike (3,205 feet), its largest and deepest lakes – Windermere and Wast Water, along with hundreds of other mountains, another 14 lakes (known for the most part as 'meres' or 'waters'), challenging crags and lovely wooded valleys.

Though it is a draw for millions, most of these keep themselves to the main tourist attractions, so the region retains many peaceful glades and windswept, isolated fells, as celebrated by the Lake Poets Wordsworth, Coleridge and Southey. Between them, this lyrical trio transformed the pervading 18th-century perception of this most northwesterly corner of England from that of an intimidating wilderness to an oasis of majestic scenery.

Cumbria is England's second-largest county in size, though its population numbers not half a million. Almost one-third of the county's 2,636 square miles lies within the boundaries of the Lake District National Park, created in 1951 to protect the area from 'inappropriate development' and to provide 'access to the land for public enjoyment'. It offers a wonderfully varied landscape, and the opportunities for enjoying the great outdoors are almost endless.

Cumbria is much more than the Lake District National Park, however. It was here that the British Celts managed to preserve their independence from the Saxons; the Norse influence can still be detected in the place names here. Not a single mile of motorway has penetrated its borders, with only the very occasional stretch of dual-carriageway. Access to the area is very easy, however, as the M6 runs right along its eastern edge. For many visitors travelling from the south into Cumbria, their first experience of the county is the area around Kendal and Kirkby Lonsdale. These ancient settlements provide an excellent introduction to the history, people, culture and economy of Cumbria. Ideally placed for the Lake District National Park and the South Cumbrian coast, it is easy to forget that this area is also close to the northern Pennines and the Yorkshire Dales National Park.

Devil's Bridge, Kirkby Lonsdale

3

•

Kirkby Lonsdale has won the Britain in Bloom competition three times, and also attracts thousands of visitors for its Victorian Fair, held on the first full weekend in September, and again in December for the Yuletide procession through streets ablaze with coloured lights and decorated Christmas trees.

•

LAKELAND WILDLIFE OASIS

Hale, Milnthorpe

One of the Lake District's premier attractions where visitors can see and, in some cases, touch a variety of wildlife.

 see page 136

KIRKBY LONSDALE

One fine day in 1875, John Ruskin came to Kirkby Lonsdale and stood on the stone terrace overlooking the valley of the River Lune. It was, he declared, 'one of the loveliest scenes in England, therefore in the world'. He was equally enthusiastic about the busy little market town – 'I do not know in all my country a place more naturally divine than Kirkby Lonsdale.'

Ruskin had been inspired to visit the town after seeing JMW Turner's painting of that view. Turner himself had come in 1816 on the recommendation of William Wordsworth. These three artists and friends made a point of going to see the **Devil's Bridge** over the Lune – a handsome, lofty structure of three fluted arches. The Devil's Bridge was reputedly built by Satan himself in three days. According to legend, an old woman, unable to cross the deep river with her cattle, had asked the Devil to build her a bridge. He agreed, but demanded in return the soul of the first creature to cross. Cumbrian cunning outwitted him, however; the old woman threw a bun across the bridge for her dog to run and fetch; thus she cheated the Devil of a human soul.

The bridge is at least 700 years old. Its exact age is a mystery but we do know that some repairs were carried out in 1275, making it certainly the oldest surviving bridge in Westmorland. By the 1920s this narrow bridge, originally designed for pack-horses, proved quite inadequate for motorised transport. A new bridge was built and this, together with one of the country's first by-pass roads, has saved this lovely old town from further destructive road-widening schemes.

Kirkby's Main Street is a picturesque jumble of houses spanning several centuries, with intriguing passages and alleyways skittering off in all directions, all of them worth exploring. It's still a pleasure to stroll along the narrow streets bearing names such as Jingling Lane, past the 16th-century weavers' cottages in Fairbank, across the **Swine Market** with its 600-year-old cross where traders have displayed their wares every Thursday for more than 700 years, past ancient hostelries to the even more venerable **St Mary's Church** with its noble Norman doorway and massive pillars. In the churchyard, a late Georgian gazebo looks across to the enchanting view of the Lune Valley as painted by Turner.

AROUND KIRKBY LONSDALE

HALE

7 miles W of Kirkby Lonsdale off the A6

This tiny village close to the Lancashire border is surrounded by woodland. It is also home to the **Lakeland Wildlife Oasis** where a wide range of animals and birds can be seen. A hands-on exhibition tells the story of evolution. Visitors can drape a snake around their neck, exchange inquisitive glances with a ruffled lemur or a meerkat up on its haunches, and admire creatures rarely seen in captivity such as flying foxes and poison arrow frogs. The Tropical Hall is the home of numerous free-flying birds, bats and butterflies; other exhibits range from leaf-cutter ants to pygmy marmosets. The Oasis was established in 1991 by Dave and Jo Marsden, who were keepers at Chester Zoo before setting up this popular family attraction, which is open throughout the year.

About 3 miles south of the town, **Leighton Hall** is actually in Lancashire but well worth a short diversion. The Hall has been described as the most beautifully situated house in the British Isles, with the dramatic panorama of the Lakeland Fells providing a striking backdrop. The elaborate neo-Gothic façade cloaks an 18th-century mansion which in turn stands on the site of the original medieval house built in 1246 by Adam d'Avranches, whose descendants still live here.

Leighton Hall is famed for its collection of Gillow furniture.

ARNSIDE

10 miles W of Kirkby Lonsdale off the B5282

This quiet town on the Kent Estuary, with its short but elegant promenade, was once a busy port with its own shipbuilding and sea salt-refining industry. As the Estuary silted up during the 19th century – a process accelerated by the construction of the striking 50-arch railway viaduct – so the port

declined. Today it is a favourite retirement destination and a peaceful holiday resort.

Inland from Arnside, down a quiet lane, **Arnside Tower** is one of the many pele towers that were built in the area in the 14th century. This particular tower dates from the 1370s and may have been part of the chain of towers designed to form a ring of protection around Morecambe Bay. Pele towers, unique to the north of England, were usually three-storey buildings; about 90 were built in the region.

BEETHAM

8 miles W of Kirkby Lonsdale on the A6

Approached through a pergola of rambling roses, the **Church of St Michael and All Angels** dates from Saxon times. Although the church was badly damaged during the Civil War, when its windows were smashed and effigies broken, a glass fragment of Henry IV in an ermine robe has survived the

•

Around Arnside there is a wonderful choice of country walks, particularly over and around Arnside Knott. This limestone headland, now a nature reserve rich in old woods and wild flowers, is part of the Arnside and Silverdale Area of Outstanding Natural Beauty. Knott comes from the Saxon word meaning 'rounded hill', which in this case rises 521 feet above sea level and gives extensive views of the Lakeland fells, the Pennines and the southern Cumbrian coast. There is a beautiful path around the headland and along the shoreline past Blackstone Point.

•

Heron Corn Mill, Near Beetham

2 THE CROSS KEYS HOTEL

Milnthorpe

The **Cross Keys** is a great place to unwind, with good food and drink and a choice between B&B and self-catering accommodation.

 see page 136

3 THE BULLS HEAD

Milnthorpe

In the centre of Milnthorpe, the **Bulls Head** is a great place to relax and enjoy good beer, good food and good company.

see page 138

4 THE BLUE BELL HOTEL

Heversham, Milnthorpe

The **Blue Bell Hotel** offers old-world charm and up-to-date comfort and convenience for both leisure and business guests.

 see page 137

centuries. During restoration work in the 1830s, a hoard of coins, minted in Norman times, was discovered inside the base of a pillar in the church. The village of Beetham is also home to an unusual 19th-century **Post Office** with a distinctive black-and-white studded door.

Just outside the village lies **Heron Corn Mill**, a restored and working watermill with fully operational grinding machinery. A fine example of a traditional corn mill which operated for trade in the Westmorland farming area, the mill ceased trading as recently as the 1950s. The situation of Heron Mill is ideal, as a natural shelf of rock in the River Bela forms a waterfall, providing the necessary head of water to drive the waterwheel. This made the site an obvious one when, in 1220, the Lords of the Manor of Haverback granted lands to the Canons of Coningshead for the construction of a mill. Also here is the **Museum of Paper Making**, which was established in 1988 to commemorate 500 years of papermaking in England.

MILNTHORPE

8 miles W of Kirkby Lonsdale on A6

Just north of the Lancashire border, Milnthorpe has been a market town since the 14th century. It originally flourished as a port on the banks of the River Bela, but the harbour has long since silted up. The mill of the town's name refers to the waterfalls that once stood alongside the river. A small folly tower on **St Andrew's Hill** was built in the 1830s by the architect George Webster as a means of occupying his idle hours while restoring the town's church.

From the small village of Sandside, 9 miles west of Kirkby on the banks of the Kent Estuary, pack-horses and drovers during the Middle Ages, together with their sheep and cattle, would set off across the treacherous sands into Cumbria rather than take the longer, inland route. Consequently many lives were lost. The route remains as dangerous today as it was then.

KENDAL

A survey a few years back by Strathclyde University revealed that the highest quality of life of any town in England was to be found in Kendal, the unofficial capital of South Lakeland. That assessment came as no surprise to the residents of this lively, bustling town, which was once one of the most important woollen textile centres in northern England. The Kendal woollen industry was founded in 1331 by John Kemp, a Flemish weaver, and it flourished and sustained the town for almost 600 years until the development of competition from the huge West Riding of Yorkshire mills during the Industrial Revolution.

Kendal's motto 'wool is my bread' reveals the extent to which the town's economy depended on the wool from the flocks of Herdwick sheep that roamed the surrounding fells. The fame of the

Kendal Castle Ruins

local wool was so great that Shakespeare refers to archers clad in Kendal Green cloth in his play *Henry IV*. These archers were the famous **Kendal Bowmen** whose lethal longbows were made from local yew trees culled from the nearby limestone crags. It was these men who clinched the English victories at Agincourt and Crécy, and fought so decisively against the Scots at the Battle of Flodden Field in 1513.

Kendal has royal connections, too. The Parr family lived at **Kendal Castle** until 1483 – their most famous descendant being Katherine Parr, the last of Henry VIII's six wives. Today, the castle's gaunt ruins stand high on a hill overlooking the town, with most of the castle wall and one of the towers still standing, and two underground vaults still complete. Castle Hill is a popular place for walking and picnics. In summer the hillside is smothered with wild flowers. From the hilltop there are spectacular views; a panorama panel here assists in identifying the distant fells.

The largest settlement in the old county of Westmorland, Kendal has always been a bustling town, from the days when it was on the main route to Scotland. Nowadays the M6 and a by-pass divert much of the traffic away from the town centre, but its narrow main streets, Highgate, Stramongate, and Stricklandgate, are always busy during the season. However, a new pedestrian priority zone through most of Highgate and Stricklandgate provides a much more pleasant ambience. The fine coaching inns of the 17th and 18th centuries, to which Bonnie Prince Charlie is said to have retreated after his abortive 1745 rebellion, still line these streets.

Anyone wandering around the town cannot help but notice the numerous alleyways, locally known as yards, that are a unique architectural town planning feature of Kendal. An integral part of the old town, there were once about

5 INFUSION ITALIAN RESTAURANT

Kendal

Infusion is a smart, stylish modern town-centre Italian restaurant serving a wide range of top-class dishes.

🍴 see page 139

6 I LOVE ORGANICS

Kendal

I Love Organics is a superb combination of coffee shop/café, health & beauty shop and beauty salon.

🍴 🏛 see page 138

7 WATERSIDE WHOLEFOOD

Kendal

Waterside Wholefood has won a strong following with its superb food, mainly organic, that can be enjoyed on the riverside premises or to take away.

🍴 see page 140

7

8   DICKIE DOODLES

Kendal

Open every evening from 8 till late, **Dickie Doodles** is a magnet for lovers of good music and well-kept ales.

    see page 141

9   THE RING O' BELLS

Kendal

The **Ring o' Bells** offers the best of hospitality, good wholesome food and well-kept ales in traditional surroundings.

    see page 142

10   LYNDHURST GUEST HOUSE

Kendal

Lyndhurst Guest House is a very friendly, relaxing base for a holiday in a quiet riverside setting close to Kendal's amenities.

    see page 140

150 of them leading off the main streets. In the late 18th century and early 19th century, when the woollen industry expanded, families worked together weaving, dyeing and tanning, all of which were carried out in the yards.

A local product well worth sampling is **Kendal Mint Cake**, a tasty, sugary confection which is cherished by climbers and walkers for its instant infusion of energy. Another once-popular local medication, **Kendal Black Drop**, is sadly no longer available. 'A more than commonly strong mixture of opium and alcohol', Kendal Black Drop was a favourite of poets Samuel Taylor Coleridge and Thomas de Quincey.

Kendal's excellent sporting facilities include the **Lakes Leisure Centre**, which offers a wide selection of indoor activities; Kendal Wall, which is one of the highest indoor climbing facilities in the country; two local golf courses and a driving range. Drama, music and the visual arts are represented in a regularly changing programme of exhibitions, live music, theatre productions and craft workshops at the **Brewery Arts Centre**. The Centre also houses Kendal's cinemas, which present a mixture of mainstream, classic and art house films.

A number of interesting museums and galleries are also located in Kendal. The **Museum of Lakeland Life** takes as its theme the traditional rural trades of the region, and together with the **Abbot Hall Art Gallery** forms part of a complex within Abbot Hall Park. The museum, in re-created farmhouse rooms, contains a wide variety of exhibits, including Arthur Ransome memorabilia, craft workshops, a Victorian street scene, artefacts from the Arts and Crafts movement, nautical displays and Captain Flint's Locker, a pirate-themed activity area for children and families. The Gallery, in an elegant Georgian villa, houses a collection of society portraits by the locally born George Romney, and watercolour scenes by Ruskin and Turner, as well as works by 20th-century and contemporary artists such as Walter Sickert, Ben Nicholson, Lucien Freud and Bridget Riley. **Kendal Museum**, founded in 1796, is one of the oldest museums in the country and contains outstanding displays of archaeology, natural history, geology and local history (open Thursday, Friday and Saturday 12 noon - 5pm). Based on the collection first exhibited by William Todhunter in the late 18th century, the Museum takes visitors on a journey from prehistoric times, a trip which includes an interactive exhibit recounting the story of Kendal Castle.

The famous fellwalker and writer, Alfred Wainwright, whose handwritten guides to the Lakeland hills will be found in the backpack of any serious walker, was honorary clerk here between 1945 and 1974. Many of his original drawings are on display.

Adjacent to the elegant Georgian Abbot Hall and Museum

is the 13th-century **Parish Church** of Kendal, 'the Church of the Angels', one of the widest in England, with five aisles and a peal of 10 bells. Among the many interesting things to see are the carved reredos of the Parr Chapel, the stained glass windows, and the sculpture *The Family of Man* by Josephina de Vasconcellos. The church also contains a sword that is said to have belonged to Robert Philipson, a Cavalier during the Civil War. While away fighting in Carlisle, Cromwell's supporters laid siege to Philipson's house at Windermere. On his return, the Cavalier attacked the Kendal church when he thought the Roundheads would be at prayer. Riding his horse right into the church, he found it empty save for one innocent man, whom he despatched with his trusty sword.

Perhaps the most unusual attraction in Kendal is the **Quaker Tapestry Exhibition** at the Friends Meeting House in the centre of the town. This unique exhibition of 77 panels of community embroidery explores Quaker history from the 17th century to the present day. These colourful, beautifully crafted tapestries are the work of some 4,000 people aged between 4 and 90, from 15 countries. A Quaker costume display, embroidery demonstrations, workshops, courses and a large-screen video programme combine to provide a fascinating insight into the Quaker movement and its development (on tour during the winter).

Countryside Near Kendal

AROUND KENDAL

LEVENS

5 miles S of Kendal off the A590

At the southern tip of Scout Scar, overlooking the Lyth Valley and the lower reaches of the River Kent, stands **Levens Hall** with its unique topiary gardens. The superb Elizabethan mansion (described as 'one of the wonders of Lakeland') developed from a 14th-century pele tower. The gardens were first laid out in 1694, and were the work of Colonel James Grahme, a keen gardener who purchased the hall in 1688 and employed a Frenchman, Guillaume Beaumont, to create the amazing topiary work (Beaumont also redesigned the gardens at Hampton Court for James II). The fame of the Levens Hall gardens spread quickly, and ever since they

11 THE GARDEN HOUSE HOTEL & RESTAURANT

Kendal

The **Garden House** is an elegant, quiet and civilised hotel with a bar, restaurant and 12 en suite guest rooms.

see page 143

9

Levens Hall

12 THE STATION INN

Oxenholme, nr Kendal

The **Station Inn** is a fine Victorian hostelry offering excellent food, cask ales, en suite bedrooms and an adventure playground in the large garden.

🍴 🛏 see page 144

13 THE WHEATSHEAF

Brigsteer

The **Wheatsheaf** is a particularly pleasant village hostelry offering good food and drink and excellent B&B accommodation.

🍴 🛏 see page 145

have been a popular attraction. Today there are more than 90 individual specimens, some almost 20 feet high, with the ancient yew trees cut into often surreal shapes. The topiary is by no means the only attraction in the grounds, however, which also include a Fountain Garden created in 1994 to mark the tercentenary of the gardens. The interior of the house is equally rewarding – a wealth of period furniture, fine panelling and plasterwork, a dining room with walls covered in goatskin, and paintings by Rubens, Lely and Cuyp. The Hall is said to be haunted by three ghosts: a black dog, a lady in pink, and a gypsy woman who, legend has it, put a curse on the family saying that they would have no heir until the River Kent ceased to flow and a white fawn was born in the park. In fact, after many years without a direct heir, in 1896 the River Kent froze over, a white fawn was seen, and a son and heir was born. A major location for the BBC-TV serial

Wives and Daughters, the Hall's other attractions include a collection of working steam engines, a tea room, gift shop and plant centre.

Only a couple of miles north of Levens Hall, just off the A591, is another stately old residence, **Sizergh Castle**, the impressive home of the Strickland family since 1239 (although the property is now administered by the National Trust). Originally a pele tower built to withstand border raiders, the house has been added to and altered over the intervening centuries to provide the family, as times became less violent, with a more comfortable home. It now boasts intricately carved chimney mantels, fine oak panelling and a collection of portraits of the Stuart royal family. The castle offers an additional 'attraction' in the form of the ghost of a medieval lady. She is said to haunt the castle, screaming to be released from the room in which she was locked by her fiercely jealous husband. It was here that she starved to death while he was away in battle. More reliable (and less gruesome!) attractions at Sizergh are the well laid-out gardens and 1,500 acres of grounds which provide superb views over the Lakeland fells.

BRIGSTEER

3 miles SW of Kendal off A591

This tiny hamlet lies under the limestone escarpment of Scout Scar. From this pretty settlement the road leads into the National Trust property of **Brigsteer Woods** where, as the climate is milder here due to its sheltered position, there are wild daffodils in spring.

BURNESIDE

2 miles N of Kendal off the A591

The remains of an ancient stone circle can be seen close by Burneside, on **Potter Fell**. By the 15th century Burneside was a settled agricultural area, and a rich variety of mills sprang up along the River Sprint – corn, cotton, wool, bobbin and the original rag paper mill at **Cowan Head**. There has been a settlement at Burneside since Stone Age times.

The River Sprint, which meets the River Kent just south of Burneside, has its own remarkably beautiful Longsleddale Valley which curves past Garnett Bridge deep into the high fell country. A bridle path climbs from the head of the valley into Kentmere, another spectacularly beautiful walk.

GRAYRIGG

5 miles NE of Kendal on the A685

This is a fine village with a cluster of almshouses, cottages and a simple church found in a lovely rural setting. It was the birthplace of Francis Howgill (1610-69), who was responsible for introducing founding Quaker father George Fox to the **Westmorland Seekers**, a group of radical Christians from the area.

SEDBERGH

In 1974 Sedbergh was brusquely removed from the West Riding of Yorkshire and became part of Cumbria. However, it still lies within the Yorkshire Dales National Park – the surrounding scenery certainly belongs to the Dales, as the mighty **Howgill Fells**, great pear-shaped drumlins shaped by glaciers that soar to more than 2,200 feet (670 metres), attest. **Winder Hill**, which provides a dramatic backdrop to the little market town, is half that height, but with its sleek grassy flanks and domed top, seems much loftier. Four valleys and four mountain streams meet here. For centuries Sedbergh (pronounced Sedber) has been an important centre for cross-Pennine travellers. Long ago, the stage-coach would have been used frequently by the boys attending Sedbergh's famous **Public School**. Its founder was Roger Lupton, a Howgill boy who rose to become Provost of Eton: he established the school because he felt that one was desperately needed 'in the north country amongst the people rude in knowledge'. In later years Wordsworth's son studied here, and Coleridge's son, Hartley, became a master. The school's extensive grounds, through which visitors are welcome to wander, seem to place the old-world town within a park.

This impression is reinforced if you follow the path beside the River Rawthey to **Brigflatts**. Close to where George Fox stayed overnight with his friend Richard Robinson is the oldest **Quaker Meeting House** in the north of England. Built in 1675, and still with its original oak interior, this beautiful, simple building has changed little over the years.

14 CROSTHWAITE HOUSE

Crosthwaite, nr Kendal

Crosthwaite House offers a superb setting, a civilised ambience and excellent amenities.

♭ *see page 147*

15 WILF'S CAFÉ

Staveley, nr Kendal

Wilf's Café is a splendid café overlooking the River Kent, serving a daytime selection of fresh, wholesome snacks and meals.

⎯ *see page 146*

16 THE DUKE WILLIAM

Staveley, nr Kendal

The **Duke William** is a traditional village pub with a cosy ambience and a wide variety of food to eat in or take away.

⎯ *see page 147*

17 THE GALLERY COFFEE HOUSE

Sedbergh

The Gallery is a busy, high-class coffee house serving a day-long variety of snacks, light meals, cakes and pastries.

see page 148

18 STONE CLOSE TEA ROOM & GUEST HOUSE

Dent

Stone Close offers a traditional tea room and B&B rooms in a quiet, picturesque village setting.

see page 148

This area is filled with Quaker history and **Firbank Knott**, on nearby Firbank Fell, can be said to be the birthplace of Quakerism: it was here, in 1652, that the visionary George Fox gave his great sermon to inspire a huge gathering from the whole of the north of England. This meeting was to lead to the development of the **Quaker Movement**. The simple boulder on the fell, from which Fox delivered his momentous words, is marked by a plaque and is now known as **Fox's Pulpit**.

In 2006, Sedbergh was recognised as **England's Book Town**. The booktown movement, which started in Hay on Wye in Wales 40 years ago, is now an international phenomenon with towns, based on a love of books and trading in books, springing up from England and all over Europe to as far afield as Malaysia. In Sedburgh a number of bookshops and other businesses based on writing, reading and publishing have been brought together, the main aim being to concentrate on selling hard-to-find second-hand books. Sedburgh now has a two-week Festival of Books and Drama that takes place at the end of August/beginning of September each year and in 2007 the Festival of Ideas, an event that brings philosophy and matters of current interest such as politics, religion and green issues to the public, has been established. Throughout the year the Book Town Literary Trust offers talks, courses and performances to help promote the

love and use of language for everyone to enjoy. Many of the town's older buildings have survived, in particular the stone-built cottages on both sides of the cobbled yard known as **The Folly**, just off Main Street, which have not only survived unscathed but remain dwellings rather than having been converted to other uses. Much of the heart of Sedbergh has been deemed a Conservation Area.

To the east of town, on a small wooded hilltop, lies **Castlehaw**, the remains of an ancient motte-and-bailey castle. Built by the Normans in the 11th century, the castle guarded the valleys of the River Rawthey and the River Lune against the marauding Scots. Also just outside town, on the A683 Garsdale road, is **Farfield Mill** Heritage and Arts Centre, where spinners, weavers, potters, woodcarvers and other craftspeople use traditional skills to produce high-quality goods, all of it for sale in the shop. Also on site are an arts and crafts gallery, a heritage display depicting the history of the mill, and a riverside restaurant. The mill is accessible to all visitors, with disabled facilities and a lift to all three levels.

AROUND SEDBERGH

DENT

4 miles SE of Sedbergh off the A684

This charming village, the only one in Dentdale – one of Cumbria's finest dales – has a delightful cobbled main street with tall cottages lining the road. Visitors to this tranquil place will find it hard to believe that, in the 18th century, Dent was of greater importance than nearby Sedbergh. The impressive **St Andrew's Church** is Norman in origin, though it underwent almost complete renovation in the early 15th century. Inside can be seen a Jacobean three-decker pulpit that is still in use and also the local marble which paves the chancel.

Farming has dominated the local economy for many years, though knitting, too, has played its part. During the 17th and 18th centuries the women and children on whom this work fell became known as the '**Terrible Knitters of Dent**', which may sound uncomplimentary but in fact, at that time, meant quite the opposite (like 'wicked' today!). Large amounts of dressed wool were turned by the knitters into stockings and gloves which were then exported out of the dale to local towns. Dent's most famous son is the 'Father of Geology', Adam Sedgwick. Born the son of the local vicar in 1785, Sedgwick went on to become the Woodwardian Professor of Geology at Cambridge University and also a friend of Queen Victoria and Prince Albert. The fountain of pinkish Shap granite in the village centre is Dent's memorial to the great geologist.

Dent stone, with no iron pyrites likely to cause sparks, was popular for the millstones used in gunpowder works. The little valley of Dentdale winds from the village up past old farms and hamlets to **Lea Yeat** where a steep lane

hairpins up to Dent Station, almost 5 miles from the village. This is a marvellous place to begin a ramble into Dentdale or over the Whernside. In the shadow of Whernside itself, **Whernside Manor** is a famous house with associations with the slave trade. Dent is the highest railway station in Britain, over 1,100 feet above sea level, and it lies on the famous Settle-Carlisle railway line.

GARSDALE

5 miles E of Sedbergh on the A683

Lying just north of Dentdale, Garsdale is both a dale and a village, both overlooked by the dramatic **Baugh Fell**. The River Clough follows down the dale from Garsdale Head, the watershed into Wensleydale where a row of Midland Railway cottages lies alongside the former junction station on the Settle-Carlisle line. This is now a surprisingly busy little place during the summer months when, from time to time, preserved steam locomotives pause to take water from a moorland spring.

Waterfall at Garsdale

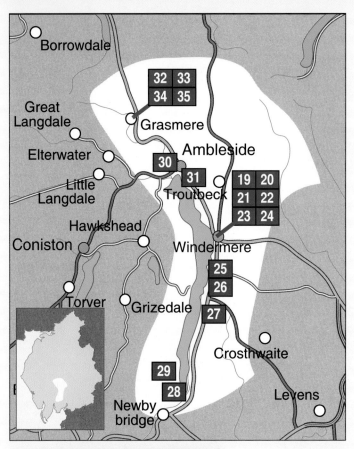

Around Windermere and Ambleside

This southeastern corner of the extensive Lake District National Park is Cumbria's best known and most popular area, with the main resort towns of Windermere, Bowness-on-Windermere and Ambleside – and, of course, Lake Windermere itself. The area is certainly busy with tourists during the summer months, but this does not in any way detract from its charm. Also, with the unpredictability of Lakeland weather, the region is well equipped with a host of indoor amusements to appeal to all ages.

The area opened up to tourism as a result of the Victorians' growing interest in the natural world and their engineering ability in providing a railway service. Thus these villages, once little more than places where the fell farmers congregated to buy and sell their livestock and exchange gossip, grew into inland resorts with fine Victorian and Edwardian villas, houses and municipal buildings.

There are also many beautiful places close to the bustling and crowded towns that provide solitude. To the southeast lies Cartmel Fell, while further north is isolated Kentmere.

Grasmere

15

19 THE COOK HOUSE

Windermere

The Cook House is a splendid new café and bistro in the heart of Windermere.

🍴 see page 149

20 THE LAKES HOTEL

Windermere

Two offerings in one: **The Lakes Hotel** is a comfortable, well-equipped B&B and is the headquarters of Lakes Supertours.

🛏 see page 150

21 THE GREY WALLS HOTEL

Windermere

The **Grey Walls** is a particularly welcoming, family-friendly base for a holiday, with en suite rooms, real ales and tasty traditional food.

🛏 🍴 see page 151

WINDERMERE

Birthwaite village no longer features on any map, thanks to the Kendal and Windermere Railway Company which built a branch line to it in 1847. With an eye on tourist traffic, and considering the name Birthwaite had little appeal, they named the station 'Windermere' even though the lake is over a mile distant. In the early days carriages and, in later years, buses linked the station with the landing stages in the village of Bowness on the shores of the lake. As the village burgeoned into a prosperous Victorian resort, it became popularly, and then officially, known by the name of its station, while Windermere Water was given the redundant prefix of Lake.

The town's Victorian heritage still predominates in the many large houses here, originally built as country retreats for Manchester businessmen – the railway made it possible for them to reach this idyllic countryside in just over two hours. Hotels, boarding houses, comfortable villas and shops sprang up around the station and spread rapidly down the hill towards the lake until Birthwaite and Bowness were linked together.

Windermere's railway is still operating, albeit now as a single track branch line. Diesel railcars run along the **Lakes Line**, providing a busy shuttle service to and from the main line at Oxenholme. The route, through Kendal, Burneside and Staveley, is a delight and provides a very pleasant alternative to the often-crowded A591. The Lakes Line is now the only surviving Railtrack line to run into the heart of the Lake District.

Within a few yards of Windermere Station, just across the busy main road, is a footpath that

Lake Windermere at Dusk

Cumbrian Mountains from Lake Windermere

leads through the woods to one of the finest viewpoints in Lakeland, **Orrest Head**. This spectacular vantage point provides a 360-degree panoramic view that takes in the ten-mile length of Windermere, the Cumbrian hills and even the fells of the Yorkshire Pennines. In a region where glorious views open up at every turn, the vista from Orrest Head remains exceptional. In Victorian times, visitors wandered through such ravishing scenery carrying, not cameras, but small, tinted mirrors mounted in elaborate frames. Arriving at a picturesque spot, they placed themselves with their back to the view, held the mirrors above them and so observed the view framed, as in a painting. The image they saw recalled the romantic landscapes of Claude Lorraine: the mirrors, accordingly, were known as **Claude Glasses**.

AROUND WINDERMERE

BOWNESS-ON-WINDERMERE

2 miles S of Windermere on the A592

It is from this attractive but seasonally very busy town right on the edge of Windermere that most of the lake cruises operate. Lasting between 45 and 90 minutes, the cruises operate daily and provide connections to the **Lakeside & Haverthwaite Steam Railway**, the **Fell Foot Country Park** and the **Visitor Centre** at Brockhole – this centre (also easily reached by road) is idyllically situated in 30 acres of gardens and grounds and has two floors of interactive exhibitions. There are evening wine/champagne cruises during the summer months, and rowing boats and self-drive motor boats

---

22   THE ARCHWAY

Windermere

The **Archway** is a super B&B in a quiet, attractive location close to the centre of Windermere.

see page 150

23   DENEHURST GUEST HOUSE

Windermere

Denehurst is a friendly, civilised guest house with attractive bedrooms and bumper breakfasts.

see page 153

24   GLENVILLE HOUSE

Windermere

Glenville House is a handsome residence in traditional Lakeland stone, a lovely B&B base between the town centre and the Lake at Bowness.

see page 152

Bowness-on-Windermere

Aunty Val's is one of the most popular tea rooms in the region, a favourite both with local residents and with visitors from near and far.

¶ see page 153

are also available for hire all year round.

Not only is **Windermere** the largest lake in Cumbria but it is, at 11 miles long, the largest in England. Formed in the Ice Age by the action of moving glaciers, the lake is fed by the Rivers Brathay and Rothay at the northern end, while the outlet is into the River Leven, at Newby Bridge. Windermere is actually a public highway or, more correctly, waterway, and this stretch of water, with its thickly wooded banks and scattered islands, has been used since Roman times as a means of transport. Later, the monks of Furness Abbey fished here for pike and char. The name 'Windermere', however, comes from Viking times and is derived from *Vinand's Mere*, *Vinand* being the name of a Nordic chief.

Roman Legionnaires used Lake Windermere for transporting stone to their fort at *Galava*, near present-day Ambleside at the head of the lake

Across from Bowness, the lake is almost divided in two by **Belle Island,** which is believed to have been inhabited by the Romans. During the Civil War it was owned by Colonel Phillipson (the Royalist supporter who disgraced himself by riding into Kendal Parish Church), whose family had to withstand an 80-day siege, successfully, while the Colonel was away on another campaign. In 1774 the island was bought by a Mr English, who constructed the round house which, at the time, caused such consternation that he sold the property and the island to Isabella Curwen, who planted the surrounding trees.

Fishermen find great enjoyment practising their skills on this well-stocked lake. Once considered a great delicacy in the 17th and 18th centuries, the char, a deep-water trout, is still found here – though catching it is a special art.

Away from the marinas and car parks is the old village where **St Martin's Church** is of particular interest. It has a magnificent east window filled with 14th and 15th century glass, and an unusual 300-year-old carved wooden figure of St Martin depicted sharing his cloak with a beggar.

On the lake shore just to the north of the village is the **Windermere Steamboat Centre**. Housed here is a unique collection

Belle Island

of Lake Windermere's nautical heritage. The exhibits, mainly Victorian and Edwardian craft, include *Dolly*, the oldest mechanically-powered boat in the world, and Beatrix Potter's rowing boat. The 'Swallows and Amazons' exhibition features guided tours of *Esperance*, Arthur Ransome's inspiration for Captain Flint's houseboat. The Museum grounds also include a model boat pond, shop, tea room and picnic area.

Just down the road from the Steamboat Museum is the Old Laundry Visitor Centre, the home of **The World of Beatrix Potter**, one of the most popular visitor attractions in the country. Here visitors can enjoy fascinating re-creations of the Lakeland author's books, complete with the sounds, sights and even the smells of the countryside. The year 2002 saw the centenary of the publication of the first *Tale of Peter Rabbit*, and to mark the occasion the Peter Rabbit Centenary springs to life every 15 minutes and features some previously unpublished illustrations from the stories. Open all year, the complex also includes the Tailor of Gloucester Tea Room (children's menu and colouring sheets available) and the Beatrix Potter shop.

About a mile and a half south of Bowness, just off the A5074 on the B5360, **Blackwell** is a treasure trove of the Arts and Crafts Movement. Completed in 1900, it is the largest and most important surviving masterpiece of the architect MH Baillie Scott (1865-

1945). Inspired by Lakeland flora and fauna, he designed every last detail of this outstanding house, creating a symphony of Art Nouveau stained glass, oak panelling, intricate plasterwork and fanciful metalwork. From the gardens there are wonderful views of Windermere and the Coniston fells.

WINSTER

4 miles S of Windermere on the A5074

This charming hamlet has an old post office, originally built in the early 17th century as a cottage, that is much photographed. South from the village runs the Winster Valley, which provided Wordsworth with one of his favourite walks. It was at **Low Ludderburn**, a couple of miles to the south, that Arthur Ransome settled in 1925 and here that he wrote his classic children's novel *Swallows and Amazons*. The house is still there, but is not open to the public.

While living here, Ransome discovered the peaceful St Paul's churchyard at **Rusland** and decided that was where he wanted to be buried. When he passed away in 1967, he was duly buried here, to be joined later by his second wife Eugenia.

WITHERSLACK

9 miles S of Windermere off the A590

On the edge of the village is the **Latterbarrow Reserve** of the Cumbrian Wildlife Trust, a relatively small reserve that is home to some 200 species of flowering plants and ferns. Butterflies and

26   MAY COTTAGE

Bowness-on-Windermere

May Cottage, close to lake; charming Victorian house with en suite bedrooms; super breakfasts; parking; leisure facilities.

 see page 153

27   BLACKWELL

Bowness-on-Windermere

A magnificent example of Arts & Crafts architecture, and housing an important collection of Arts & Crafts furniture and artefacts.

 see page 154

28 THE AQUARIUM OF THE LAKES

Lakeside, Newby Bridge

The UK's largest collection of freshwater fish can be seen in a variety of naturally themed habitats.

  see page 154

birds, including the spotted flycatcher, are a common sight among the plants that grow in the thin soil between the rocky outcrops. Further from the village is **Witherslack Hall**, once the summer residence of the Earls of Derby, now a school.

NEWBY BRIDGE

8 miles S of Windermere on the A592

The bridge here crosses the River Leven which runs from the southern tip of Windermere to Morecambe Bay. According to geologists, the mass of end moraines seen here show clearly that the village lay at the southernmost point of Windermere, since they were deposited by the glacier while it paused, having carved out the lake. Today, however, the village is some distance from the water's edge, which can be reached on foot, by car or by taking the steam train on the Lakeside & Haverthwaite Railway.

One mile north of the village, **Fell Foot Country Park** (National Trust) is a delightful 18-acre site of landscaped gardens and woodland laid out in late-Victorian times. Admission is free (although there's a car parking charge), and the grounds include picnic areas, a children's adventure playground, a splendid rhododendron garden, a gift shop and a tea room with outside tables where you can watch the lake traffic and also the steam trains chugging into Lakeside on the western bank. Rowing boats can be hired at the piers from which

there are regular ferries across to Lakeside, and pleasure cruises operate during the summer school holidays.

BACKBARROW

9 miles S of Windermere on the A592

This small village in the valley of the River Leven, which drains Windermere, was a hive of industry at one time. In 1711, the most ambitious iron furnace in Cumbria was built here; its remains can still be seen, along with the relics of the heyday of water power in the village.

LAKESIDE

10 miles S of Windermere off the A590

Located at the southwestern tip of Windermere, Lakeside sits beneath gentle wooded hills. It's the northern terminus of the **Lakeside & Haverthwaite Railway**, a 4-mile route through the beautiful Leven Valley which was once part of a line stretching to Ulverston and Barrow-in-Furness. Throughout the season, hard-working steam locomotives chug along the track, their departure times set to coincide with boat arrivals from Bowness – a joint boat and train return ticket is available. Nearby lies the **Aquarium of the Lakes** with the largest collection of freshwater fish in the UK and also a number of playful otters and diving ducks. A unique attraction for visitors is to walk along a re-creation of Windermere's lake bed along an underwater tunnel. The Aquarium of the Lakes is Britain's only freshwater aquarium. There's also a shop and a café.

A mile or so north of Lakeside, **Stott Park Bobbin Mill** (English Heritage) is a must for anyone interested in the area's industrial heritage. One of the best preserved in the country, it's a genuine working 19th-century mill and stands in a lovely woodland setting at the southern end of the Lake. Visitors can join the inclusive 45-minute tour, watch wooden bobbins being made as they were 200 years ago, and browse over the informative exhibition.

INGS

3 miles E of Windermere off the A591

A pleasant little village set alongside the River Gowan, Ings owes its fine Georgian church and charming almshouses to a certain Robert Bateman, who was born here in the late 1600s. Wordsworth commemorated Bateman in a poem that recounts how the villagers made a collection so that the young boy could travel to London. He prospered greatly, became a major ship owner and devoted a sizeable portion of his wealth to the benefit of his native village. Sadly, he never saw the completed church: less than a year after building began, he was murdered by pirates.

TROUTBECK BRIDGE

1 mile NE of Windermere on the A591

This small village in the valley of Trout Beck takes its name from the bridge here over the Beck, just before the water runs into Windermere. During the 17th century, **Calgarth Hall** was owned by Myles Phillipson, a local Justice of the Peace who wished to gain possession of nearby farmland. He duly invited the landowner and his wife to a banquet at the Hall and then, having hidden a silver cup in their luggage, accused them of stealing.

At the resulting trial, Phillipson, who was the presiding judge, sentenced the couple to death as well as appropriating their land. As she was led away, the wife placed a curse on the judge, saying that not only would his victims never leave him but that his family would also perish in poverty. The couple were executed, but their skulls reappeared at Calgarth Hall and, no matter what Phillipson did (including burning them and throwing them into Lake Windermere) the skulls kept returning to the Hall. Moreover, the Phillipson family grew poorer and poorer. Finally, in 1705, the family died out altogether.

TROUTBECK

3 miles NE of Windermere off the A592

Designated a conservation area, Troutbeck has no recognisable centre, as the houses and cottages are grouped around a number of wells and springs which, until recently, were the only form of water supply. Dating from the 16th, 17th and 18th centuries, the houses retain many of their original features, including mullioned windows, heavy cylindrical chimneys and, in some cases, exposed spinning galleries, and are of great interest to lovers of vernacular architecture. **Troutbeck**

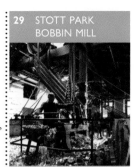

29 STOTT PARK BOBBIN MILL

Ulverston
Guided tours are offered at this working historic mill.

🏛 see *page 154*

•

Just north of Troutbeck Bridge, on the A592 Patterdale road, lies the Lakeland Horticultural Society's Holehird. Run by volunteers, it primary aim is to promote knowledge on the cultivation of plants, shrubs and trees, especially those suited to Lakeland conditions. Highlights include the borders in the walled garden, the many specimen trees, the summer-autumn heathers and the National Collections of astilbes and hydrangeas.

•

Townend, Troutbeck

Inside St Cuthbert's Church in Kentmere is a bronze memorial to Bernard Gilpin, who was born at Kentmere Hall in 1517 and became Archdeacon of Durham Cathedral. Known as the 'Apostle of the north', he was also a leader of the Reformation, and in 1558 he travelled to London to face charges of heresy against the Roman Catholic Church. During the journey Gilpin fell and broke his leg, but while he was recovering Catholic Queen Mary died and was succeeded by Protestant Queen Elizabeth. The new Queen restored Gilpin to favour and saved him from being burnt at the stake.

Church, too, is worthy of a visit as there is a fine east window, dating from 1873, that is the combined work of Edward Burne-Jones, Ford Maddox Brown and William Morris.

However, perhaps the best-known building at Troutbeck is **Townend** (National Trust), another enchanting example of Lake District vernacular architecture. Built in 1626, the stone-and-slate house contains some fine carved woodwork, books, furniture and domestic implements collected by the Browne family, wealthy farmers who lived here for more than 300 years until 1944. Open from April to October the house runs a regular 'living history' programme, so if you visit on a Thursday you can meet Mr George Browne – circa 1900.

Another notable resident of Troutbeck was 'the Troutbeck Giant' – Thomas Hogarth, uncle of the painter William Hogarth.

KENTMERE

8 miles NE of Windermere off the A591

This hamlet, as its name implies, lies in part of the valley that was once a lake, later drained to provide precious bottom pasture land. A large mill pond remains to provide a head of water on the River Kent for use at a paper mill.

The beautiful valley of the River Kent is best explored on foot. A public footpath runs up its western side, past Kentmere Hall (now a privately owned farmhouse). Following the river southwards, the **Dales Way** runs down into Kendal and on into the Yorkshire Dales.

BROCKHOLE

3 miles NW of Windermere off the A591

The **Lake District Visitor Centre** at Brockhole provides enough activities for a full family day out. Lake cruises depart from the jetty here for 45-minute circular trips – groups of 20 or more can organise their own private boat. The gardens and grounds were the work of Thomas H Mawson, a Lancastrian who trained in London and set up in business in Windermere in 1885. He soon became fashionable, and landscaped the gardens of many wealthy industrialists. Within the beautifully landscaped grounds at Brockhole visitors can join an organised walk accompanied by one of the gardening team, while their children can enjoy the well-equipped adventure playground. There are also lakeside picnic areas and a rare breeds centre. Brockhole itself is a fine Victorian mansion, originally built for a Manchester silk merchant. Here visitors can watch an audio-visual presentation about the area, browse in the gift shop (which stocks an excellent range of books, guides and maps), or take a break in the comfortable café which has an outdoor terrace overlooking the lake. Home baking to traditional Cumbrian recipes is the speciality, and many dishes feature local produce. There is good wheelchair access to all parts of the Visitor Centre and most of the grounds.

AMBLESIDE

5 miles NW of Windermere on the A591

Standing less than a mile from the head of Lake Windermere, Ambleside is one of the busiest of the Lakeland towns, a popular centre for walkers and tourers, with glorious walks and drives radiating from the town in all directions. Ambleside offers a huge choice of pubs, restaurants, cafés, hotels and guest houses, as well as art galleries, two 2-screen cinemas and a mix of traditional family-run shops supplemented by a modern range of retailers in the **Market Cross Centre**. Because of its many shops specialising in outdoor clothing, the town was recently described as 'the anorak capital of the world'. It would certainly be hard to find a wider selection anywhere of climbing, camping and walking gear.

Many of Ambleside's buildings are constructed in the distinctive grey-green stone of the area that blends in well with the green of the fields and fells all around. The centre of the town is a conservation area; its most picturesque building perhaps being **The Bridge House**, a tiny cottage perched on a packhorse bridge across Stock Ghyll. Today it's a National Trust shop and information centre, but during the 1850s it was the home of Mr and Mrs Rigg and their six children. The main room of this one-up, one-down residence measures just 13 feet by 6 feet, so living chez Rigg was decidedly cosy. The **Armitt Museum** and Library is dedicated to the area's history since Roman times and to its most famous literary luminaries, John Ruskin and Beatrix Potter. Among the highlights are Beatrix Potter's early watercolours – exquisite studies of fungi and mosses – and a fascinating collection of photographs by Herbert Bell, an Ambleside chemist who became an accomplished photographer.

The popular panoramic view of Ambleside, looking north from the path up **Loughrigg Fell**, reveals the town cradled within the apron of the massive Fairfield Horseshoe, which rises to nearly 3,000 feet. Within

30 MELROSE GUEST HOUSE

Ambleside

The owners of the **Melrose Guest House** provide a friendly home-from-home atmosphere close to Ambleside's amenities and attractions.

see page 155

Bridge House, Ambleside

Waterhead, Ambleside

the townscape itself, the most impressive feature is the rocket-like spire, 180 feet high, of **St Mary's Church**. The church was completed in 1854 to a design by Sir George Gilbert Scott, the architect of London's St Pancras Station and the Albert Memorial. Inside the church is a chapel devoted to the memory of William Wordsworth, and an interesting 1940s mural depicting the ancient ceremony of rush-bearing. The mural was painted by Gordon Ransome of the Royal College of Art during the Second World War,

when the college was evacuated to the town. The rush-bearing ceremony dates back to the days when the floor of the church was covered by rushes, and is still enacted on the first Saturday in July. Some 400 children process through the town bearing colourful decorated rushes and singing the specially-commissioned Ambleside Rushbearer's Hymn.

A few weeks later every July, the famous **Ambleside Sports** take place, an event distinguished by the variety of local traditional sports it features. In addition to carriage-driving, ferret- or pigeon-racing, and tugs of war, the Sports include Cumberland and Westmorland wrestling (a little like Sumo wrestling but without the rolls of fat), fell-racing and hound-trailing.

Another experience not to be missed while at Ambleside is a boat cruise on Lake Windermere to Bowness. There are daily departures from the pier at **Waterhead**, about a mile south of the town. At Bowness there are connections to other lakeland attractions and, during the summer months, evening wine cruises. Rowing boats and self-drive motor boats can also be hired. Just to the west of the pier is **Borrans Park**, a pleasant lakeside park with plenty of picnic spots, and to the west of the park, the site of Galava Roman Fort. There is little to be seen of the fort, but the setting is enchanting. Also well worth a visit is nearby **Stagshaw Gardens**

(National Trust), a spring woodland garden which contains a fine collection of shrubs, including some impressive rhododendrons, azaleas and camellias. Parking is very limited and vehicular access is hazardous, so it's best to park at Waterhead car park and walk.

Perhaps the most unusual visitor attraction in Ambleside is the **Homes of Football**, described by the *Sunday Times* as a national treasure. It began as a travelling exhibition of football photographs and memorabilia, but now has a permanent home in Lake Road. Photographer Stuart Clarke recorded games and grounds at every kind of venue from the Premier League down to amateur village teams. There are now 60,000 photographs on file and a massive selection on show, framed and for sale.

From Ambleside town centre, a steep road climbs sharply up to the dramatic **Kirkstone Pass** and over to Ullswater. The pass is so called because of the rock at the top which looks like a church steeple. Rising to some 1,489 feet above sea level, the road is the highest in the Lake District and, though today's vehicles make light work of the climb, for centuries the Pass presented a formidable obstacle. The severest incline, known as **The Struggle**, necessitated passengers to alight from their coach and make their way on foot, leaving the horses to make the steep haul with just the empty coach.

RYDAL

7 miles NW of Windermere on the A591

In 1813, following the deaths of their young children Catherine and Thomas, William and Mary

Rydal Water

Wordsworth were too grief-stricken to stay on at the Old Rectory in Grasmere. They moved a couple of miles down the road to **Rydal Mount**, a handsome house overlooking tiny **Rydal Water**. By now, the poet was well established and comparatively prosperous. A salaried position as Westmorland's Distributor of Stamps (a tax official) supplemented his earnings from poetry. Although Wordsworth only ever rented the house, it is now owned by his descendants and has been open to the public since 1970. The interior has seen little change, retaining a lived-in atmosphere. It contains first editions of the poet's work and many personal possessions, among them the only surviving portrait of his beloved sister, Dorothy.

William Wordsworth was a keen gardener, and the 4-acre garden at Rydal Mount remains very much as he designed it.

GRASMERE

9 miles NW of Windermere on the A591

In 1799, Wordsworth described Grasmere as 'the loveliest spot that man hath ever found'. Certainly Grasmere enjoys one of the finest settings in all Lakeland, its small lake nestling in a natural scenic amphitheatre beside the compact, rough-stone village.

For lovers of Wordsworth's poetry, Grasmere is the pre-eminent place of pilgrimage. They come to visit **Dove Cottage** where Wordsworth lived in dire poverty from 1799 to 1808, obliged to line the walls with newspaper for warmth. The great poet shared this very basic accommodation with his wife Mary, his sister Dorothy, his sister-in-law Alice and, as almost permanent guests, Coleridge and De Quincey. (Sir Walter Scott also stayed, though he often sneaked off to the Swan Hotel for a dram, since

Dove Cottage, Grasmere

the Wordsworths were virtually teetotal.) Located on the outskirts of the village, Dove Cottage has been preserved intact: next door is an award-winning museum dedicated to Wordsworth's life and works. Dove Cottage, Rydal Mount (another of the poet's homes near Grasmere), and his birthplace, Wordsworth House at Cockermouth, are all owned by the **Wordsworth Trust** which offers a discount ticket covering entrance to all three properties.

In 1808 Wordsworth moved to **The Rectory** (private) opposite St Oswald's Church. In his long poem *The Excursion*, he describes the house and its lovely garden beside the River Rothay. The church, too, is remembered in the same poem:

Not raised in nice proportions was the pile
But large and massy, for duration built,
With pillars crowded and the roof upheld
By naked rafters intricately crossed,
Like leafless underboughs in some thick
wood.

In 1850 the Poet Laureate was buried beneath yew trees he himself had planted in **St Oswald's** churchyard. He was joined here by his sister Dorothy in 1885, and his wife Mary in 1889. In Grasmere town cemetery is the grave of

William Archibald Spooner, sometime Warden of New College, Oxford. He gave his name to Spoonerisms, in which the initial letters of two words are transposed, with amusing results. Here are a few of his gems, some genuine, others perhaps apocryphal, such as '*You have hissed all my mystery lessons*' and '*Yes indeed: the Lord is a shoving leopard.*' Spooner spent many holidays in Grasmere with his wife at her house, How Foot.

Like Ambleside, Grasmere is famous for its **Sports**, first recorded in 1852, which still take place in late August. The most celebrated event in the Lake District, they attract some 10,000 visitors and feature many pursuits unique to Cumbria, such as Cumberland and Westmorland wrestling as well as the more straightforward, if arduous, fell-running.

Collectors of curiosities who happen to be travelling north on the A591 from Grasmere should look out for the vintage black-and-yellow AA telephone box on the right-hand side of the road. Still functioning, **Box 487** has been accorded Grade II listed building status by the Department of the Environment.

34 DALE LODGE HOTEL

Grasmere

Dale Lodge Hotel has earned its fine reputation for its real ales, superb food, glorious setting and beautifully appointed gust bedrooms.

see page 158

35 OAK BANK HOTEL

Grasmere

Oak Bank Hotel is a classic Victorian house in the very heart of the Lake District, with first-class accommodation and food.

see page 159

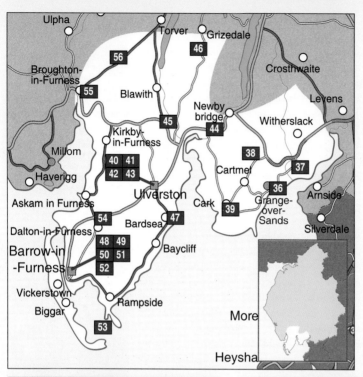

The Cartmel & Furness Peninsulas

The southernmost coast of Cumbria is sometimes overlooked by visitors, but this is a great pity as it has much to offer, including a rich history as well as some truly splendid scenery. Lying between the lakes and mountains of the Lake District and the sandy estuaries of Morecambe Bay, this is an area of gentle moorland, craggy headlands, scattered woodlands and vast expanses of sand.

It was once a stronghold of the Cistercian monks, whose influence can still be seen in the buildings and fabric of the landscape. This was Cumbria's ecclesiastical centre, and several monasteries remain. Two in particular are well worth visiting today: Cartmel Priory and Furness Abbey.

Before the great boom of the local iron-ore mining industry, the peninsular villages and market towns relied on farming and fishing and, before some of the river estuaries silted up, there was also some import and export trade. The rapid growth of Barrow-in-Furness, which will be forever linked with the shipbuilding industry, changed the face of much of the area, but as the iron industry declined, so too did the town.

The arrival of the railways in the mid-19th century saw the development of genteel resorts such as Grange-over-Sands overlooking the treacherous sands of Morecambe Bay. Grange is still an elegant little town and has been spared the indignity of vast amusement parks and rows of slot machines, retaining its character as a quiet and pleasant holiday centre.

Grange-Over-Sands

29

36 BLACKROCK HOLIDAY FLATS

Grange-over-Sands

Blackrock Holiday Flats comprise two self-catering flats and a cottage, each sleeping two in cosy comfort facing Morecambe Bay.

see page 161

37 WOODLANDS HOTEL & PINE LODGES

Grange-over-Sands

B&B and self-catering guests enjoy high levels of comfort, service and food in beautiful, secluded surroundings.

see page 160

GRANGE-OVER-SANDS

Grange, as it's known locally, is an attractive little town set in a natural sun-trap on the north shore of Morecambe Bay. Much of its Victorian charm can be credited to the **Furness Railway Company** which developed the town after building the Lancaster-to-Whitehaven line in 1857. At that time, the whole of the Cartmel and Furness Peninsulas were part of Lancashire, a detached area whose main link with the rest of the county was the dubious route across Morecambe Sands. The railway provided a safe alternative to this hazardous journey. At Grange the company built an elegant mile-long promenade (now traffic free) and set out the colourful ornamental gardens. Prosperous merchants built grand country homes here, and it wasn't long before local residents began referring to their town as 'the Torquay of the North'.

Though Grange doesn't have a beach to rival that of its neighbour across Morecambe Bay, it does enjoy an exceptionally mild climate, the mildest in the northwest, thanks to the Gulf Stream. It is still a popular place, particularly with people who are looking for a pleasant and quiet place to retire. It was a favourite with Beatrix Potter, who recorded that on one visit to the town she met a 'friendly porker', a meeting that inspired *The Tale of Pigling Bland*. There's no connection, of course, but today the town boasts a butcher's shop, Higginsons, which has been voted the Best Butcher's Shop in England.

The route to Grange, across the sands of **Morecambe Bay**, is a treacherous one, though it was used not only by the Romans but also by the monks of Furness Abbey and, later, even by stage coaches looking to shorten their journey time. Avoiding the quicksands of the bay, which have taken many lives over the centuries, is a difficult task. Back in the 16th century, the Duchy of Lancaster appointed an official guide to escort travellers over the shifting sands, and also provided him with a house at Grange. The town still has an official guide who takes groups on a three-hour walk across the bay. The sands are extremely dangerous since 'the tide comes in with the merciless speed of a galloping horse' – a crossing should never be attempted without the help of a qualified guide.

Away from the hotels, shops and cafés of the town there are

Morecambe Bay

some lovely walks, and none is more pleasant than the path behind Grange which climbs through magnificent limestone woodlands rich in wildflowers. The path finally leads to the 727 feet **Hampsfell Summit** and **The Hospice**, a little stone tower from which there are unforgettable views over the bay and, in the opposite direction, the craggy peaks of the Lake District. The Hospice was provided by Grange's Vicar, the Reverend Thomas Remington, in 1834 to provide a refuge for travellers who found themselves stranded on the fell overnight. An external flight of stairs leads to a flat roof and, as the Vicar observed in a poem attached to the wall:

The flight of steps requireth care,
The roof will show a prospect rare.

AROUND GRANGE-OVER-SANDS

LINDALE

2 miles NE of Grange-over-Sands off the A590

This small village was the birthplace of a man who defied the scepticism of his contemporaries and built the first successful iron ship. 'Iron Mad' John Wilkinson also built the first cast-iron barges, and later created the castings for the famous Iron Bridge at Coalbrookdale. After his death in 1808 he was buried in an iron coffin (naturally) in an unmarked grave, and the lofty **Wilkinson Obelisk** to his memory that stands near the village crossroads is also cast in iron. The

admirers who erected it, however, omitted to provide the iron column with a lightning conductor. A few years later it was struck to the ground by a lightning bolt. The obelisk lay neglected in shrubbery for some years, but has now been restored and towers above the village once again. Just outside Lindale, at **Castle Head**, is the imposing house that Wilkinson built by the River Winster.

CARTMEL

2 miles W of Grange-over-Sands off the B5278

One of the prettiest villages in the Peninsula, Cartmel is a delightful cluster of houses and cottages set around a square from which lead winding streets and arches into back yards. The village is dominated by the famous **Cartmel Priory**, founded in 1188 by Augustinian canons. According to legend, it was originally intended to be sited on nearby Mount Bernard, until St Cuthbert appeared in a vision to the monastic architect and ordered him to build the Priory

> •
>
> *Grange is the starting point of the Cistercian Way, an interesting 33-mile long footpath through Furness to Barrow. 'Grange' or 'Graunge' came from the French word for 'granary': the monks of nearby Cartmel Priory stored their grain here until Henry VIII dissolved the monasteries in 1537.*
>
> •

38   THE BYRE

Field Broughton

With its excellent location and superb self-catering facilities, **The Byre** is a great spot for a holiday.

📧   see page 161

Cartmel Priory Church

In the southwest corner of the Church of St Mary and St Michael is a door known as Cromwell's Door. The holes in it are said to have been made by indignant parishioners firing at Parliamentarian soldiers who had stabled their horses in the nave. Cromwell's troops were certainly in the area in 1643 and, to further establish the story, fragments of lead were found in the wood during restoration work in 1955. Other features of interest include the glorious 45 feet high east window (inspired by York Minster), the 14th-century tomb of Lord and Lady Harrington, a fine Jacobean screen and some floor tablets referring to people who had drowned trying to cross the sands of Morecambe Bay. By the chancel screen are two sculptures by Josephina de Vasconcellos – one of St Michael, the other depicting the flight to Egypt.

between two springs of water, one flowing north and the other south. The next morning, water was found to be trickling in two different directions from the foundation stones, and it is here that the church stands today.

Like all monastic institutions, Cartmel Priory was disbanded with the Dissolution and several of its members were executed for participating in the Pilgrimage of Grace. Today, substantial remains of the 12th-century Gatehouse (National Trust) survive, but the rest of the Priory was cannibalised to build many of the village's cottages and houses. After the Dissolution, only the south aisle of the **Church of St Mary and St Michael** was still standing. In 1620, George Preston of Holker began restoring the entire building; the richly carved black oak screens and stall canopies date from this restoration. St Mary & St Michael's has recently been described as 'the most beautiful church in the northwest'.

Cartmel is also famous for its attractive **Racecourse**, set beside the River Eea, on which National Hunt meetings are held in May, July and August. Located close to the village, the course must be one of the most picturesque in the country; it is certainly one of the smallest.

FLOOKBURGH

3 miles SW of Grange-over-Sands on the B5277

An ancient Charter Borough, Flookburgh is still the principal

fishing village on Morecambe Bay. Roads from the square lead down to the shore where fishermen still land their catches of cockle, shrimps and (less often nowadays) flukes, the tasty small flat fish from which the village takes its name. In **Coach House**, Winder Lane, is an unusual attraction in the form of a miniature village. Some 120 buildings made of local Coniston slate are accurate down to the last detail.

Ducky's Farm Park provides a fun day out for all the family with a variety of animals to see and stroke as well as a wide range of other activities including donkey rides.

CARK-IN-CARTMEL

3 miles SW of Grange-over-Sands on the B5278

Cumbria's premier stately home, **Holker Hall** is one of many belonging to the Cavendish family, the Dukes of Devonshire. An intriguing blend of 16th-century Georgian and Victorian architecture, a visitor-friendly place with no restraining ropes keeping visitors at a distance, a fire burning in the hearth and a lived-in, family atmosphere. There's an impressive cantilevered staircase, a library with some 3,500 leather-bound books (plus a few dummy covers designed to hide electricity sockets) and an embroidered panel said to be the work of Mary, Queen of Scots.

Each year, Holker's 25 acres of award-winning gardens host the **Holker Garden Festival** which has been hailed as the 'Chelsea of the North'. The gardens are the pride of Lord and Lady Cavendish, who developed the present layout from the original 'contrived natural landscape' of Lord George Cavendish over 200 years ago. The Great Holker Lime and the stunning spring display of rhododendrons are among the delights not to be missed. Here, too, are a wonderful rose garden, an azalea walk and a restored Victorian rockery. Lord and Lady Cavendish have put their pride of Holker into words: 'If you gain from your visit a small fraction of the pleasure that we ourselves get from them, then the work of generations of gardeners will not have been in vain.' The gardens at Holker Hall have featured in BBC-TV's *An English Country Garden.*

The Holker Hall estate contains a wide variety of other attractions: formal gardens, water features, a 125-acre deer park, picnic and children's play areas, a gift shop and café. Also within the grounds is the **Lakeland Motor Museum**, which as well as boasting a completely restored 1920s garage, has more than 100 vehicles on show among well over 20,000 well-presented exhibits. The cars may hold centre stage, but there's a great deal more, including 'magnificent motorbikes, superb scooters, bygone bicycles and triumphant tractors'. Housed in a quaint former Shire horse stable and its courtyard, the Lakeland Motor Museum also honours leading figures from the world of motoring, among them Walter Owen Bentley, Frederick Henry Royce, Henry Ford, Colin Chapman and Alec Issigonis. A

special exhibit is devoted to the attempts of Sir Malcolm and Donald Campbell to beat the world water speed record on Coniston Water.

ULVERSTON

It was way back in 1280 that Edward I granted Ulverston its market charter. Over 700 years later, colourful stalls still crowd the narrow streets and cobbled market square every Thursday and Saturday. It's a picturesque scene, but a walk up nearby **Hoad Hill** is

39 THE ENGINE INN

Cark-in-Cartmel

The **Engine Inn** is a cheerful local, an excellent restaurant and a comfortable B&B.

see page 162

Holker Hall Gardens

40 THE STAN LAUREL INN

Ulverston

The **Stan Laurel** is a delightful pub with B&B open for food and drink every session, named after Ulverston's most famous son.

 see page 163

41 THE DEVONSHIRE ARMS

Ulverston

The **Devonshire Arms** is a convivial pub close to the town centre, serving real ales, keg beers and good wholesome food.

see page 163

42 THE KINGS ARMS HOTEL

Ulverston

The **Kings Arms** is a convivial local with good home cooking, B&B rooms and a nearby self-catering cottage.

 see page 164

rewarded with an even more striking view of the town. The great expanse of Morecambe Bay with a backdrop of the Pennines stretches to the south, the bulk of Ingleborough lies to the east, Coniston Old Man and the Langdale Pikes lie to the west and north. Crowning another hill, to the north of the town centre, is the **Barrow Monument**, a 100 feet replica of the Eddystone Lighthouse erected in 1850 to honour Sir John Barrow. An explorer, diplomat and author, Sir John served as Lord of the Admiralty for more than 40 years, and it was his naval reforms that contributed to England's success in the Napoleonic Ward.

Hoad Hill, Ulverston

A famous son of Ulverston was Stanley Jefferson, born at number 3, Argyle Street on June 16th, 1890. Stanley is far better known to the world as Stan Laurel. His 30-year career in more than 100 comedy films with Oliver Hardy is celebrated in the town's **Laurel and Hardy Museum** in Upper Brook Street. The museum was founded in 1976 by the late Bill Cubin, who devoted his life to the famous duo and collected an extraordinary variety of memorabilia, believed to be the largest in the world. Everything is here, including letters, photographs, personal items and even furniture belonging to the two greats of cinema comedy. A large extension has been added to the modest 17th-century house and there is also a small cinema showing films and documentaries throughout the day. The museum is open seven days a week all year round except during January.

Another great man associated with the town is George Fox, founder of the Quakers. Despite an extremely rough reception from the citizens of Ulverston when he preached here in the 1650s, Fox later married Margaret, widow of Judge Fell of nearby **Swarthmoor Hall**. This lovely late 16th-century manor house, set in extensive gardens, was the birthplace of the Quaker movement and was for a time George and Margaret's home and the first settled centre of the Quaker movement.

Ulverston itself, with its fascinating alleys and cobbled streets, is a delightful place to wander around. The oldest building in the town is the **Church of St Mary** which dates, in parts, from 1111. Though it was restored and rebuilt in the mid-19th century and the chancel was added in 1903, it has retained its splendid Norman door and some magnificent stained glass, including a window designed by the painter Sir Joshua Reynolds. The present tower dates from the reign of Elizabeth I, as the original steeple was destroyed during a storm in 1540.

Ulverston also boasts England's shortest, widest and deepest **Canal**. Visitors can follow the towpath walk alongside, which runs dead straight for just over a mile to Morecambe Bay. Built by the famous engineer John Rennie and opened in 1796, the canal ushered in a half-century of great prosperity for Ulverston as an inland port. At its peak, some 600 large ships a year berthed here, though those

good times came to an abrupt end in 1856 with the arrival of the railway. The railway company's directors bought the canal and promptly closed it.

The town's other attractions include **The Lakes Glass Centre**, which features the high-quality Heron Glass and Cumbria Crystal. Also at the Centre is the **Gateway to Furness Exhibition**, providing a colourful snapshot of the history of the Furness Peninsula.

The open area to the north of Ulverston, known as **The Gill**, is the starting point for the 70-mile Cumbria Way. The route of the Cumbria Way was originally devised by the Lake District area of the Ramblers Association in the mid-1970s, and provides an exhilarating journey through a wonderful mix of natural splendour and fascinating heritage. The first section is the 15-mile walk to Coniston.

AROUND ULVERSTON

HAVERTHWAITE

5 miles NE of Ulverston off the A590

Haverthwaite is the southern terminus of the **Lakeside & Haverthwaite Railway**, a branch of the Furness railway originally built to transport passengers and goods to the steamers on Lake Windermere. It was one of the first attempts at mass tourism in the Lake District. Passenger numbers peaked in the 1920s, but the general decline of rail travel in the 1960s led to the railway's closure in

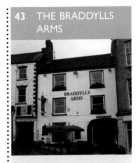

43 THE BRADDYLLS ARMS

Ulverston

The **Braddylls Arms** is open all day for drinks and snacks and all year for B&B accommodation.

🍽 🛏 see page 165

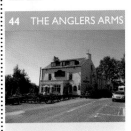

44 THE ANGLERS ARMS

Haverthwaite, Ulverston

Ten real ales and great food bring visitors from near and far to the **Anglers Arms**.

🍽 see page 166

45 THE ROYAL OAK

Spark Bridge, Nr Ulverston

The **Royal Oak** attracts visitors from near and far with a varied menu of home-cooked dishes and three luxuriously appointed B&B rooms.

🍴 🛏 see page 167

46 THE EAGLES HEAD

Satterthwaite, nr Ulverston

Owners and head chef combine to make the **Eagles Head** a great place to enjoy real ales and top-notch food.

🍴 see page 168

47 THE BRADDYLLS ARMS

Bardsea

Great views of the Bay accompany a drink or a meal at the **Braddylls Arms**. Also en suite B&B rooms.

🍴 🛏 see page 169

1967. However, a group of dedicated rail enthusiasts rescued this scenic stretch, restored its engines and rolling stock to working order and now provide a full service of steam trains throughout the season.

SWARTHMOOR

1 mile S of Ulverston off the A590

This small village of whitewashed cottages, now almost entirely incorporated into Ulverston, also has a curious 16th-century hall. **Swarthmoor Hall** stands in well-kept gardens and, although a cement rendering disguises its antiquity, the mullion windows and leaded panes give a clue to its true age. It was built in around 1586 by George Fell, a wealthy landowner. It was his son, Judge Thomas Fell, who married Margaret Askew, who, in turn, became a follower of George Fox after hearing him preach in 1652. At that time, many people were suspicious of Fox's beliefs, but Margaret was able to persuade her husband to use his position to give Fox protection and shelter, and the Hall became the first settled centre of the Quaker Movement. Missionaries were organised from here and the library was stocked with both Quaker and anti-Quaker literature. Judge Fell died in 1658 and, 11 years later, Margaret married George Fox. Swarthmoor Hall is open during the summer and offers visitors a fascinating insight into the history of the early Quakers.

LINDAL-IN-FURNESS

3 miles SW of Ulverston on the A590

The **Colony Country Store** combines the aromatic character of an old-fashioned country general stores with the cost-cutting advantages of a Factory Shop. There's a huge range of textiles, glassware, ceramics and decorative accessories for the home, but the Colony is also Europe's leading manufacturer of scented candles, supplying millions of scented and dinner candles every year to prestigious shops around the world. From a viewing gallery visitors can watch the traditional skills of hand-pouring and dipping being used to create a variety of candle styles.

GREAT URSWICK

3 miles S of Ulverston off the A590

The ancient village **Church of St Mary and St Michael** is noted for its unusual and lively woodcarvings that were created by the Chipping Campden Guild of Carvers. As well as the figure of a pilgrim to the left of the chancel arch, there are some smaller carvings in the choir stall of winged children playing musical instruments. Also worthy of a second look is the 9th-century wooden cross which bears a runic inscription.

Lying between Great Urswick and Bardsea and overlooking Morecambe Bay is **Birkrigg Common**, a lovely area of open land. On the east side of the common is the **Druid's Circle**, with two concentric circles made up of 31 stones, some of them 3 feet high.

The cremated remains found around the site in 1921 indicated that it was used for burials.

BARDSEA

2 miles S of Ulverston off the A5087

The village stands on a lovely green knoll overlooking the sea and, as well as having a charming, unhurried air about it, there are some excellent walks from here along the coast either from its Country Park or through the woodland.

Just up the coast, to the north, lies **Conishead Priory**, once the site of a leper colony that was established by Augustinian canons in the 12th century. After the Dissolution, a superb private house was built on the site and the guide service was continued by the Duchy of Lancaster. In 1821, Colonel Braddyll demolished the house and built in its place the ornate Gothic mansion that stands here today. He was also responsible for the atmospheric ruined folly on **Chapel Island** that is clearly visible in the estuary. The monks from Conishead Priory used to act as guides across the dangerous Cartmel Sands to Lancashire.

Latterly, **Conishead Priory** has been a private house, a hydropathic hotel, a military hospital and a rest home for Durham miners; it is now owned by the Tibet Buddhist Manjushri Mahayana Buddhist Centre, who came here in 1977. During the summer months visitors are welcome to the house, which is open for tours, and there is a delightful woodland trail to follow

through the grounds. A new Buddhist temple was opened in 1998, based on a traditional design which symbolises the pure world (Mandala) of a Buddha.

BARROW-IN-FURNESS

Undoubtedly the best introduction to Barrow is to pay a visit to the **Dock Museum** (free admission), an impressive glass-and-steel structure which hangs suspended above a Victorian Graving Dock (see panel). It was James (later Sir James) Ramsden who established the first Barrow Iron Ship Company in 1870, taking advantage of local steel-production skills. In 1896 the firm was acquired by **Vickers**, a name forever linked with Barrow, and for a number of years was the largest armaments works in the world. Sir James was also the General Manager of the Furness Railway and the town's first mayor. At the Ramsden Square roundabout is a statue to Sir James, and at the next roundabout is a statue of HW Schneider, one of the men who developed the Furness iron mines and was involved in the Barrow Haematite Steel Company.

Today, Barrow is the Peninsula's prime shopping centre, with all the familiar High Street stores mingling with local specialist shops, and the largest indoor market in the area which is open on Mondays, Wednesdays, Fridays and Saturdays.

48 THE COFFEE BEAN

Barrow-in-Furness

The **Coffee Bean** is a popular, family-friendly place for a daytime snack or meal.

🍴 see page 169

49 THE RAMS HEAD HOTEL

Barrow-in-Furness

The **Rams Head** is a cheerful, convivial hostelry on a corner site open from noon to midnight. Seven letting bedrooms.

🍴 🛏 see page 169

50 THE DUKE OF EDINBURGH HOTEL & BAR

Barrow-in-Furness

High-quality accommodation has recently been added to the **Duke of Edinburgh**, which serves a fine selection of real ales and home-cooked food.

🛏 🍴 see page 170

51 THE COFFEE SHOP

Dock Museum, Barrow-in-Furness

The **Coffee Shop** in the Dock Museum provides an excellent break while visiting one of the North of England's best attractions.

🍴 see page 170

52 THE DOCK MUSEUM

Barrow-in-Furness

A superb modern museum tracing the history of Barrow as it developed from a tiny fishing hamlet to a major iron, steel and shipbuilding centre.

 see page 171

Barrow is also the western starting point of the **Cistercian Way**, a 33-mile-walk to Grange-over-Sands through wonderfully unspoilt countryside. En route it passes Furness Abbey in the Vale of Deadly Nightshade, prehistoric sites on the hills surrounding Urswick Tarn and many other historical places of interest. The Way is marked on public roads and footpaths, and a fully descriptive leaflet is available from Tourist Information Centres.

AROUND BARROW-IN-FURNESS

GLEASTON

3 miles E of Barrow-in-Furness off the A5087

This village is typical of the small, peaceful villages and hamlets that can be found in this part of the peninsula. Here, standing close by the ruins of **Gleaston Castle**, can be found **Gleaston Water Mill**. The present buildings date from 1774, with the massive original wooden gearing still in place. The machinery is operational most days – an 18 feet water-wheel and an 11 feet wooden pit wheel serviced by an intriguing water course. Evening tours with supper are available by prior arrangement. To reach Gleaston Water Mill, follow the signs from the A5087. Guided talks, walks and tours can be arranged.

FOULNEY ISLAND

5 miles E of Barrow-in-Furness off the A5087

The island, like its smaller neighbour Roa Island, is joined to the mainland by a causeway. The

Gleaston Castle Ruins

site of the local lifeboat station, the island is small and sheltered from the Irish Sea by Walney Island.

PIEL ISLAND

5 miles SE of Barrow-in-Furness via foot ferry from Roa Island

Though this tiny island was probably visited by both the Celts and the Romans, its first recorded name is Scandinavian – *Fotheray*, from the Old Norse meaning 'fodder island'. In 1127 the islands were given to the Savignac Monks by King Stephen; the order merged with the Cistercian monks in the middle of the 12th century. The monks of Furness Abbey used Piel Island as a warehouse and storage area.

Piel Castle, on the island, was a house fortified in the early part of the 14th century and at the time it was the largest of its kind in the northwest. Intended to be used as one of the abbey's warehouses and to offer protection from raiders, in later years the castle also proved to be a useful defence against the King's Customs men, and a prosperous trade in smuggling began. The castle has, over many years, been allowed to fall into ruin and now presents a stark outline on the horizon.

One of the most exciting events in Piel's history occurred on 4th June 1487 when a man claiming to be the Earl of Warwick, one of the Princes in the Tower allegedly murdered by Richard III, landed on the island. If true, the Earl was indisputably the true King of England. In reality, this 'Earl of Warwick' was later proved to be

Lambert Simnel, the son of a joiner. Supported by an army of German and Irish mercenaries, Simnel set out across Furness to march on London. However, when he arrived in the capital it was as the prisoner of Henry VII, who had defeated Simnel's troops at Stoke.

WALNEY ISLAND

2 miles W of Barrow-in-Furness on the A590

This 10-mile-long island is joined to the Furness Peninsula by a bridge from Barrow docks and is home to two important nature reserves situated at either end of the island. **North Walney National Nature Reserve** covers some 350 acres within which are a great variety of habitats including sand dunes, heath, salt marsh, shingle and scrub. As well as having several species of orchid and over 130 species of bird either living or visiting the reserve, there is also an area for the preservation of the Natterjack toad, Britain's rarest amphibian. Unique to the Reserve is the Walney Geranium, a plant that grows nowhere else in the world. North Walney also boasts a rich prehistoric past, with important archaeological sites from Mesolithic, Neolithic, Bronze and Iron Age times. **South Walney Nature Reserve** is home to the largest nesting ground of herring gulls and lesser black-backed gulls in Europe.

Walney Island's southernmost tip, **Walney Point**, is dominated by a 70ft lighthouse which was built in 1790 and whose light was, originally, an oil lamp.

53   PIEL CASTLE

Piel Island, Barrow in Furness

Impressive 14th century castle ruins, reached by small boat to Piel Island.

 see page 170

54 THE RED LION INN

Dalton-in-Furness

The **Red Lion** scores in all aspects: great hospitality, Cask Marque ales, fine food, excellent rooms for B&B.

🍴 🛏 see page 171

DALTON-IN-FURNESS

5 miles N of Barrow-in-Furness off the A590

Lying in a narrow valley on the part of Furness that extends deep into Morecambe Bay, it is difficult to imagine that this ancient place was once the leading town of Furness and an important centre for administration and justice. The 14th-century pele tower, **Dalton Castle**, was built with walls 6 feet thick to provide a place of refuge for the monks of Furness Abbey against Scottish raiders and it still looks very formidable. Over the centuries, in its twin role as both prison and court, it has been substantially altered internally although it still retains most of its original external features. It is now owned by the National Trust and houses a small museum with an interesting display of 16th and 17th-century armour, along with exhibits about iron mining, the Civil War in Furness, and the life and work of George Romney, the 18th-century portrait painter.

Dalton became established as a market town in the 13th century when the Cistercians began to hold fairs and markets in the town. Indeed, the influence of the monks was great here as, before the Dissolution, it was the Abbot who held court and administered justice. Not surprisingly, Dalton's decline coincided with the departure of the monks and also with the growing importance of Ulverston and Greenodd as ports.

The red sandstone **Church of St Mary** was designed by the celebrated Victorian architects Paley and Austin. In the graveyard lies George Romney, best known in his day for his many portraits of Nelson's mistress, Lady Hamilton, with whom he formed a romantic attachment in spite of having a wife in Kendal. His grave is marked with the inscription *pictor celeberrimus*. Also worth seeking out in the graveyard is the plaque which outlines the devastating effect of the bubonic plague which swept through the town in 1662. Of the total population at the time of 612, no fewer than 320 fell victim to the plague.

Visitors to Dalton will find that it is time well spent looking around the many fascinating façades in and close to the market place, such as the unique, cast-iron shop front at **No 51, Market Street**. In the market place itself is an elegant, **Victorian Drinking Fountain** with fluted columns supporting a dome of open iron work above the pedestal fountain. Nearby stand the market cross and the slabs of stone

Pele Tower, Dalton-in-Furness

that were used for fish-drying in the 19th century.

From the mostly pedestrianised Tudor Square, visitors can board a bus to the award-winning **South Lakes Wild Animal Park** which has been designated the Region's Official Top Attraction by the Cumbria Tourist Board. It's the only place in Britain where you can see rare Amur and Sumatran tigers (the world's biggest and smallest tigers). At feeding time (2.30pm each day) they climb a 20 feet vertical tree to 'catch' their food. Ring-tailed lemurs wander freely through the park, visitors can walk with emus and hand-feed the largest collection of kangaroos in Europe. The 17 acres of natural parkland are also home to some of the rarest animals on earth, among them the red panda, maned wolves and tamarin monkeys as well as some 150 other species from around the world, including rhinos, giraffes, tapirs, coatis and the ever-popular meerkats. Other attractions include a Safari Railway, adventure play area, many picnic spots, a gift shop and café.

To the south of the town lies **Furness Abbey** (English Heritage), a magnificent ruin of eroded red sandstone set in fine parkland, the focal point of south Cumbria's monastic heritage. Among the

Furness Abbey

atmospheric remains can still be seen the canopied seats in the presbytery and the graceful arches overlooking the cloister, testaments to the abbey's former wealth and influence. Furness Abbey stands in the **Vale of Deadly Nightshade**, a shallow valley of sandstone cliffs and rich pastureland. The abbey itself was established in 1123 at Tulketh, near Preston, by King Stephen. Four years later it was moved to its present site and, after 20 years, became absorbed into the Cistercian Order. Despite its remoteness Furness Abbey flourished, with the monks establishing themselves as guides across the treacherous sands of Morecambe Bay. Rich endowments

of land, including holdings in Yorkshire and Ireland, led to the development of trade in products such as wool, iron and charcoal. Furness Abbey became the second wealthiest monastery in Britain, after Fountains Abbey in Yorkshire. After the Dissolution in 1537, the abbey became part of Thomas Cromwell's estate and it was allowed to decay into a picturesque and romantic ruin. It is now owned by English Heritage, who have a small Interpretative Centre nearby detailing its history. Off the A595 Dalton-to-Askam road, **Sandscale Haws** is one of the most important sand dune systems in Britain, supporting an outstanding variety of fauna.

GRIZEBECK

15 miles N of Barrow-in-Furness on the A595/A5092

This small village on the edge of the Lake District National Park nestles against the flanks of the **Furness Fells**. Although it stands at the junction of roads leading to the Furness Peninsula and the South Cumbria coast, the village and the area around is peaceful and unhurried, offering the visitor an inviting alternative to some of the busier and more crowded Lakeland towns.

BROUGHTON-IN-FURNESS

19 miles N of Barrow-in-Furness on the A595/A593

At the heart of this attractive, unspoilt little town is the **Market Square** with its tall Georgian houses, commemorative obelisk of 1810, village stocks, fish slabs and some venerable chestnut trees. The old Town Hall, occupying the whole of one side, dates back to 1766 and now houses the town's Tourist Information Centre and the Clocktower Gallery, which exhibits paintings, ceramics, mirrors and glassware. On August 1st each year, Broughton's Lord of the Manor comes to the Square to read out the market charter granted by Elizabeth I, while Councillors dispense pennies to any children in the crowd.

One of the town's famous short-term residents was Branwell Brontë, who was employed here as a tutor at **Broughton House**, a splendid double-fronted, three-storey town house just off the Square. Branwell apparently found time both to enjoy the elegance of the town and to share in whatever revelries were in train. Wordsworth often visited Broughton as a child. Throughout his life he loved this peaceful corner of Lakeland and celebrated its charms in some 150 poems; his 20th-century poetical successor, Norman Nicholson, was similarly enchanted.

Some of the Lake District's finest scenery – the Duddon Valley, Furness Fells, Great Gable and Scafell – are all within easy reach, and about 3 miles west of the town is **Swinside Circle**, a fine prehistoric stone circle, some 60 feet in diameter, containing 52 close-set stones and two outlying 'portal' or gateway stones.

Swinside Circle

About 3 miles north of the town, the peaceful hamlet of **Broughton Mills** will attract followers of the Coleridge Trail. During the course of his famous 'circumcursion' of Lakeland in August 1802, the poet stopped to refresh himself at the **Blacksmith's Arms** where he 'Dined on Oatcake and Cheese, with a pint of Ale, and 2 glasses of Rum and water sweetened with preserved Gooseberries'. The inn, built in 1748, is still there and barely changed since Coleridge's visit.

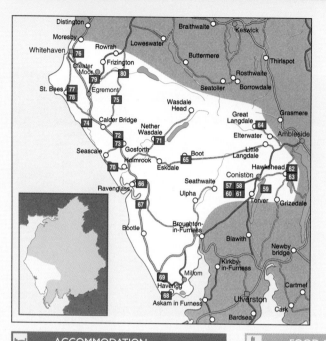

Coniston & South West Cumbria

Three distinct areas lie within the southwest quarter of Cumbria. The enchanting scenery around Coniston Water and its environs is very much on the tourist trail, and also has strong literary connections. John Ruskin, the 19th-century author, artist and critic, made his home at Brantwood on the shore of Coniston; the lake is also the setting for many of the adventures recounted in *Swallows and Amazons* as told by Arthur Ransome. Wordsworth went to school in Hawkshead, where the desk he defaced with his name can still be seen. But probably the most popular of Coniston's literary denizens is Beatrix Potter, who, after holidaying at Near Sawrey as a child, later bought a house at Hill Top as well as many acres of farms which she bequeathed to the National Trust. Further west is Cumbria's 'Empty Quarter', a vast terrain of magnificent mountains and desolate fells beloved of climbers and walkers. England's highest mountain, Scafell Pike, rises here; the country's deepest lake, Wast Water, sinks to a depth of some 200 feet and is surrounded by sheer cliffs soaring up to 2,000 feet. The village of Wasdale Head claims to have the smallest church in England.

Bordering this untamed landscape is the narrow coastal strip stretching from Whitehaven down to Millom, which has its own identity as well as a quiet charm. The coastline is dominated by small 18th and 19th century iron-mining communities set between the romantic outline of the Lakeland fells and the grey-blue waters of the Irish Sea. The famous Ravenglass and Eskdale Railway carries many visitors from the coast up one of Cumbria's most picturesque valleys. There are also several genteel Victorian resorts along the coast, including the popular village of Seascale.

Old Man of Coniston

Coniston

In a glorious setting at the foot of the Old Man of Coniston, the **Black Bull** is renowned for its home-brewed ales, hearty food and comfortable accommodation.

see page 173

CONISTON

Beatrix Potter, John Ruskin, Arthur Ransome, Sir Donald Campbell – all had strong connections with **Coniston Water**, the third largest and one of the most beautiful of the central Cumbrian lakes. Beatrix Potter lived at Sawrey near Lake Windermere, but she owned the vast **Monk Coniston** estate at the head of Coniston Water. On her death she bequeathed it to the National Trust, a body she had helped to establish and to which she devoted much of her time and fortune.

Ruskin came to Coniston in 1872, moving into a house he had never seen. Brantwood, on the eastern side of the lake, is open to the public and enjoys superb views across the water to the great

crumpled hill of the **Old Man of Coniston**, 800 metres high. From its summit there are even more extensive vistas over Scotland, the Isle of Man, and on a clear day as far as Snowdonia.

Arthur Ransome's *Swallows and Amazons* has delighted generations with its tales of children's adventures set in and around the Lake District. As a child he spent his summer holidays near Nibthwaite at the southern end of the lake and recalled that he was always 'half-drowned in tears' when he had to leave. Later he bought a house overlooking Coniston Water and many locations in his books can be recognised today: **Peel Island**, for example, at the southern end of the lake, is the Wildcat Island of his books.

Sir Donald Campbell's associations with the lake were both glorious and tragic. In 1955 he broke the world water speed record here; 12 years later, when he was attempting to beat his own record, his boat, **Bluebird**, struck a log while travelling at 320 mph. In March 2001 his widow was present as the tailfin of the boat was at last hauled up to the surface. For 34 years the 15ft rear section had lain on a bed of silt, 140 feet down and right in the middle of the lake. Sir Donald's body was later recovered and was buried on September 12th, 2001 in the village cemetery – an event that was comparatively little covered by the media, who were obviously concerned with the tragic events in the United States the day before.

Coniston Water

Nowadays, boats on Coniston Water are restricted to a 10-mph limit – an ideal speed if you're travelling in the wonderful old steamship, the **Gondola**. So called because of its high prow, which enabled it to come in close to shore to pick up passengers, *Gondola* was commissioned by Sir James Ramsden, General Manager of the Furness Railway Company and first Mayor of Barrow, and was launched on Coniston Water in 1859. She retired in 1936, but found a new career as a houseboat in 1945. Abandoned after a storm in the 1960s, she was saved by a group of National Trust enthusiasts and restored and rebuilt by Vickers Shipbuilding. She was relaunched in 1980. Up to 86 passengers can now travel in opulent comfort on her regular trips around the lake. Coniston Launch also offers lake cruises in its two timber launches, and at the boating centre craft of every kind are available to rent.

Coniston village was once an important copper mining centre, and was also widely known for the beautiful decorative green slate, quarried locally, which is used on so many of the public buildings. The great bulk of the Old Man of Coniston overlooks the village; it was from this mountain, and some of the surrounding hills, that copper was extracted. Mined from the days of the Romans, the industry's heyday in Coniston was in the 18th and 19th centuries but, with the discovery of more accessible deposits, the industry went into decline and the village

returned to pre-boom peacefulness. At 2,631 feet, the Old Man of Coniston is a considerable climb, but many make the effort and the summit can be bustling with fell-walkers enjoying the glorious views.

Just south of the village and beside the lake is **Coniston Hall**, the village's oldest building. Dating from the 16th century, it was the home of the Le Fleming family, the largest landowners in the area. Coniston's most famous inhabitant was, however, John Ruskin, the 19th-century author, artist, critic, social commentator and one of the first conservationists. He lies buried in Coniston churchyard and the **Ruskin Museum** nearby contains many of his studies, pictures, letters and photographs as well as his collection of geological specimens. Visitors can also see a pair of his socks, his certificate of matriculation from Oxford, and his funeral pall made of Ruskin lace embroidered with wild flowers. The lace was so called because Ruskin had encouraged the revival of flax hand-spinning in the area. Lace pieces made to his own designs and based on the sumptuous ruffs worn by sitters in portraits by Titian, Tintoretto and Veronese were attached to plain linen to make decorative cushions, table covers and bedspreads – many of these are on display.

From the jetty at Coniston, a short ferry trip takes you to John Ruskin's home, **Brantwood**, which occupies a beautiful setting on the eastern shores of Coniston Water. It was his home from 1872 until his

58 THE CROWN INN

Coniston

The **Crown Inn** is a stylishly appointed hotel a short walk from Coniston Water: real ales, good food, 12 comfortable bedrooms

see page 174

59 BRANTWOOD

Coniston

The home of John Ruskin from 1872 until his death in 1900, this beautifully situated house retains many of Ruskins personal belongings and is well worth a visit.

see page 176

60 THE SUN HOTEL

Coniston

Character and quality combine at a high level at the **Sun Inn**, a welcoming hotel with a classic Lakeland pub next door.

see page 175

61 THE SHIP INN

Bowmanstead, nr Coniston

The Ship is a traditional country inn with cosy accommodation, good food and drink and glorious flower displays outside.

see page 176

•

Every Thursday during the season there are lace-making demonstrations at Brantwood, and readings from Ruskin's works are performed regularly in the study. There's also a well-stocked bookshop, a craft gallery and 250 acres of grounds where there are well-marked nature trails and where a theatre season is held during the summer.

•

death in 1900. When he arrived for the first time he described the house, which he had bought for £1,500 without ever seeing it, as 'a mere shed'. He spent the next 20 years extending the house, adding another 12 rooms, and laying out the gardens. The view from the Turret Room he had built was, Ruskin declared, 'the best in all England'.

Visitors today can wander around rooms filled with Ruskin's watercolours, paintings by Turner (who was one of his heroes), see his study which is lined with wallpaper he designed himself, and watch a 20-minute video which provides a useful introduction to his life and works.

AROUND CONISTON

GRIZEDALE

3 miles SE of Coniston off the B5285

The village lies at the heart of the 9,000-acre **Grizedale Forest** which was acquired by the Forestry Commission in 1934 and is famous for its Sculpture. The Commission's original intention of chiefly cultivating the forest for its timber met with much resistance and, over the years, many pathways have been opened and a variety of recreational activities have been encouraged. The forest, too, is famously the home of some 80 tree sculptures commissioned since 1977. All are created from natural materials found in the forest, and made by some of Britain's best-known contemporary artists, including Andy Goldsworthy, as

well as by artists from all over the world. The great beauty of these sculptures is their understated presence: there are no signposts pointing to the exhibits; visitors are left entirely on their own to discover these wonders – though there is a printed map obtainable from the Grizedale Forest Visitor Centre. The Centre vividly illustrates the story of the forest as well as showing how the combination of wildlife, recreation and commercial timbering work together.

NEAR SAWREY

4 miles E of Coniston on the B5285

Though this little village will not be familiar to many visitors to the Lake District, its famous inhabitant, Beatrix Potter, almost certainly will be. After holidaying here in 1896, the authoress fell in love with the place and, with the royalties from her first book, *The Tale of Peter Rabbit*, she purchased **Hill Top** in 1905. After her marriage in 1913 to a local solicitor, she actually lived in another house in the village, Castle Cottage (private), and used the charming 17th-century cottage as her study. Oddly, she wrote very little after the marriage, spending most of her time dealing with the management of the farms she had bought in the area.

Following Beatrix Potter's death in 1943, the house and the land she had bought on the surrounding fells became the property of the National Trust. In accordance with Beatrix Potter's will, Hill Top has remained exactly as she would have known it.

One of the most popular Lakeland attractions, Hill Top is full of Beatrix Potter memorabilia, including some of her original drawings. The house is very small, so it is best avoided at peak holiday times. **Tarn Hows**, part of the 4,000-acre Monk Coniston estate bought and sold on to the National Trust, was created to resemble a Swiss lake and is very rich in flora and fauna – it has been designated a Site of Special Scientific Interest.

HAWKSHEAD

3 miles E of Coniston on the B5285

There are more Beatrix Potter connections in the enchanting little village of Hawkshead. Her solicitor husband, William Heelis, worked from an office in the Main Street here, and this has now been transformed into **The Beatrix Potter Gallery**. The gallery features an exhibition of her original drawings and illustrations alongside details of the author's life.

Situated at the head of **Esthwaite Water**, enjoying glorious views of Coniston Old Man and Helvellyn, Hawkshead has a history that goes back to Viking times. Its name is Norse in origin, derived from *Haukr*, who built the original settlement. It's a delightful village of narrow cobbled lanes with a pedestrianised main square dominated by the Market House, or Shambles, and another square linked to it by little snickets and arched alleyways which invite exploration. The poet Norman Nicholson observed that 'The whole village could be fitted into

the boundaries of a large agricultural show; yet it contains enough corners, angles, alleys and entries to keep the eye happy for hours.'

Hawkshead was once an important market town serving the surrounding area; at that time most of the land here was owned by the monks of Furness Abbey. The only building in Hawkshead to survive from monastic times is the Courthouse, to the north of the village, part of a medieval manor house built by the monks.

The **Church of St Michael & All Angels**, with its massive 15th-century tower, seems rather grand for the village but it too was built at a time when Hawkshead was a wealthy town. Inside, there are some remarkable wall paintings from the late 1600s and also look out for the 'Buried in Woolen' affidavit near the vestry door. In 1666 the Government had decreed that corpses must not be buried in shrouds made from 'flaxe, hempe, silke or hair, or other than what is made of sheeps wool onely'. The idea was to help maintain the local woollen industry, and this was one way of ensuring that even the dead got to help out. The church is the focal point of the annual Lake District Summer Music Festival and a popular venue for concerts and recitals. In the churchyard is a war memorial erected in 1919 and modelled on the ancient runic cross at Gosforth.

Some lovely walks lead from Hawkshead to **Roger Ground** and Esthwaite Water, possibly the least

Hawkshead has specific Wordsworth connections. Hawkshead Grammar School was founded in 1585 by Edwin Sandys, Archbishop of York, and between 1779 and 1787 the young William Wordsworth was a star pupil. The earliest of his surviving poems was written to celebrate the school's 200th year. The school is open from Easter to September, and visitors can inspect the classrooms during the summer holidays, see the desk where William carved his name and have a look around the headmaster's study. Ann Tyson's Cottage, where Wordsworth lodged while he attended the school, has also survived. It stands in Wordsworth Street and is now a guest house.

62 QUEENS HEAD HOTEL

Hawkshead

Top-quality food based on the best local produce and a choice of B&B or self-catering accommodation in a fine family-run hotel.

🛏 🍴 see page 177

63 IVY HOUSE HOTEL & RESTAURANT

Hawkshead

A handsome Georgian house offering top-quality food and accommodation.

 see page 177

64 THE OLD DUNGEON GHYLL HOTEL

Great Langdale

The **Old Dungeon Ghyll Hotel** is a perfect base for walkers, climbers and tourists, with a truly magnificent setting at the head of the Great Langdale Valley.

see page 178

frequented of the Lakes, and also to the nearby hamlet of **Colthouse** where there's an early Quaker Meeting House built around 1690. Esthwaite Water was much loved by Wordsworth, as he shows in his poem

The Prelude: My morning walks were early; oft before the hours of school I travelled round our little lake, five miles Of pleasant wandering. Happy time!

GREAT LANGDALE

9 miles N of Coniston on the B5343

One of the most dramatic of the Lake District waterfalls is **Dungeon Ghyll**, which tumbles 60 feet down the fellside. Nearby is the well known Old Dungeon Ghyll Hotel, which makes an excellent starting point for walks in this spectacularly scenic area where the famous peaks of Crinkle Crags, Bowfell and the Langdale Pikes provide some serious challenges for hikers and ramblers. The 'dungeon' is actually a natural cave.

SEATHWAITE

5 miles W of Coniston via minor road off the A593

A mere 5 miles or so from Coniston as the crow flies, by road Seathwaite is nearly three times as far. It stands in one of the Lake District's most tranquil and least-known valleys, **Dunnerdale**. Wordsworth captured its natural beauty in a sequence of sonnets. In his poem *The Excursion*, he wrote about the Reverend Robert Walker, the curate of Seathwaite. Nicholas, or 'Wonderful Walker' as Wordsworth referred to him, served the church here for some 67 years though he also filled various other jobs such as farm labourer and nurse as well as spinning wool and making his own clothes. Fell-walkers and hikers who prefer to escape the masses will delight not only in the solitude of this glorious valley but also in the wide variety of plant, animal and birdlife that have made this haven their home.

HARDKNOTT PASS

5 miles W of Coniston off the A593

Surrounded by the fell of the same name, this pass is one of the most treacherous in the Lake District yet it was used by the Romans for the road between their forts at Ambleside (*Galava*) and Ravenglass (*Glannaventa*). Of the remains of Roman occupation, **Hardknott Fort** on a shoulder of the fell, overlooking the Esk Valley, is the most substantial and also

Hardknott Fort

provides some of the grandest views in the whole of the Lake District. The walls of the fort, known as *Mediobogdum*, still stand up to 2 metres high, and within them the foundations of the commander's house, headquarters building and granary can be seen.

BOOT

8 miles W of Coniston off the A595

Lying at the eastern end of the **Ravenglass and Eskdale Railway,** this is a wonderful place to visit whether arriving by train or car. A gentle walk from the station at Eskdale brings you to this delightful village with its pub, post office, museum, waterfall and nearby St Catherine's Church in its lovely secluded riverside setting. Perhaps because of the rugged walking country to the east, the village is well supplied – with both a campsite and bunkhouse available.

ESKDALE GREEN

10 miles W of Coniston off the A595

One of the few settlements in this beautiful and unspoilt valley, the village lies on the route of the Ravenglass and Eskdale Railway. Further up the valley lies a group of buildings that make up **Eskdale Mill** where cereals have been ground since 1578, when it is recorded that the brothers Henry and Robert Vicars were the tenants, paying an annual rent of eight shillings (40p). The original machinery for grinding oatmeal is in full working order and operated daily.

RAVENGLASS

Lying as it does at the estuary of three rivers – the Esk, the Mite, and the Irt – as well as enjoying a sheltered position, it is not surprising that Ravenglass was an important port from prehistoric times. The Romans built a naval base here around AD 78 which served as a supply point for the military zone around Hadrian's Wall. They also constructed a fort, **Glannaventra,** on the cliffs above the town, which was home to around 1,000 soldiers. Little remains of Glannaventra except for the impressively preserved walls of the Bath House. Almost 12 feet high, these walls are believed to be the highest Roman remains in the country. In the 1700s Ravenglass was a base for smugglers bringing contraband in from coastal ships – tobacco and French brandy.

Today the estuary has silted up but there are still scores of small boats and the village is a charming resort, full of atmosphere. The layout has changed little since the 16th century; the main street is paved with sea pebbles and leads up from a shingle beach. Once, iron-ore was brought to the estuary by narrow-gauge railway from the mines near Boot, in Eskdale, about 8 miles away.

One of the town's major attractions is the 15-inch narrow-gauge **Ravenglass and Eskdale Railway** which runs for 7 miles up the lovely Mite and Esk River valleys. Better known as 'La'al Ratty', it was built in 1875 to

65 DALE VIEW

Boot, Eskdale

Dale View offers a lovely location for B&B guests in unspoilt Eskdale.

see page 179

Power for the two waterwheels at Eskdale Mill is provided by Whillan Beck, which surges down from England's highest mountains, the Scafell range. Visitors can enjoy a picnic in the picturesque mill grounds, browse in the gift shop or explore the Mill's history in the informative exhibition. Eskdale Mill may be reached by crossing a 17th-century packhorse bridge over the beck.

•

Originally part of the estate, Muncaster Water Mill can be traced back to 1455, though it is thought that the site could be Roman. The situation is certainly idyllic, with the mill race still turning the huge wooden water wheel and the Ravenglass & Eskdale Railway running alongside.

•

66 MUNCASTER CASTLE

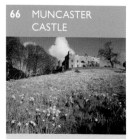

Ravenglass

View the unique treasures here at Muncaster and wander through the spectacular gardens.

 see page 179

67 THE BROWN COW INN

Waberthwaite

The **Brown Cow** is a delightful inn open all day for an excellent choice of food and drink.

see page 180

52

transport ore and quarried stone from the Eskdale Valley, and opened the following year for passenger traffic. Since then the railway has survived several threats of extinction. The most serious occurred at the end of the 1950s when the closure of the Eskdale granite quarries wiped out the railway's freight traffic at a stroke. However, at the auction for the railway in 1960 a band of enthusiasts outbid the scrap dealers and formed a company to keep the little railway running.

Today, the company operates 12 locomotives, both steam and diesel, and 300,000 people a year come from all over the world to ride on what has been described as 'the most beautiful train journey in England'. The La'al Ratty is still the best way to explore Miterdale and Eskdale, and enchants both young and old alike. There are several stops along the journey, and at both termini there is a café and a souvenir shop. At the Ravenglass station there is also a museum which brings to life the history of this remarkable line and the important part it has played in the life of Eskdale.

A mile or so east of Ravenglass stands **Muncaster Castle**, which has been in the ownership of the Pennington family since 1208. In 1464 the Penningtons gave shelter to King Henry VI after his defeat at the Battle of Hexham. On his departure Henry presented them with his enamelled glass drinking bowl, saying that as long as it remained unbroken the

Penningtons would survive and thrive at Muncaster. Apart from the many treasures, the stunning Great Hall, Salvin's octagonal library and the barrel ceiling in the drawing room, Muncaster is also famous for its gardens. The collection of species rhododendrons is one of the finest in Europe, gathered primarily from plant-hunting expeditions to Nepal in the 1920s, and there are also fine azaleas, hydrangeas and camellias as well as many unusual trees.

For many visitors the chief attraction is the **World Owl Centre**, where many endangered owl species are bred. Snowy owls have become great favourites on the back of the Harry Potter craze, and many visitors have enquired about keeping them as pets. The staff at the Centre have to point out that the snowy owl is a mighty predator with a 5-feet wingspan. Mighty as he is, he is not the mightiest of the owls at the Centre: that honour goes to the Eurasian eagle owl, whose full splendour can be seen at the daily demonstrations. Muncaster's latest attraction is the Meadow Vole Maze (these little creatures are the staple diet of barn owls, and visitors can find out what it's like to be a vole on the run from a hungry owl).

AROUND RAVENGLASS

WABERTHWAITE

4 miles S of Ravenglass on the A595

No visit to west Cumbria is complete without the inclusion of a trip to RG Woodall's shop. Found in the heart of this village, Richard Woodall is world famous for his sausages, in particular for the Waberthwaite Cumberland Sausage, and is the proud possessor of a Royal Warrant from the Queen.

BOOTLE

7 miles S of Ravenglass on the A595

This ancient village is particularly picturesque and quaint. The river Annas flows beside the main road and then dives under the village on its way to the sea. High up on **Bootle Fell**, to the southeast of the village, lies one of the best stone circles in Cumbria. Over the years, many of the 51 stones that make up the **Swinside Stone Circle** have fallen over. When it was originally constructed and all the stones were upright, it is likely, as they were also close together, that the circle was used as an enclosure.

SILECROFT

10 miles S of Ravenglass off the A595

Perhaps of all the villages in this coastal region of the National Park, Silecroft is the perfect example. Just a short walk from the heart of the village is the beach, which extends as far as the eye can see. On the horizon lies the distant outline of the Isle of Man. There is also a Site of Special Scientific Interest close by, a tract of coastal scrubland which provides the perfect habitat for the rare Natterjack toad.

MILLOM

13 miles S of Ravenglass on the A5093

This small and peaceful town

Millom Church and Castle

stands at the mouth of the River Duddon with the imposing **Black Combe Fell** providing a dramatic backdrop. Originally called Holborn Hill, the present-day name was taken from nearby **Millom Castle** which is now a private, working farm. Like many neighbouring towns and villages in Furness, Millom was a small fishing village before it too grew with the development of the local iron industry. **Millom Folk Museum** tells the story of the town's growth and there is also a permanent memorial here to Norman Nicholson (1914-1987) who is generally regarded as the best writer on Lakeland life and customs since Wordsworth himself. Nicholson's book *Provincial Pleasures* records his affectionate memories of Millom, the town where he spent all his life. Other displays include a full-scale reproduction of a drift and cage from nearby Hodbarow mine. South of Millom, at Haverigg, is the **RAF Millom Museum** situated in the former

---

68   QUIET COTTAGE

Haverigg, nr Millom

Quiet Cottage is a cosy self-catering cottage close to the beach, an RSPB sanctuary and an RAF Museum.

🛏 *see page 180*

---

69   BANKFIELD HOUSE COUNTRY HOUSE & RESTAURANT

Kirkstanton, nr Millom

Set in 5 acres of beautiful countryside, **Bankfield** has earned its fine reputation for good wholesome food and comfortable, characterful accommodation.

🛏 🍴 *see page 181*

70 THE VICTORIA HOTEL

Drigg

The **Victoria** is a friendly hotel a mile from the coast, with good home cooking and excellent rooms for B&B

 see page 182

71 STRANDS HOTEL

Nether Wasdale, nr Santon Bridge

Strands Hotel offers great hospitality, great food and comfortable B&B rooms in a picturesque village close to Scafell and Wast Water.

 see page 183

72 THE LION & LAMB HOTEL

Gosforth

The **Lion & Lamb** is both a convivial local meeting place and a comfortable B&B base for tourists.

 see page 184

Officers Mess. Visitors to the site will find a fascinating collection of over 2,000 photographs of the wartime activities of the RAF in the area, various artefacts connected with the period and a number of items recovered from local crash sites. The museum also has a fine collection of aero engines including a Rolls Royce Merlin, a Westland Whirlwind helicopter, the cockpit section of a De Havilland Vampire jet trainer and an example of the HM14 or Flying Flea. The Duddon Estuary is an important site for wildlife, and the RSPB site at **Hodbarrow** is home not only to birds but to many kinds of flora and fauna. **Hodbarrow Beacon**, which still stands, was built in 1879 as a lighthouse to assist vessels taking iron ore from the mines to destinations in Europe.

HOLMROOK

2 miles N of Ravenglass on the A595

Situated on the banks of the River Irt, where it is possible to fish for both salmon and sea trout, this small village also lies on the Ravenglass and Eskdale Railway line. Though the village Church of St Paul is not of particular note, inside there is not only a 9th-century cross of Irish style but also memorials to the Lutwidges, the family of Lewis Carroll.

DRIGG

2 miles N of Ravenglass on the B5343

The main attractions here are the sand dunes and the fine views across to the Lakeland mountains

and fells. There is an important nature reserve, **Drigg Dunes**, on the salt marshes that border the River Irt but – take note, adders are common here. The reserve is home to Europe's largest colony of black-headed gulls.

SANTON BRIDGE

3 miles NE of Ravenglass off the A595

The churchyard of **Irton Church**, reached from Santon Bridge via an unclassified road, from the Holmebrook to Santon Bridge road, offers the visitor not only superb views of the Lakeland fells to the west but also the opportunity to see a beautiful Celtic Cross, in excellent condition, dating from the early 9th centruy. Though the original runic inscription has been eroded away over time, the fine, intricate carving can still be seen. The Bridge Inn here plays host each November to the 'World's Biggest Liar' competition (see Gosforth below).

SEASCALE

4 miles N of Ravenglass on the B5343

One of the most popular seaside villages in Cumbria, Seascale enhanced its resort status in 2000 by restoring the **Victorian Wooden Jetty** to mark Millennium Year. Stretching out into the Irish Sea, it provides the starting point for many walks, including the Cumbrian Coastal Way which passes along the foreshore. This fine sandy beach enjoys views over to the Isle of Man and the Galloway Mountains of Scotland while, behind the village, the entire length of the western Lakeland hills presents an impressive panorama.

Two Victorian buildings stand out: the **Water Tower**, medieval in style and with a conical roof, and the old **Engine Shed** which is now a multi-purpose Sports Hall.

GOSFORTH

5 miles N of Ravenglass on the A595

On the edge of this picturesque village, in the graveyard of **St Mary's Church**, stands the tallest ancient cross in England. Fifteen feet high, the **Viking Cross** towers above the huddled gravestones in the peaceful churchyard. Carved from red sandstone and clearly influenced by both Christian and pagan traditions, the cross depicts the crucifixion, the deeds of Norse gods and Yggdrasil, the World Ash Tree that Norsemen believed supported the universe. The interior of the church also contains some interesting features. There's a **Chinese Bell**, finely decorated with Oriental imagery, which was captured in 1841 at Anunkry, a fort on the River Canton, some delightful carved faces on the chancel arch and a collection of ancient stones the most notable of which dates from Saxon times and depicts the Lamb of God trampling on the serpents of pagan faith.

A major attraction in this appealing village is **Gosforth Pottery**, where Dick and Barbara Wright produce beautifully crafted work and also give pottery lessons.

To the east of Gosforth runs Wasdale, the wildest of the Lake District valleys but easily accessible

by road. The road leads to **Wast Water**, which is just 3 miles long but is the deepest lake in England. The southern shores are dominated by huge screes some 2,000 feet high that plunge abruptly into the lake; they provide an awesome backdrop to this tranquil stretch of water. A lake less like Windermere would be hard to find, as there are no motorboats ploughing their way up and down the lake. This is very much the country of walkers and climbers, and from here there are many footpaths up to some of the best fells in Cumbria.

Wasdale Head, just to the north of the lake, is a small, close-knit community with a far-famed Inn that has provided a welcome refuge for walkers and climbers since the mid-1800s who have been out discovering Wasdale and the lake. **Wasdale Church** is claimed to be the smallest in England – although this title is hotly disputed by Culbone in Somerset and Dale Abbey in Derbyshire. The church was built in the 14th century and it is hidden away amidst a tiny copse of evergreen trees. Local legend

Viking Cross, Gosforth

73 GOSFORTH HALL HOTEL

Gosforth

Gosforth Hall is a grand 17th century residence offering first-class accommodation, excellent food and drink and wonderful Western Lakes hospitality.

see page 185

74 THE WHITE MARE

Beckermet, nr Calder Bridge

The **White Mare** is a convivial country hotel, inn and restaurant in a quiet village a short drive from the sea.

see page 186

suggests that the roof beams came from a Viking ship and it is certainly true that until late Victorian times, the church had only an earth floor and few seats.

As well as the deepest lake and the smallest church, Wasdale also boasts the highest mountain, **Scafell Pike** (3,205 feet) – and the world's biggest liars. This latter claim goes back to the mid-1800s when Will Ritson, 'a reet good fibber', was the publican at the inn. Will enthralled his patrons with tall stories of how he had crossed foxes with eagles to produce flying foxes and had grown turnips so large he could hollow them out to make a comfortable residence. In the same spirit, the 'World's Biggest Liar' Competition takes place every November, usually at the Bridge Inn at Santon Bridge, when contestants from all over the country vie in telling the most enormous porkies.

Sca Fell, about a mile away, is 'only' 3,162 feet, though getting from one to the other by a direct route isn't straightforward. The easiest routes are either via Lord's Rake on the Wasdale side or by

Egremont Castle

descending and then re-ascending via Foxes Tarn on the Eskdale side.

CALDER BRIDGE
7 miles N of Ravenglass on the A595

From this small 19th-century settlement there is an attractive footpath to **Calder Abbey**. It was founded by monks of Savigny in 1134 but amalgamated with the Cistercians of Furness Abbey when it was ransacked by the Scots a few years later. After the Dissolution the monastery buildings lapsed slowly into the present-day romantic ruin. Part of the tower and west doorway remain, with some of the chancel and transept, but sadly these are unsafe and have to be viewed from the road. Monk's Bridge, the oldest packhorse bridge in Cumbria, was built across the River Calder for the monks. To the northeast of the village, the River Calder rises on Caw Fell.

EGREMONT
12 miles N of Ravenglass on the A595

This pretty town is dominated by **Egremont Castle** with walls 20 feet high and an 80 feet tower. It stands high above the town, overlooking the lovely River Ehen to the south and the marketplace to the north. The castle was built between 1130 and 1140 by William de Meschines on the possible site of a former Danish fortification. The most complete part still standing is a Norman arch that once guarded the drawbridge entrance. Nearby is an unusual four-sided sundial and the stump of the old market cross dating from the early 13th century. The Castle grounds are now a park to be enjoyed by the townspeople, open from early morning to dusk.

Egremont's prosperity was based on the good quality of its local iron ore, and in the **Florence Mine Heritage Centre** visitors can join an underground tour and discover why the miners became known as the Red Men of Cumbria. Jewellery made from the ore can be bought at the **Lowes Court Gallery**, in Main Street. It is housed in an 18th century listed building and was established in 1972 to promote the appreciation of the visual arts in Cumbria. The Gallery aims to show high-standard traditional and contemporary arts and crafts by emerging and established artists from Cumbria and bordering counties. In September every year the town celebrates its **Crab Fair**. Held each year on the third Saturday in September, the Fair dates back more than seven centuries – to 1267 in fact, when Henry III granted a Royal Charter for a three-day fair to be held on 'the even, the day and the morrow after the Nativity of St Mary the Virgin'. The celebrations include the 'Parade of the Apple Cart' when a wagon loaded with apples is driven along Main Street with men on the back throwing fruit into the crowds. Originally, the throng was pelted with crab apples – hence the name Crab Fair – but these are considered too tart for modern taste, so nowadays more palatable

varieties are used. The festivities also feature a greasy pole competition (with a pole 30 feet high), a pipe-smoking contest, wrestling and hound-trailing. The highlight, however, is the **World Gurning Championship** in which contestants place their heads through a braffin, or horse collar, and vie to produce the most grotesque expression. If you're toothless, you start with a great advantage!

WHITEHAVEN

The first impression of Whitehaven is of a handsome Georgian town, but it was already well established in the 12th century as a harbour used by the monks of nearby St Bees Priory. After the Reformation the land was acquired and developed by the Lowther family in order to expand the coal industry. Whitehaven's growth in those years was astonishing by the standards of the time – it mushroomed from a hamlet of just six thatched cottages in 1633 to a sizeable, planned town with a population of more than 2,000 by 1693. Its 'gridiron' pattern of streets, unusual in Cumbria, will be familiar to American visitors, and the town boasts some 250 listed buildings. By the mid-1700s, Whitehaven had become the third-largest port in Britain, its trade based on coal and other cargo business, including importing tobacco from Virginia, exporting coal to Ireland, and transporting emigrants to the New World. When the large iron steamships arrived,

75 THE RED LION HOTEL

Egremont
The **Red Lion** is a friendly place that's open all day for drinks, lunchtime and dinner for meals and all year round for B&B accommodation.

🍴 🛏 *see page 187*

•

A legend concerning the castle is related in Wordsworth's poem, The Horn of Egremont. Apparently, a great horn hanging in the castle could only be blown by the rightful lord. In the early 1200s the rightful lord, Eustace de Lucy, was on a Crusade to the Holy Land together with his brother Hubert. The dastardly Hubert arranged with local hit men to have Eustace drowned in the Jordan. Hubert returned to Egremont, but during the celebration feast to mark his inheritance a mighty blast on the horn was heard. The hit men had reneged on the deal: Eustace was still alive. Hubert prudently retired to a monastery.

•

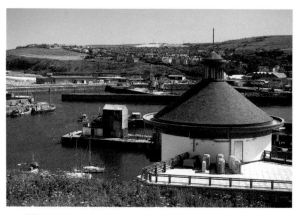

Whitehaven

76   THE BEACON

Whitehaven

Home to the town's museum collection, there is also a changing exhibition programme

 see page 191

museum's collection, is one of the masterpieces of English glass-making and is probably the finest example of its kind in existence. Also here are the **Harbour Gallery**, with an ongoing arts programme, and the **Met Office Gallery**, where visitors can monitor, forecast and broadcast the weather. They can also learn about the 'American Connection' and John Paul Jones' attack on the town in 1778, or settle down in the cinema to watch vintage footage of Whitehaven in times past. John Paul Jones had been an apprentice seaman at Whitehaven before going to the New World, where he became well known in the War of Independence. In 1777 he became Captain of the privateer *The Ranger* and led a raid on Whitehaven with the intention of firing the ships in the harbour. Thwarted by light winds, the party raided the fort and spiked the guns, then managed to damage only three ships before retreating under fire. The museums at The Beacon trace the social, industrial and maritime heritage of the area.

however, the harbour's shallow draught halted expansion and the port declined in favour of Liverpool and Southampton. For that reason much of the attractive harbour area – now full of pleasure craft and fishing smacks – and older parts of the town remain largely unchanged.

The harbour and its environs have been declared a Conservation Area, and here visitors will find **The Beacon**, where, through a series of innovative displays, the history of the town and its harbour are brought to life. Looking a bit like a small lighthouse, the museum deals with the history of the whole of Copeland (the district of Cumbria in which Whitehaven lies) with special emphasis on its mining and maritime past. The displays reflect the many aspects of this harbour borough with a collection that includes paintings, locally-made pottery, ship models, navigational instruments, miners' lamps and surveying equipment. The Beilby 'Slavery' Goblet, part of the

There's more history at **The Rum Story**, which tells the story of the town's connections with the Caribbean. The display is housed in the original 1785 shop, courtyards, cellars and bonded warehouses of the Jefferson family, the oldest surviving UK family of rum traders. Visitors can learn about the various processes involved in the making of rum, travel through realistic re-creations of far-off villages, and experience the sights, sounds and smells of life on board the trading ships, many of which participated in a trade then considered acceptable but nowadays, of course, abhorrent: the trade in human 'cargo', or slaves.

As well as the elegant Georgian buildings that give the town its air of distinction, there are two fine parish churches that are worth a visit. Dating from 1753, **St James' Church** has Italian ceiling designs and a beautiful Memorial Chapel (dedicated to those who lost their lives in the two World Wars, and also the local people who were killed in mining accidents) while the younger **St Begh's Church**, which was built in the 1860s by EW Pugin, is striking with its sandstone walls. In the graveyard of the parish church of **St Nicholas** is buried Mildred Gale, the grandmother of George Washington. In 1699, this widow and mother of three married George Gale, a merchant who traded from Whitehaven to Maryland and Virginia. Her sons were born in Virginia but went to school in Appleby. When their mother died they returned to Virginia; one of them, Augustin, became the father of George Washington, first President of the United States.

Whitehaven is interesting in other ways. The grid pattern of streets dating back to the 17th century gives substance to its claim to be the first planned town in Britain. Many of the fine Georgian buildings in the centre have been restored and **Lowther Street** is a

particularly impressive thoroughfare. Also of note is the **Harbour Pier** built by the canal engineer John Rennie and considered to be one of the finest in Britain. There is a fascinating walk and a nature trail around **Tom Hurd Rock**, above the town.

AROUND WHITEHAVEN

ST BEES

3 miles S of Whitehaven on the B5343

St Bees Head, a red sandstone bluff, forms one of the most dramatic natural features along the entire coast of northwest England. Some 4 miles long and 300 feet high, these towering, precipitous cliffs are formed of St Bees sandstone, the red rock that is so characteristic of Cumbria. Far out

77 THE MANOR HOUSE INN & COAST 2 COAST BAR

St Bees

The **Manor House Inn & Coast 2 Coast Bar**: a super family welcome, real ales, great food and en suite guest bedrooms.

see page 188

South Head, St Bees

59

78 HARTLEYS BEACH
SHOP

St Bees

Open daily for snacks, beverages and superb ice cream, **Hartleys Beach Shop** is one of the most popular snacking places in the whole region.

 see page 189

An anonymous resident of St Bees has also achieved fame of a kind. In 1981, archaeologists excavating a ruined chapel discovered a lead-lined coffin containing one of the best preserved medieval bodies in England. It was the corpse of a local lord who had died during the Crusades. Some of the artefacts including a shroud and hair found with the body can be seen in St Bees Church, together with pictures of the body and the setting in which it was found.

to sea, on the horizon, can be seen the grey shadow of the Isle of Man and, on a clear day, the shimmering outline of the Irish coast. From here the 190-mile **Coast-to-Coast Walk** starts on its long journey across the Pennines to Robin Hood's Bay in North Yorkshire.

Long before the first lighthouse was built in 1822, there was a beacon on the headland to warn and guide passing ships away from the rocks. The present 99 feet high lighthouse dates from 1866-7, built after an earlier one was destroyed by fire.

St Bees Head is now an important **Nature Reserve** and the cliffs are crowded with guillemots, razorbills, kittiwakes, gulls, gannets, and skuas. Bird watchers are well provided for with observation and information points all along the headland. There is a superb walk of about 8 miles along the coastal footpath around the headland from St Bees to Whitehaven. The route passes Saltam Bay and Saltam Pit, which dates from 1729 and was the world's first undersea mineshaft. The original lamp house for the pit has been restored and is now used by HM Coastguard.

St Bees itself, a short walk from the headland, is a small village which lies huddled in a deep, slanting bowl in the cliffs, fringed by a shingle beach. The village is a delightful place to explore, with its main street winding up the hillside between old farms and cottages. It derives its name from St Bega, daughter of an Irish king who, on the day she was meant to marry a Norse prince, was miraculously transported by an angel to the Cumbrian coast.

According to legend, on Midsummer Night's Eve, St Bega asked the pagan Lord Egremont for some land on which to found a nunnery. Cunningly, he promised

Norman Doorway, Priory Church, St Bees

60

her only as much land as was covered by snow the following morning. But on Midsummer's Day, 3 square miles of land were blanketed white with snow, and here she founded her priory. (Incidentally, this 'miracle' snowfall is a not an uncommon feature of a Cumbrian summer on the high fells.)

The Priory at St Bees grew in size and importance until it was destroyed by the Danes in the 10th century: the Benedictines later re-established the priory in 1129. **The Priory Church of St Mary and St Bega** is all that is now left, and although it has been substantially altered there is still a magnificent Norman arch and a pre-Conquest, carved Beowulf Stone on a lintel between the church and the vicarage, showing St Michael killing a dragon. The most stunning feature of all is much more modern, a sumptuous Art Nouveau metalwork screen. In the south aisle is a small museum.

Close by the church are the charming Abbey Cottages and **St Bees School** with its handsome clock-tower. The original red sandstone quadrangle bears his coat-of-arms and the bridge he gave to the village is still in use. Among the school's most famous alumni is the actor and comedian Rowan Atkinson, creator of the ineffable Mr Bean. St Bees School was founded in 1583 by Edmund Grindal, Archbishop of Canterbury under Elizabeth I, and the son of a local farmer.

CLEATOR MOOR

3 miles SE of Whitehaven on the B5295

The name of this once-industrial town derives from the Norse words for cliff and hill pasture. Cleator developed rapidly in the 19th century because of the insatiable demand during the Industrial Revolution for coal and iron ore. As the Cumbrian poet Norman Nicholson wrote:

> *From one shaft at Cleator Moor*
> *They mined for coal and iron ore.*
> *This harvest below ground could show*
> *Black and red currants on one tree.*

Cleator is surrounded by delightful countryside, and little evidence of the town's industrial past is visible. There is, however, a thriving business nearby – the **Kangol Factory Shop** in Cleator village which stocks a huge range of hats, scarves, bags, caps and golf wear.

ENNERDALE BRIDGE

7 miles E of Whitehaven off the A5086

Wordsworth described Ennerdale's church as 'girt round with a bare ring of mossy wall' – and it still is. The bridge here crosses the River Ehen, which, a couple of miles upstream runs out from **Ennerdale Water**, one of the most secluded and inaccessible of all the Cumbrian lakes. The walks around this tranquil lake and through the quiet woodlands amply repay the slight effort of leaving the car at a distance.

79   GROVE COURT HOTEL

Cleator

Grove Court is a beautifully appointed hotel in a former village school, with great food and excellent B&B rooms.

see page 190

80   THE SHEPHERDS ARMS HOTEL

Ennerdale Bridge

The **Shepherd Arms Hotel** is a lovely place for a drink and a meal, and a pleasant base for w a walking or touring holiday

see page 191

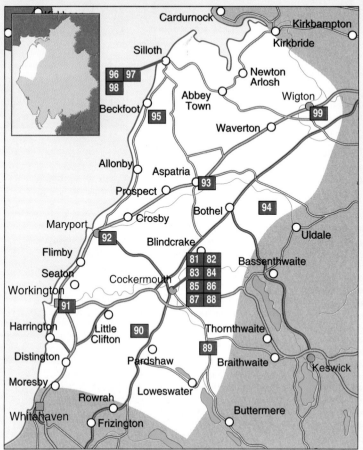

The North Cumbrian Coast

The North Cumbrian coast, from Workington in the south to the Solway Firth in the north, is one of the least-known parts of this beautiful county but it certainly has a lot to offer. It is an area rich in heritage, with a network of quiet country lanes, small villages, old ports, and seaside resorts. The coast's largest town, Workington, on the site of a Roman fort, was once a large port, prospering on coal, iron and shipping. It later became famous for fine-quality steel, and though its importance has declined, it is still the country's largest producer of railway lines. Further up the coast is Maryport, again a port originally built by the Romans.

However, Maryport has not gone down the industrial route to the extent of its neighbour and, as well as being a quaint and picturesque place, it is also home to a fascinating museum dedicated to the town's maritime past. A short distance inland lies Cockermouth on the edge of the Lake District National Park, a pretty market town with some elegant Georgian buildings. However, most visitors will be more interested to see and hear about the town's most famous son, the poet William Wordsworth, who was born here in 1770.

The northernmost stretch of coastline, around the Solway Firth, is an area of tiny villages with fortified towers standing as mute witness to the border struggles of long ago. These villages were the haunt of smugglers, wildfowlers, and half-net fishermen. What is particularly special about this coastline is its rich birdlife. The north Cumbrian coast was also the setting for Sir Walter Scott's novel *Redgauntlet*, and the fortified farmhouse by the roadside beyond Port Carlisle is said to be the 'White Ladies' of the novel.

Maryport

81 THE KINGFISHER INN

Cockermouth

The **Kingfisher** is a traditional town inn serving excellent food in the bar, the dining room or in the secluded riverside garden.

see page 192

82 WELLINGTON JERSEYS ICE CREAM & THE OLD STACKYARD TEA ROOMS

Cockermouth

Superb ice cream, hot and cold snacks and meals, local produce and crafts: all available at **Wellington Farm** in a lovely rural setting.

see page 193

83 ROOK GUEST HOUSE

Cockermouth

Rook Guest House provides an excellent B&B base close to the Castle.

see page 194

COCKERMOUTH

Cockermouth fully earns its designation as a 'gem town' recommended for preservation by the Department of the Environment. A market town since 1226, Cockermouth has been fortunate in keeping unspoilt its broad main street, lined with trees and handsome Georgian houses, and dominated by a statue to the Earl of Mayo. The Earl was Cockermouth's MP for ten years from 1858 before being appointed Viceroy of India. His brilliant career was brutally cut short when he was stabbed to death by a convict at a prison settlement he was inspecting on the Andaman Islands.

But Cockermouth boasts two far more famous sons. Did they ever meet, one wonders, those two young lads growing up in Cockermouth in the 1770s, both of them destined to become celebrated for very different reasons? The elder boy was Fletcher Christian, who would later lead the mutiny on the *Bounty*; the younger lad was William Wordsworth, born here in 1770 at Lowther House on Main Street, an imposing Georgian house now maintained by the National Trust. Now known as **Wordsworth House**, it was built in 1745 for the Sheriff of Cumberland and then purchased by the Earl of Lowther; he let it to his land agent, John Wordsworth, William's father. All five Wordsworth children were born here, William on 7th April

1770. Many of the building's original features survive, among them the staircase, fireplace, and fine plaster ceilings. A few of the poet's personal effects are still here and the delightful walled garden by the River Cocker has been returned to its Georgian splendour. The garden is referred to in *The Prelude*.

Wordsworth was only eight years old when his mother died and he was sent to school at Hawkshead, but later he fondly recalled walking at Cockermouth with his sister Dorothy, along the banks of the rivers Cocker and Derwent to the ruined castle on the hill. Built in 1134 by the Earl of Dunbar, **Cockermouth Castle** saw plenty of action against Scottish raiders (Robert the Bruce himself gave it a mauling in 1315), and again during the Wars of the Roses; in the course of the Civil War it was occupied by both sides in turn. Mary, Queen of Scots, took refuge at the castle in 1568 after her defeat at the Battle of Langside. Her fortunes were so low that she was grateful for the gift of 16 ells (about 20 yards) of rich crimson velvet from a wealthy merchant. Part of Cockermouth Castle is still lived in by the Egremont family; the remainder is usually only open to the public during the Cockermouth Festival in July.

Opposite the Castle entrance, **Castlegate House** is a fine Georgian house, built in 1739, which hosts a changing programme of monthly exhibitions of the work of Northern and Scottish artists - paintings, sculptures, ceramics and glass. To the rear of the house is a charming walled garden that is open from time to time during the summer.

Jennings Brewery offers visitors a 90-minute tour which ends with the option of sampling some of their ales – Cumberland Ale, Cocker Hoop or the intriguingly named Sneck Lifter. The last independent brewing company in Cumbria, Jennings have been brewing traditional beers since the 1820s. Today there are more than 100 Jennings pubs across the north of England. In addition to the tours, Jennings has a shop selling gifts and leisure wear, the latter boldly emblazoned with the names of its various brews.

A short walk from the Brewery brings you to the **Kirkgate Centre**,

Cockermouth Castle

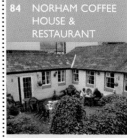

84 NORHAM COFFEE HOUSE & RESTAURANT

Cockermouth

Norham Coffee House & Restaurant is a popular for customers of all ages, with a day-long menu of tasty home-cooked dishes.

see page 194

85 THE BUSH HOTEL

Cockermouth

Well-kept Jennings Ales head the list of refreshments at the **Bush Hotel**, a friendly, lively drinking place in the centre of town.

see page 195

86 ALFIE'S CAFÉ

Cockermouth

Alfie's is a friendly, bustling café serving a good range of snacks, meals and hot and cold drinks.

see page 196

87 JUNIPERS RESTAURANT & CAFÉ BAR

Cockermouth

A magnet for all lovers of good food and a great place to meet for a drink.

¶   see page 196

88 GRAYSONSIDE

Cockermouth

In the heart of the Cumbrian countryside, **Graysonside** offers quality, space and comfort with the bonus of glorious views.

⊨   see page 197

which is housed in a converted Victorian primary school. Run by volunteers, the Centre offers a wide range of events and activities including live music, amateur and professional drama, films, dance, workshops, exhibitions of art and local history.

Two visitor attractions stand either side of Wordsworth House in the Main Street. The **Printing House Museum** occupies a building dating back to the 16th century and follows the progress of printing from its invention by Johann Gutenberg in 1430 to the end of the letterpress era in the 1960s, when computers took over. On display is a wide range of historical presses and printing equipment, the earliest being a Cogger Press dated 1820. Visitors are offered the opportunity to gain hands-on experience by using some of the presses to produce cards or keepsakes.

Just south of the town, the Lakeland Sheep & Wool Centre provides an introduction to life in the Cumbrian countryside with the help of a spectacular visual show, numerous breeds of sheep and a wide variety of exhibits. The Centre also hosts indoor sheepdog trials and sheep-shearing demonstrations.

AROUND COCKERMOUTH

BRIGHAM

2 miles W of Cockermouth off the A66

St Bridget's Church, which was probably founded as part of a nunnery, contains many interesting features, including pre-Norman carved stones, a rare 'fish window' and a window dedicated to the Reverend John Wordsworth, son of William and vicar of Brigham for 40 years. One of the tombs in the graveyard is that of Charles Christian, the father of Fletcher Christian, the *Bounty* mutineer. Fletcher himself was baptised in the church on the day of his birth, as it was thought unlikely that he would survive.

BRIDEKIRK

2 miles N of Cockermouth off the A595

The village **Church** contains one of the finest pieces of Norman sculpture in the country, a carved font with a runic inscription and a mass of detailed embellishments. It dates from the 12th century and the runic inscription states that:

> *Richard he me wrought*
> *And to this beauty eagerly me brought.*

Richard himself is shown on one side with a chisel and mallet. Not only is this a superb example of early English craftsmanship but it is exceedingly rare to find a signed work. Ancient tombstones stand round the walls of this cruciform church and inside it has unusual reredos of fleur-de-lys patterned tiles.

HIGH & LOW LORTON

5 miles SE of Cockermouth on the B5289

The yew tree that Wordsworth wrote about in his poem *Yew Trees* is still there, behind the village hall of High Lorton. It was in the shade of its branches that the Quaker George Fox preached to a large gathering under the watchful eye of Cromwell's soldiers. In Low Lorton, set beside the River Cocker, is **Lorton Hall** (private) which is reputed to be home to the ghost of a woman who carries a lighted candle. Less spectral guests in the past have included King Malcolm III of Scotland, who stayed here with his queen while visiting the southern boundaries of his Kingdom of Strathclyde of which this area was a part.

EAGLESFIELD

2 miles SW of Cockermouth off the A5086

This small village was the birthplace of Robert Eaglesfield, who became confessor to Queen Philippa, Edward III's Queen. He was also the founder of Queen's College, Oxford, where he was buried in 1349. Even more famous is **John Dalton**, who was born here in 1766. The son of Quaker parents, Dalton was teaching at the village school by the time he was 12. Despite having had no formal education himself, he became one of the most brilliant scientists, naturalists, and mathematicians of his age and was the originator of the theory that all matter is composed of small indestructible particles called atoms. He was also the first to recognise the existence of colour blindness. He suffered from it himself, and in medical circles it is known as Daltonism.

A memorial to the remarkable John Dalton now marks the house where he lived in Eaglesfield.

WORKINGTON

The largest town on the Cumbrian coast, Workington stands at the mouth of the River Derwent and on the site of the Roman fort of **Gabrosentum**. Its prosperity was founded on the three great Cumbrian industries – coal, iron and shipping. As early as 1650 coal was being mined here and, by the end of the 18th century, Workington was a major port exporting coal as well as smelting iron ore. Many of the underground coal seams extended far out to sea. In later years, Workington became famous for its fine quality steel, especially after Henry Bessemer developed his revolutionary steel-making process here in 1850. The seat of the Curwen family for over 600 years, **Workington Hall** has an interesting history. Originally built around a 14th-century pele tower, the hall was developed over the years with extensive alterations being made in the 18th century by the then-lord of the manor, John Christian Curwen. Now a stabilised ruin, it has several commemorative plaques which give a taste of the hall's history.

John Christian Curwen travelled throughout Britain and Europe to research and develop a better and more profitable way of farming. His results were adopted worldwide and are still being used today

The most famous visitor to Workington was Mary, Queen of Scots, who sought refuge here when she fled from Scotland in

89   THE OLD VICARAGE

Low Lorton

The Old Vicarage is a small, friendly country house hotel set in wooded grounds in the lovely Vale of Lorton.

see page 198

90   THE OLD POSTING HOUSE

Cockermouth

A 300-year-old hostelry, extended and modernised to provide excellent eating and accommodation.

see page 199

91   THE TRAVELLERS REST

Workington

Families are made very welcome at the **Travellers Rest**, a really happy pub on Workington's High Street.

see page 197

The Theatre Royal in Workington was built by John Smith in 1845. In the 1920s it became the town's first cinema. Local people called it 'pennymacs'. This closed in the 1930s although the 'Playgoers' bought the theatre and continue giving regular performances.

1568. She stayed for a few days, during which time she wrote the famous letter to her cousin Elizabeth I bemoaning her fate, 'for I am in a pitiable condition ... having nothing in the world but the clothes in which I escaped,' and asking the Queen 'to have compassion on my great misfortunes'. The letter is now in the British Museum.

Workington's **Church of St John the Evangelist** is a very grand affair built at enormous expense in 1823 to give thanks for the defeat of Napoleon at Waterloo. It is a copy of St Paul's, Covent Garden, and its walls were built with stones from the local Schoose and Hunday quarries. The interior was splendidly restored by Sir Ninian Comper in 1931. St Michael's is the ancient parish church, restored after a fire in 1994.

The **Helena Thompson Museum**, situated on Park End Road, is a fascinating place to visit with its displays telling the story of Workington's coal-mining, shipbuilding and iron and steel industries for which the town became internationally renowned. The Georgian Room gives an insight into the variety of decorative styles which were popular between 1714 and 1830, with displays of beautiful cut-glass tableware, porcelain from China and period pieces of furniture. Bequeathed to the town by the local philanthropist Miss Helena Thompson, MBE, JP, the museum was opened in 1949 and contains

some of her own family heirlooms. One particularly interesting exhibit is the Clifton Dish, a locally-produced 18th-century piece of slipware pottery, while further displays demonstrate the links between this local industry and the famous Staffordshire pottery families. Fashion fans will be interested in the display of women's and children's dresses from the 1700s to the early 1900s, together with accessories and jewellery.

The centre of Workington has been transformed in a major redevelopment scheme. Among the many new features is an intriguing interactive mechanical clock that moves and chimes between 9am and 10pm.

Workington is at the start of the C2C cycle route that runs to Sunderland and Newcastle. A short distance south of town is **Harrington Reservoir Nature Reserve**, a haven for wildlife with a rich variety of wild flowers, insects, butterflies, birds and animals. To the north, behind the ultra-modern Dunmail Park Shopping Centre, **Siddick Ponds** is another important wildlife site, with a wide variety of wildlife throughout the year, butterflies, dragonflies and small mammals.

NORTH AND EAST OF WORKINGTON

MARYPORT

6 miles NE of Workington on the A596

Dramatically located on the Solway Firth, Maryport is a charming

Alauna Roman Earthworks, Maryport

92 THE LAKE DISTRICT COAST AQUARIUM

Maryport

A fascinating collection of local fish, shellfish and invertebrates. A cafe, gift shop and amusements make this an ideal day out.

 see page 200

Cumbrian coastal town rich in interest and maritime history. The old part is full of narrow streets and neoclassical, Georgian architecture that contrast with sudden, surprising views of the sea. Some of the first visitors to Maryport were the Romans, who built a clifftop fort here, **Alauna**, which is now part of the Hadrian's Wall World Heritage Site. The award-winning **Senhouse Roman Museum** tells the story of life in this outpost of the Empire. Housed in the striking Naval Reserve Battery, built in the 1880s, the museum holds the largest collection of Roman altars from a single site in Britain. Other highlights include a reconstruction of the shrine from the fort's headquarters and interpretive panels describing the fort, the Roman coastal defences and the Senhouse family – it was John Senhouse of Netherall who started the collection way back in the 1570s. Modern Maryport dates from the 18th century when another Senhouse, Humphrey, a local landowner, developed the harbour at what was then called Ellenfoot to export coal from his mines, and named the new port after his wife, Mary. Over the next century it became a busy port as well as a ship-building centre; boats had to be launched broadside because of the narrowness of the harbour channel. The town declined, along with the mining industry, from the 1930s onwards. It nevertheless attracted the artist LS Lowry, who was a frequent visitor and loved painting the harbour. Today Maryport is enjoying a well-earned revival, with newly restored Georgian quaysides, clifftop paths, sandy beaches and a harbour with fishing boats.

The town's extensive maritime history is preserved in the vast array of objects, pictures and models on display at the **Maritime Museum** overlooking the harbour,

93 BRANDRAW HOUSE

Aspatria

Brandraw House is a friendly B&B home-from-home in a quiet setting above the Ellen Valley.

see page 200

94 SNITTLEGARTH LODGES

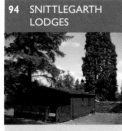

Snittlegarth, Ireby, Wigton

Snittlegarth Lodges provide luxurious self-catering accommodation in a quiet rural setting of woods, walks and wildlife.

see page 201

sited on the first plot of land developed by the Senhouse family when they created the new town and the harbour. Housed in another of Maryport's more interesting and historic buildings, the former Queen's Head public house, the museum tells of the rise and fall of the harbour and docks. Other exhibits include a brass telescope from the *Cutty Sark* and the town's connections with the ill-fated liner, the *Titanic*, and with Fletcher Christian, instigator of the mutiny on the *Bounty*. The *Titanic* was part of the fleet of the White Star Line, which was founded by a Maryport man, Thomas Henry Ismay. Fletcher Christian was also a local man, being born at Brigham, near Cockermouth in 1764.

Close to the Maritime Museum in Maryport is the **Lake District Coast Aquarium** where a series of 45 spectacular living habitat re-creations introduce visitors to the profusion of marine life found in the Solway Firth – thornback rays (which can be touched), some small sharks, minuscule sea horses, colour-changing cuttlefish, spider crabs and the comically ugly tompot blenny among them. Open all year, the Aquarium also has a gift shop and a quayside café that enjoys superb views of the harbour and the Solway.

DEARHAM

7 miles NE of Workington off the A594

This village has a very beautiful church with open countryside on three sides. The chancel of **Dearham Church** is 13th century,

and the church has a fortress tower built for the protection of men and beasts during the Border raids. There are also some interesting relics within the church including the Adam Stone, dating from AD 900, which depicts the fall of man (with Adam and Eve hand in hand above a serpent), an ancient font carved with mythological beasts, a Kenneth Cross showing the legend of the 6th-century hermit brought up by seagulls, and a magnificent wheel-head cross carved with Yggdrasil, the Norse Tree of the Universe.

ASPATRIA

14 miles NE of Workington on the A596

Lying above the shallow Ellen Valley, Aspatria's main interest for most visitors lies in the elaborate **Memorial Fountain** to 'Watery Wilfred', Sir Wilfred Lawson MP (1829-1906), a lifelong crusader for the Temperance Movement and International Peace. According to one scribe, writing about Sir Wilfred Lawson, 'No man in his day made more people laugh at Temperance meetings.'

Also worth a visit is the much-restored **Norman Church** that is entered through a fine avenue of yew trees. Inside are several ancient relics including a 12th-century font with intricate carvings, a Viking hogback tombstone, and a grave cover with a pagan swastika-like engraving. Like many other churches in the area, the churchyard contains a holy well in which it is said St Kentigern baptised his converts.

GILCRUX

10 miles NE of Workington off the A596

From this village there are particularly good views across the Solway Firth to Scotland and it is well worth visiting for the 12th-century **Church of St Mary** which is believed to be the oldest building in the district. Standing on a walled mound and with a buttressed exterior, it has a thick-walled chancel. The village is remarkable for the number of its springs, at least five of which have never failed even in the driest summers.

ALLONBY

11 miles N of Workington on the B5300

This traditional Solway village is backed by the Lake District fells and looks out across the Solway Firth to the Scottish hills. Popular with wind-surfers, the village has an attractive shingle and sand beach that received Seaside Awards in 1998 and 2005. The Allerdale Ramble and the Cumbrian Cycle Way both pass close by, and the village is also on the **Smuggler's Route** trail. Smuggling seems to have been a profitable occupation around here.

In the early 1800s, Allonby was a popular sea-bathing resort. The former seawater baths, built in 1835 and now Grade II listed buildings, still stand in the old **Market Square**. In those days, the upper floor was in popular use as a ballroom for the local nobility.

HOLME ST CUTHBERT

14 miles N of Workington off the B5300

This inland hamlet is also known as Rowks because, in the Middle Ages, there was a chapel here dedicated to St Roche. The present church dates from 1845 but it contains an interesting torso of a medieval knight wearing chain mail. Found by schoolboys on a nearby farm, the hollowed-out centre of the torso was being used as a trough. It seems to be a 14th-century piece and could be a representation of Robert the Bruce's father, who died at Holm Cultram Abbey.

Northeast of the hamlet, and enveloped among low hills, is a lovely 30-acre lake known as **Tarns Dub**, which is a haven for birdlife. A couple of miles to the southwest, the headland of **Dubmill Point** is popular with sea anglers. When the tide is high and driven by a fresh westerly wind, the sea covers the road with lashing waves.

BECKFOOT

16 miles N of Workington on the B5300

At certain times and tides, the remains of a prehistoric forest can be seen on the sand beds here and, to the south of the village, is the site of a 2nd-century Roman fort known as **Bibra**. According to an inscribed stone found here, it was once occupied by an Auxiliary Cohort of 500 Pannonians (Spaniards) and surrounded by a large civilian settlement. The small stream flowing into the sea was used in World War I as a fresh water supply by German U-boats.

Allonby still keeps much of its Georgian and early Victorian charm with cobbled lanes, alleyways and some interesting old houses. It was also an important centre for herring fishing, and some of the old kippering houses can still be seen. Allonby was the birthplace of Joseph Huddart, hydrographer and inventor of various ships' safety measures. He is buried at St Martin's in the Fields, London.

95   THE GINCASE

Mawbray Hayrigg, nr Silloth

Farmhouse tearoom, craft barn, gallery and farm park – all in one location a mile from the Solway Coast.

🏛 see page 201

96 SILLOTH CAFÉ

Silloth-on-Solway

Fish & chips head the menu at a popular café in a pleasant seaside resort.

 see page 203

97 NITH VIEW GUEST HOUSE

Silloth-on-Solway

Location, hospitality, comfort and facilities all excel at **Nith View Guest House** on the seafront at Silloth.

 see page 202

98 TANGLEWOOD CARAVAN PARK

Silloth-on-Solway

Tanglewood is a family-run caravan park in a pleasant setting a mile from Silloth.

 see page 204

SILLOTH

18 miles N of Workington on the B5300

This charming old port and Victorian seaside resort is well worth exploring. With the coming of the railways in the 1850s, Silloth developed as a port and railhead for Carlisle. The Railway Company helped to develop the town and had grey granite shipped over in its own vessels from Ireland to build the handsome church which is such a prominent landmark. The town's name is derived from 'Sea Lath' – sea because of its position and lath being a grain store, used by monks from nearby Holm Cultram Abbey.

The region's bracing air and low rainfall helped to make Silloth a popular seaside resort. Visitors today will appreciate the invigorating but mild climate, the leisurely atmosphere, and the glorious sunsets over the sea that inspired Turner to record them for posterity. The town remains a delightful place to stroll, to admire the sunken rose garden and the pinewoods and 2 miles of promenades. Silloth's 18-hole championship golf course was the home course of Miss Cecil Leitch (1891-1978), the most celebrated lady player of her day. Another keen golfer was the great contralto Kathleen Ferrier. She lived for several years in Eden Street, Silloth, above the bank where her husband was the manager. A plaque on the wall records her stay here between 1936 and 1941.

One of the most popular attractions is the **Solway Coast Discovery Centre**, where Auld Michael the Monk and Oyk the Oystercatcher guide visitors through 10,000 years of Solway Coast history.

Silloth-on-Solway

WIGTON

The pleasant market town of Wigton has adopted the title 'The Throstle Nest of all England' – throstle being the northern term for a thrush. The story is that a Wigton man returning home from the trenches of the Great War crested the hill and on seeing the familiar cluster of houses, churches, farms and the maze of streets, yards and alleys, exclaimed 'Awa' lads, it's the throstle's nest of England.'

For centuries Wigton has been the centre of the business and social life of the Solway coast and plain, its prosperity being based on the weaving of cotton and linen. It has enjoyed the benefits of a Royal Charter since 1262 and the market is still held on Tuesdays and Fridays. Horse sales are held every April (riding horses and ponies) and October (Clydesdales, heavy horses and ponies). Today, most of the old town is a Conservation Area and, particularly along the **Main Street**, the upper storeys of the houses have survived in an almost unaltered state. On street corners, metal guards to prevent heavy horse-drawn wagons damaging the walls can also still be seen.

One feature of the town that should not be missed is the magnificent **Memorial Fountain** in the Market Place. Its gilded, floriate panels are set against Shap granite and surmounted with a golden cross. It was erected in 1872 by the philanthropist George Moore in memory of his wife, Eliza Flint Ray, with whom he fell in love when he was a penniless apprentice. Bronze reliefs show four of her favourite charities – giving clothes to the naked, feeding the hungry, instructing the ignorant, and sheltering the homeless. The bronzes were created by Thomas Woolner, the pre-Raphaelite sculptor.

Wigton boasts a couple of interesting literary connections. Charles Dickens and Wilkie Collins stayed at The King's Arms Hotel in 1857, during the trip described in *The Lazy Tour of Two Idle Apprentices*, and the author and broadcaster Melvyn Bragg (now Lord Bragg) was born here. The town, often disguised as Thurston, features in several of his novels, and sequences for the television dramatisation of *A Time to Dance* were set and filmed in Wigton.

One mile south of Wigton are the scant remains of the Roman fort of **Olenacum**; most of its stones were removed to rebuild Wigton in the 18th and 19th centuries.

AROUND WIGTON

SKINBURNESS

11 miles W of Wigton off the B5302

A lively market town, in the Middle Ages Skinburness was used by Edward I in 1299 as a base for his navy when attacking the Scots. A few years later a terrible storm destroyed the town; what survived became a small fishing hamlet.

99   THE HARE & HOUNDS

Wigton
New tenants have made the **Hare & Hounds** one of Wigton's favourite spots for a drink, a snack and a meal.

see page 203

From nearby **Grune Point**, the start of the **Allerdale Ramble**, there are some tremendous views over the Solway Firth and the beautiful, desolate expanse of marshland and sandbank. Grune Point, which was once the site of a Roman fort, now forms part of a designated Site of Special Scientific Interest notable for the variety of its birdlife and marsh plants.

ABBEYTOWN

5 miles W of Wigton on the B5302

As its name suggests, Abbeytown grew up around the 12th-century **Abbey of Holm Cultram** on the River Waver and many of the town's buildings are constructed of stone taken from the Abbey when it fell into ruins. Founded by Cistercians in 1150, the Abbey bore the brunt of the constant feuds between the English and the Scots. In times of peace the community prospered and soon became one of the largest suppliers of wool in the North. Edward I stayed here in 1300 and again, in 1307, when he made Abbot Robert De Keldsik a member of his Council. After Edward's death the Scots returned with a vengeance and in 1319 Robert the Bruce sacked the Abbey, even though his own father, the Earl of Carrick, had been buried there 15 years earlier.

The final blow came in 1536 when Abbot Carter joined the Pilgrimage of Grace, the ill-fated rebellion against Henry VIII's seizure of Church lands and property. The rebellion was put down with ruthless brutality and the red sandstone **Church of St Mary** only survived because local people pointed out that the building was necessary to provide protection against Scottish raiders. It is still the parish church and was restored in 1883, a strange yet impressive building with the original nave shorn of its tower, transepts and chancel. The east and west walls are heavily buttressed, and a porch with a new roof protects the original Norman arch of the west door. Within the church buildings is a room, opened by Princess Margaret in 1973, which contains the gravestones of Robert the Bruce's father and that of Mathias and Juliana De Keldsik, relations of Abbot Robert. A fire in June 2006 destroyed the roof of the church, and it is hoped that work to replace the roof will start towards the end of 2007. Near the church there are some lovely walks along the River Waver, which is especially rich in wildlife.

NEWTON ARLOSH

5 miles NW of Wigton on the B5307

Situated on the **Solway Marshes**, the village was first established by the monks of Holm Cultram Abbey in 1307 after the old port at Skinburness had been destroyed by the sea. The village's name means 'the new town on the marsh'. Work on the church did not begin until

1393, but the result is one of the most delightful examples of a Cumbrian fortified **Church**. In the Middle Ages there was no castle nearby to protect the local population from the border raids and so a pele tower was added to the church. As an additional defensive measure, the builders created what is believed to be narrowest church doorway in the country, barely 2 feet 7 inches across and a little over 5 feet high. The 12-inch arrow-slot east window is also the smallest in England. After the Reformation, the church became derelict but was finally restored in the 19th century. Inside there is a particularly fine eagle lectern carved out of bog oak.

Fortified Church, Newton Arlosh

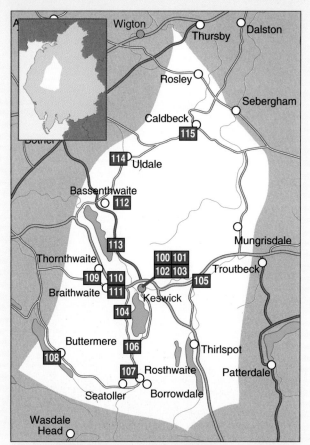

Keswick & The Northern Lakes

For many visitors this part of the county is classic Lakeland, the scenery dominated by the rounded, heather-clad slopes of the Skiddaw range to the north of Keswick, and the wild, craggy mountains of Borrowdale, to the south. Yet, despite this area's popularity, there are still many hidden places to discover and many opportunities to leave the beaten track.

The major town, Keswick, on the shores of Derwent Water, is a pleasant Lakeland town that has much to offer the visitor. The lake too, is interesting as, not only is it in a near perfect setting, but it is unusual in having some islands – in this case four. It was the view over the lake, from Friar's Crag, that formed one of John Ruskin's early childhood memories.

However, there is much more to this part of Cumbria than scenic appeal. The area is rich in history and there is frequent and significant evidence of Roman occupation. Castlerigg Stone Circle can be found here. The industrial heritage is also important, and many of the villages in the region relied on coal mining and mineral extraction for their livelihood.

But it is the wonderful, dramatic scenery that makes this area of the Lake District so special. Not only are

there several charming and isolated lakes within easy reach of Keswick, but Buttermere, considered by connoisseurs to be the best of all, lies only a few miles away. Not all the lakes, however, are what they first appear to be: Thirlmere, for example, is a 19th-century reservoir constructed to supply Manchester's growing thirst.

The Lakeland Fells are home to Herdwick sheep, one of the country's hardiest breeds. Their coarse fleece cannot be dyed, but Herdwick sheep of various ages yield wool in a variety of subtle shades of grey and black which produces an unusual and very durable tweed-like weave used for carpet-making and insulation.

Blencartha, Threlkeld

KESWICK

'Above it rises Skiddaw, majestic and famous, and at its door is Derwentwater, the lake beyond compare.'

For generations, visitors to Keswick have been impressed by the town's stunningly beautiful setting, surrounded by the great fells of Blenctathra, Saddleback, Helvellyn and Grizedale Pike.

Tourism, now the town's major industry, actually began in the mid-1700s and was given a huge boost, first by local clergyman Dr John Brown, and then by the Lakeland Poets in the early 1800s. By the 1780s the area was the most fashionable tourist destination in Europe, and the arrival of the railway in 1865 firmly established Keswick as the undisputed 'capital' of the Lake District with most of the area's notable attractions within easy reach. In a letter of 1752 Dr Brown wrote, 'The perfection of Keswick rests on three circumstances: beauty, horror and immensity.'

The grandeur of the lakeland scenery is of course the greatest draw but, among the man-made features, one not to be missed is the well-preserved **Castlerigg Stone Circle**. About a mile to the east of the town, the 38 standing stones, some of them 8 feet high, form a circle 100 feet in diameter. They are believed to have been put in place some 4,000 years ago and occupy a hauntingly beautiful position. Beautiful, but forbidding, as evoked by Keats in his poem *Hyperion*:

A dismal cirque of Druid stones,
upon a forlorn moor,
When the chill rain begins at shut of eve.
In dull November,
and their chancel vault,
The Heaven itself,
is blinded throughout night.

Keswick old town developed along the banks of the broad River Greta, with a wide main street leading up to the attractive **Moot Hall**. Built in 1813, the Hall has been at various times a buttermarket, courthouse and prison, Town Hall and now houses the Tourist Information Centre. A little further south, in **St John's Street**, the church of that name was built in the very same year as the Moot Hall and its elegant spire provides a point of reference from all around the town. In the churchyard is the grave of Sir

Keswick

Castlerigg Stone Circle

100 LITTLEFIELD

Keswick

Littlefield provides charm and hospitality for B&B guests close to the centre off Keswick.

🛏 *see page 205*

Hugh Walpole, whose once hugely popular series of novels, *The Herries Chronicle* (1930-33), is set in this part of the Lake District.

In the riverside Fitz Park is the town's **Museum & Art Gallery** which is well worth a visit not just to see original manuscripts by Wordsworth and other Lakeland poets but also for the astonishing 'Rock, Bell and Steel Band' created by Joseph Richardson of Skiddaw in the 19th century. It's a kind of xylophone made of 60 stones (some a metre long), 60 steel bars and 40 bells. Four musicians are required to play this extraordinary instrument.

Surrounded by a loop of the River Greta to the northwest of the town is a museum which must be pencilled in on any visit to Keswick. This is the **Cumberland Pencil Museum**, which boasts the 6-feet long 'Largest Pencil in the World'. The 'lead' used in pencils (not lead at all but actually an allotrope of carbon) was accidentally discovered by a Borrowdale shepherd in the 16th century, and Keswick eventually became the world centre for the manufacture of lead pencils. The pencil mill here, established in 1832, is still operating – though the wadd, or lead, is now imported.

Other attractions in the town centre include the **Cars of the Stars Museum**, ideal for movie buffs since it contains such gems as Laurel and Hardy's Model T Ford, James Bond's Aston Martin, Chitty Chitty Bang Bang, Batman's Batmobile, Lady Penelope's pink Rolls-Royce FAB 1, the Mad Max car, and Mr Bean's Mini. There are film set displays and vehicles from series such as *The Saint*, *Knightrider*, *Bergerac* and *Postman Pat*, and Del Boy's 3-wheel Reliant from *Only Fools and Horses* is here, too. **The Teapottery** makes and sells a bizarre range of practical teapots in the shape of anything from an upright piano to an Aga stove.

A short walk from the town

101 RUMOURS

Keswick

Rumours is a great place to relax, meet friends dine and drink. Open long hours every day.

🍴 *see page 206*

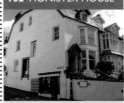

102 HONISTER HOUSE

Keswick

Honister House provides a fine B&B base in the heart of Keswick, with super breakfasts to start the day.

🛏 *see page 205*

103 LAKESIDE TEA GARDENS

Keswick

Lakeside Tea Gardens: equally popular with locals and visitors for its excellent home cooking.

 see page 207

104 THE SWINSIDE INN

Newlands Valley, Keswick

The **Swinside Inn** is an ideal place for a drink, a meal or a leisurely Lakeland holiday.

 see page 207

105 THRELKELD MINING MUSEUM

Threlkeld, nr Keswick

A fascinating museum containing artefacts from the local mines and a unique collection of mining machinery.

 see page 208

centre, along Lake Road, leads visitors to the popular **Theatre by the Lake**, which hosts a year-round programme of plays, concerts, exhibitions, readings and talks. Close by is the pier from which there are regular departures for cruises around Derwentwater and ferries across the lake to Nichol End where you can hire just about every kind of water craft, including your own private cruise boat. One trip is to the National Trust's **Derwent Island House**, an Italianate house of the 1840s on a wooded island.

Another short walk will bring the visitor to **Friar's Crag**. This famous view of Derwent Water and its islands, now National Trust property, formed one of John Ruskin's early childhood memories, inspiring in him 'intense joy, mingled with awe'. Inscribed on his memorial here are these words: 'The first thing which I remember as an event in life was being taken by my nurse to the brow of Friar's Crag on Derwentwater.' The Crag is dedicated to the memory of Canon Rawnsley, the local vicar, who was one of the founder members of the National Trust, which he helped to set up in 1895. Hardwicke Drummond Rawnsley, born at Shiplake, Oxfordshire in 1851, was a man of many parts – noted athlete at Balliol, writer, poet, traveller, vicar of Crosthwaite, Canon Carlisle, campaigner for the protection of footpaths. Keswick is host to several annual festivals, covering films, Cumbrian literature, jazz and beer. And on the first

Sunday in December a colourful 'Christmassy' Fayre is held in the Market Place.

AROUND KESWICK

GREAT CROSTHWAITE

1½ miles NW of Keswick on the A66

In the churchyard of St Kentigern stands the grave of Robert Southey (1774-1843), one of the most distinguished of the Lake Poets.

THRELKELD

3 miles E of Keswick off the A66

From Keswick there's a delightful walk along the track bed of the old railway line to the charming village of Threlkeld, set in a plain at the foot of mighty **Blencathra**. The village is the ideal starting point for a number of mountain walks, including an ascent of Blencathra, one of the most exciting of all the Lake District mountains. Also known as Saddleback and a smaller sister of Skiddaw to the west, the steep sides ensure that it looks every inch a mountain. Threlkeld is famous for its annual sheepdog trials, though its economy was built upon the several mines in the area and the granite quarry to the south. At **Threlkeld Quarry & Mining Museum** visitors can browse through the collection of vintage excavators, old quarry machinery and other mining artefacts, wander through the locomotive shed and machine shop, or join the 40-minute tour through a re-created mine. The museum has interpretive displays of Lakeland geology and quarrying, and is used as a teaching facility by several university geology departments.

Threlkeld Mining Museum has perhaps the finest collection of small mining and quarrying artefacts – everything from wedges, chisels and drills to candles, clogs and kibbles (large iron buckets used to transport ore).

MATTERDALE END

8 miles E of Keswick on the A5091

This tiny hamlet lies at one end of Matterdale, a valley that is an essential stop on any Wordsworth trail – for it was here, on April 15th 1802, that he and his sister saw that immortal

host of golden daffodils,
Beside the lake,
beneath the trees,
Fluttering and dancing in the breeze.

THIRLMERE

4 miles S of Keswick off the A591

This attractive, tree-lined lake, one of the few in the Lakes that can be driven around as well as walked around, was created in the 1890s by the Manchester Corporation. More than 100 miles of pipes and tunnels still supply the city with water from Thirlmere. At first there was no public access to the lake shore, but today these have been opened up for recreational use with car parks, walking trails and picnic places.

The creation of the huge **Thirlmere Reservoir**, 5 miles long, flooded the two hamlets of **Armboth** and **Wythburn**. All that remains of these places today is Wythburn chapel towards the southern end.

BORROWDALE

Runs S from Keswick via the B5289

'The Mountains of Borrowdale are perhaps as fine as anything we have seen,' wrote John Keats in 1818. Six miles long, this brooding, mysterious valley, steep and narrow with towering crags and deep woods, is generally regarded as the most beautiful in the Lake District. Just to the south of Derwent Water are the **Lodore Falls**, where the Watendlath Beck drops some 120 feet before reaching the lake. In woodland owned by the National Trust, lies the extraordinary **Bowder Stone** which provides an irresistible photo-opportunity for most visitors. A massive 50 feet square and weighing almost 2,000 tons, it stands precariously on one corner, apparently defying gravity. A wooden staircase on one side provides easy access to the top. South of Grange village, the valley narrows into the 'Jaws of Borrowdale'. Castle Crag, the western mandible of the Jaws, has on its summit the remains of the defensive ditches of a Romano-British fort.

From Seatoller, the B5289 slices through the spectacular **Honister Pass**, overlooked by the dramatic 1,000-feet-high Honister Crag. At the top of the pass, the 18th-century **Honister Slate Mine** has been re-opened and is once again producing the beautiful green slate that adorns so many Lakeland houses and is famous throughout the world. Buckingham Palace, The Ritz Hotel, New Scotland Yard and

Overlooking the narrow lake of Thirlmere is Helvellyn, Wordsworth's favourite mountain and one that is also very popular with walkers and climbers today. At 3,116 feet, it is one of the four Lakeland fells over 3,000 feet high, and the walk to the summit should not be undertaken lightly – but those reaching the summit will be rewarded with some spectacular views. The eastern aspect of the mountain is markedly different from the western, as it was here that the Ice Age glaciers were sheltered from the mild, west winds.

106 THE GRANGE CAFÉ

Grange in Borrowdale

The family-run **Grange Café** is equally popular with locals and visitors for its excellent home cooking.

see page 208

107 HAZEL BANK COUNTRY HOUSE

Rosthwaite, Borrowdale, Keswick

Hazel Bank offers outstanding DB&B for the house or self-catering accommodation in a glorious setting with spectacular views.

see page 209

RAF Cranwell are among the prestigious buildings donned with this stone. Helmets and lights are provided for a guided tour through great caverns of the mine to show how a mixture of modern and traditional methods is still extracting the slate which was formed here some 400 million years ago. The monks of Furness Abbey are thought to have been the first to avail themselves of Honister Slate Mine's resources, about 500 years ago. After the tour, complimentary tea or coffee is served in the Bait Cabin beside a warm fire, and the complex also has an informative Visitor Centre (honoured as the friendliest in the North of England) and a gift shop selling the ornamental green slate.

BUTTERMERE

8 miles SW of Keswick on the B5289

Half the size of its neighbour, Crummock Water, Buttermere is a beautiful lake set in a dramatic landscape. To many connoisseurs of the Lake District landscape, this is the most splendid of them all. The walk around Buttermere gives superb views of the eastern towers of **Fleetwith Pike** and the great fell wall made up of High Crag, High Stile and Red Pike.

In the early 1800s the village became involved in one of the great scandals of the age. Mary Robinson, the daughter of a local innkeeper, had been described as a maiden of surpassing beauty in J Budworth's book *A Fortnight's Ramble in the Lakes*. She became something of a local attraction, with people flocking to the inn to admire her beauty, among them Wordsworth and Coleridge. Another was a smooth-tongued gentleman who introduced himself as Alexander Augustus Colonel Hope, MP, brother of the Earl of Hopetoun. Mary fell for his charms and married him, only to discover that her husband was really John Hatfield, a bankrupt impostor and a bigamist to boot. Hatfield was tried at Carlisle for fraud, a capital offence in those days, and Coleridge supplemented his meagre income by reporting the sensational trial for the

Buttermere

Morning Post. Hatfield was found guilty and was hanged at Carlisle gaol in 1802; Mary later married a local farmer and went on to live an uneventful and happy life.

The author, broadcaster and great supporter of Cumbria, Melvyn (Lord) Bragg, tells the story of Mary Robinson in his novel, *The Maid of Buttermere*.

Standing above the village is the small, picturesque **Church of St James**, where the special features of interest include an antique organ and a memorial to Alfred Wainwright, whose ashes were scattered on his favourite place, Haystacks, a fell near Buttermere.

LOWESWATER

10 miles W of Keswick off the B5289

Reached by narrow winding lanes, Loweswater is one of the smaller lakes, framed in an enchanting fellside and forest setting. The name, appropriately, means 'leafy lake', and eons ago it was just part of a vast body of water that included what is now Crummock Water and Buttermere. Because it is so shallow, never more than 60 feet deep, Loweswater provides an ideal habitat for wildfowl, which also benefit from the fact that this is perhaps the least-visited lake in the whole of Cumbria. To the east of the lake lies the small village of the same name, while to the north stretches one of the quietest and least-known parts of the National Park, a landscape of low fells through which there are few roads or even paths.

CRUMMOCK WATER

9 miles SW of Keswick on the B5289

Fed by both Buttermere and Loweswater, this is by far the largest of the three lakes. In this less-frequented part of western Cumbria, where there are few roads, the attractions of Crummock Water can usually be enjoyed in solitude. Best seen from the top of Rannerdale Knotts, to the east, the lake has a footpath running around it – though, in places, the going gets a little strenuous.

BRAITHWAITE

3 miles W of Keswick on the B5292

This small village lies at the foot of the **Whinlatter Pass**, another of Cumbria's dramatic routes. The summit of this steep road, the B5292, is some 1,043 feet above sea level and, on the westerly descent, there are magnificent views over Bassenthwaite Lake. The road runs through the **Whinlatter Forest Park**, the only Mountain Forest in England and one of the Forestry Commission's oldest woodlands. The park offers a wide range of activities for all ages and fitness levels, from waymarked trails to cycling, orienteering or just strolling along and admiring the views. Whinlatter Forest Park boasts a Visitor Centre, adventure playground, viewpoints, gift shop and a tearoom with a terrace overlooking the woodlands and valley. Whinlatter Forest Park is the starting point for several trails suitable for the whole family.

Many of the record numbers

108 THE FISH HOTEL

Buttermere

A family-run hotel in a glorious setting, with six real ales, good food and comfortable rooms for B&B.

see page 209

109 WHINLATTER FOREST PARK

Braithwaite

The forest provides many and varied opportunities for outdoor activities, amid exceptional scenery.

see page 210

who visit the centre come to see live footage of the Lake District ospreys, beamed to a special viewing facility, or to see the birds through high-powered telescopes at the Dodd Wood viewing point. **The Lake District Osprey Project** is a partnership of the Forestry Commission, the Lake District National Park Authority and the RSPB, whose aim is to protect the nesting ospreys and to encourage other ospreys to settle and breed in other suitable locations.

BASSENTHWAITE LAKE

4 miles NW of Keswick on the A66

Only 70 feet deep and with borders rich in vegetation, Bassenthwaite Lake provides an ideal habitat for birds – more than 70 species have been recorded around the lake. Successful breeding is encouraged by the fact that no powerboats are allowed on the lake, and some areas are off limits to boats of any kind. Also, most of the shoreline is privately owned, with public access restricted mostly to the eastern shore where the Allerdale Ramble follows the lakeside for a couple of miles or so.

At the northern end of the lake, at Coalbeck Farm, **Trotters World of Animals** is home to many hundreds of animals – rare breeds, traditional farm favourites, endangered species, birds of prey and reptiles. In addition to the ring-tailed lemurs, wallabies, racoons and gibbons, there are rough-coated lemurs, lechwe antelope, red, fallow and sika deer and guanaco. Visitors to the 25-acre site can bottle-feed baby animals, cuddle bunnies, meet Monty the python, take a tractor trailer ride, watch the birds of prey demonstrations, find a quiet picnic spot or sample the fare on offer in Trotters Tea Room. And for the smaller children there's an indoor soft play climbing centre.

Winner of the Good Britain Guide Cumbria Family Attraction of the Year, as a member of the National Association of Farms for Schools Trotters can cater for school groups either for an informal day out or for a structured programme based on National Curriculum requirements.

Rising grandly above Bassenthwaite's eastern shore is **Skiddaw** which, ever since the Lake District was opened up to tourists by the arrival of the railway in the 19th century, has been one of the most popular peaks to climb. Although it rises to some 3,054 feet, the climb is both safe and manageable, if a little unattractive lower down, and typically takes around two hours. From the summit, on a clear day, there are spectacular views to Scotland in the north, the Isle of Man in the west, the Pennines to the east, and to the south the greater part of the Lake District.

Also on the eastern shore is the secluded, originally Norman, **Church of St Bridget & St Bega** which Tennyson had in mind when, in his poem *Morte d'Arthur*, he describes Sir Bedivere carrying the dead King Arthur:

Bassenthwaite Lake

> *to a chapel in the fields,*
> *A broken chancel with a broken cross,*
> *That stood on a dark strait of barren land.*

This, then, would make Bassenthwaite Lake the resting place of Excalibur but, as yet, no one has reported seeing a lady's arm, 'clothed in white samite, mystic, wonderful', rising from the waters and holding aloft the legendary sword.

Set back from the lakeside, **Mirehouse** is a 17th-century building which has been home to the Spedding family since 1688. Literary visitors to the house included Tennyson, Thomas Carlyle, and Edward Fitzgerald, the poet and translator of *The Rubaiyat of Omar Khayyam*. As well as some manuscripts by these family friends, there is also a fine collection of furniture and visitors can wander around the wildflower meadow, the walled garden and the lakeside walk. The gardens are open daily from April to October but the house, because it is still a family home, is open only on Sunday and Wednesday afternoons during the season, and also on Friday afternoons during August.

ULDALE

11 miles N of Keswick off the A591

To the northeast of Bassenthwaite Lake stretches the area known

85

114 PONDEROSA GUEST HOUSE

Uldale

Ponderosa Guest House is an ideal B&B or self-catering base for a touring or walking holiday, and a convenient stopover between England and Scotland.

see page 212

115 THE SWALEDALE WATCH

Whelpo, Caldbeck

The **Swaledale Watch** offers excellent B&B rooms on a working sheep farm surrounded by glorious unspoilt countryside.

see page 213

---

locally as the 'Land Back of Skidda', a crescent of fells and valleys constituting the most northerly part of the Lake District National Park. This peaceful region is well off the tourist track and offers visitors a delightful landscape of gently undulating bare-backed fells and valleys sheltering unspoilt villages such as Uldale. Horace Walpole featured Uldale and its moorland surroundings in two of his *Herries Chronicle* novels, *Judith Paris* and *The Fortress*. This tranquil village has one additional claim to fame: it was the daughter of an Uldale farmer who eloped with and married the legendary huntsman, John Peel (see Caldbeck).

CALDBECK

13 miles N of Keswick on the B5299

Caldbeck is perhaps the best-known village in the northern Lakes because of its associations with **John Peel**, the famous huntsman who died in 1854 after falling from his horse. He is buried in the churchyard here. His ornate tombstone is decorated with depictions of hunting horns and his favourite hound. Also buried here are John Peel's wife Mary and their four children. John Peel was Master of Hounds for over 50 years, and was immortalised by his friend John Woodcutt Graves, who worked in a Caldbeck mill making the grey woollen cloth mentioned in the song, 'D'ye ken John Peel with his coat so grey?' The tune itself is based on an old Cumbrian folk song adapted by William Metcalfe, a

chorister and organist at Carlisle Cathedral.

A few paces from Peel's tomb lies 'The Fair Maid of Buttermere', mentioned earlier, whose grave bears her married name, Mary Harrison. With its picturesque church, village green, cricket pitch, pond and blacksmith's forge, Caldbeck has all the ingredients of a picture-postcard village.

There has been a **Church** here in Caldbeck since the 12th century, one of only eight in England to be dedicated to St Kentigern. The other seven are also to be found in the north of Cumbria, where Kentigern, a bishop in the Strathclyde area of Scotland who was also known as Mungo, spent his time in exile.

Some 200 years ago Caldbeck was an industrial village, with corn mills, woollen mills and a paper mill all powered by the fast-flowing 'cold stream' – the Caldbeck. **Priest's Mill**, built in 1702 by the Rector of Caldbeck, next to his church, was a stone-grinding corn mill, powered by a waterwheel which has now been restored to working order. It is open to the public and has an accompanying Mining Museum and a collection of old rural implements. The Priest's Mill buildings are also home to a gift shop and craft workshops.

HESKET NEWMARKET

13 miles N of Keswick off the B5305

Set around a well-kept village green, this pleasing little village used to have its own market, as the name suggests, and much earlier there was probably also a racecourse here, since that is what 'Hesket' meant in Old Scandinavian. It could well be the reason why the village's main street is so wide. Although the market is no longer held, Hesket hosts two important agricultural events each year: an Agricultural Show and Sheepdog Trials. There's also a vintage motor cycle rally in May.

Charles Dickens and Wilkie Collins stayed at Hesket Newmarket in the 1850s and wrote about it in their *Lazy Tour of Two Idle Apprentices*.

MUNGRISDALE

7 miles NE of Keswick off the A66

The name of the village comes from Mungo, the name by which St Kentigern was known by those close to him, and the village church, not surprisingly, is dedicated to him. Though **St**

Kentigern's Church is believed to have been established here as early as AD 552, the present building dates from 1756 and contains a fine example of a 17th-century triple-decker pulpit. A memorial on the church wall reveals an intriguing connection with Wordsworth. The tablet commemorates Raisley Calvert whose son, also called Raisley, was 'nursed by Wordsworth'. The younger Raisley was a sculptor and friend of the poet, but fell ill of consumption (tuberculosis). Wordsworth spent many hours by his bedside in Penrith hospital but Raisley passed away in 1795, leaving in his will the huge sum of £900 to his friend. The bequest was timely and enabled the poet to complete, with his friend Coleridge, the seminal poems that were published in 1798 as the *Lyrical Ballads*.

In a converted barn at the back of the Old Crown pub in Hesket Newmarket, Hesket Brewery was set up in 1988, and beer sales, which were at first limited to the pub, soon spread across Cumbria. Many awards have come the way of Hesket Brewery beers, which include Skiddaw Special Bitter, the almost black Great Cockup Porter and the pale but potent Catbells Pale Ale.

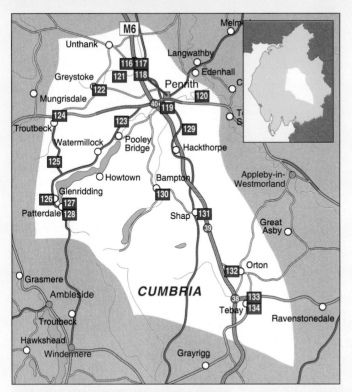

In and Around Penrith

Penrith is the most historic of Lakeland towns and was almost certainly settled long before the Romans arrived. They quickly appreciated its strategic position on the main west coast artery linking England and Scotland, and built a fort nearby, although nothing visible of it remains today. Most of the town's oldest buildings have also disappeared, victims of the incessant Border conflicts down the centuries. Penrith today is a busy place, its location close to the M6 and within easy reach not only of the Lakes but also the Border Country and the Yorkshire Dales making it a hub of this northwestern corner of England.

Only a few miles from the town, Ullswater, 8 miles long and the second longest lake in Cumbria, is also one of its most beautiful. The area around Penrith has some interesting old buildings, notably Shap Abbey and Brougham Castle, as well as two outstanding stately homes, Hutton-in-the-Forest where the Inglewood family have lived since 1605, and Dalemain, a fine mixture of medieval, Tudor and Georgian architecture which has also been inhabited by the same family for more than 300 years.

Patterdale

89

116 THE MAGIC BEAN

Penrith

A super place for enjoying the best home cooking – daytime Monday to Saturday and Saturday evening.

¶ *see page 213*

PENRITH

In Saxon times Penrith was the capital of the Kingdom of Cumbria, but after the Normans arrived the town seems to have been rather neglected – it was sacked several times by the Scots before **Penrith Castle** was finally built in the 1390s. The much-maligned Richard, Duke of Gloucester (later Richard III) strengthened the castle's defences when he was Lord Warden of the Western Marches and was responsible for keeping the peace along the border with Scotland. By the time of the Civil War, however, the castle was in a state of ruin. The Cromwellian General Lambert demolished much of what was left and the townspeople helped themselves to the fallen stones to build their own houses. Nevertheless, the ruins remain impressive, standing high above a steep-sided moat.

A short walk from the castle leads to the centre of this lively town with its charming mixture of narrow streets and wide-open spaces, such as **Great Dockray** and **Sandgate**, into which cattle were herded during the raids. Later they became market places; a market is still held every Tuesday.

Penrith has a splendid Georgian church in a very attractive churchyard, surrounded by a number of interesting buildings. The oldest part of **St Andrew's Church** dates from Norman times but the most recent part, the nave, was rebuilt between 1720 and 1722, possibly to a design by Nicholas Hawksmoor. Pevsner described it as 'the stateliest church of its time in the county'. Of particular interest is the three-sided gallery and the two chandeliers which were a gift from the Duke of Portland in 1745 – a reward for the town's loyalty during the Jacobite Rising. A tablet on the wall records the deaths of 2,260 citizens of Penrith in the plague of 1597.

The church's most interesting

Giant's Grave, Penrith

feature, however, is to be found in the churchyard, in the curious group of gravestones known as **Giant's Grave** – two ancient cross-shafts, each 11 feet high, and four 10th-century hogback tombstones which have arched tops and sharply sloping sides. They have clearly been deliberately arranged, but their original purpose is no longer known. According to a local legend the stones mark the burial place of a 5th-century King of Cumbria, Owen Caesarius. Also buried somewhere in the churchyard is Wordsworth's mother, but her grave is not marked.

Overlooking the churchyard is a splendid Tudor house, bearing the date 1563, which was at one time Dame Birkett's School. The school's most illustrious pupils were William Wordsworth, his sister Dorothy, and his future wife, Mary Hutchinson. William is also commemorated by a plaque on the wall of the Robin Hood Inn stating that he was a guest there in 1794 and again in 1795.

The **Town Hall** is the result of a 1905 conversion of two former Adam-style houses, one of which was known as Wordsworth House, as it was the home of the poet's cousin, Captain John Wordsworth.

Penrith's most spectacular visitor attraction, **Rheged Discovery Centre**, opened in Easter 2000 and dedicates itself to 'a celebration of 2,000 years of Cumbria's history, mystery and magic – as never seen before'. Named after Cumbria's Celtic

Kingdom, this extraordinary grass-covered building is also home to Britain's only exhibition dedicated to mountains and mountain adventure. It also has a giant cinema screen, speciality shops, art and craft exhibitions, restaurants and a children's play area.

The town is dominated by **Beacon Hill Pike**, which stands amidst wooded slopes high above Penrith. The tower was built in 1719 and marks the place where, from 1296, beacons were lit to warn the townsfolk of an impending attack. The beacon was last lit during the Napoleonic wars in 1804 and was seen by the author Sir Walter Scott, who was visiting Cumberland at the time. Seeing it prompted Scott to hasten home to rejoin his local volunteer regiment.

It is well worth the climb from the Beacon Edge, along the footpath to the summit, to enjoy a magnificent view of the Lakeland fells. It was on top of this hill, in 1767, that Thomas Nicholson, a murderer, was hanged. The gibbet was left on the summit and so, it is said, was Nicholson's ghost, seen in the form of a skeleton hanging from the noose.

The red sandstone from which many of Penrith's Victorian houses were built was quarried along the escarpments of Beacon Edge, and one of the old quarries, at **Cowraik**, is now a local nature reserve. In addition to the interesting variety of wildlife established down the years, it is a Site of Special Scientific Interest

117 LONSDALE BAR

Penrith

Lonsdales Bar is one of the most popular places in Penrith to meet for a drink and a meal.

🍴 see page 214

118 THE CORNER HOUSE

Penrith

Repeat visits testify to the pleasure of a stay at the **Corner House**, a lovely guest house close to the town centre.

🛏 see page 214

for the geological interest of the quarry faces. The rocks are the remnants of sand dunes formed 250 million years ago when the Eden Valley was part of a dry, sandy desert that started just north of the Equator.

AROUND PENRITH

BROUGHAM

1 mile SE of Penrith off the A66

About a mile southeast of Penrith, the substantial and imposing remains of **Brougham Castle** (English Heritage) stand on the foundations of a Roman fort. The castle was inherited in the 1640s by the redoubtable and immensely rich Lady Anne Clifford, whose patrimony as Countess of Pembroke, Dorset and Montgomery also included another five northern castles. She spent a fortune restoring them all in medieval style and, when told that Cromwell had threatened to destroy them, replied 'As often as he destroys them I will rebuild them while he leaves me a shilling in my pocket.' Brougham was Lady Anne's favourite castle and she died here in 1676 at the age of 86.

From the castle there's a delightful riverside walk to **Eamont Bridge** and the circular **Mayburgh Henge**, which dates from prehistoric times. On the huge embankment, more than 100 yards across, stands a single, large stone about 10 feet high. Close to the village, on the banks of the River Eamont, is **Giant's Cave**, the supposed lair of a man-eating giant called Isir. This local tale is linked with the legend of Tarquin, a giant knight who imprisoned 64 men in his cave and was eventually killed by Sir Lancelot. Some people also claim that Uther Pendragon, King Arthur's father, lived here and that he too ate human flesh. A nearby prehistoric earthwork has been known as **King Arthur's Round Table** for many centuries. Lady Anne also rebuilt the chapel that stands on a hill above the castle, next to **Brougham Hall**. Brougham Hall's colourful history goes back 500 years and its fame reached its height in the Victorian age, when, with its splendid appearance and its royal associations, it was dubbed 'the Windsor of the North'. The Hall today is home to a number of shops, craft workshops and a brewery. The chapel, dedicated to St Wilfred, contains a remarkable collection

Brougham Castle

of items acquired by William Brougham, later the 2nd Baron Brougham and Vaux; notable among them are French and Flemish stalls from the 16th and 17th centuries. The old parish church of Brougham is the remotely located **St Ninian's**, also known as Ninekirks, which contains some family box pews that are screened so that they look almost like cages.

MAULDS MEABURN

11 miles SE of Penrith off the A6

This charming village in the Lyvennet Valley has a large green through which the river flows, crossed by footbridges and stepping stones. As well as a fine collection of 17th and 18th-century cottages, there is also an early 17th-century Hall.

HUTTON-IN-THE-FOREST

6 miles N of Penrith on the B5305

The home of the Inglewood family since 1605, **Hutton-in-the-Forest Historic House** was originally a medieval stronghold and the **Pele Tower** still exists. Among the notable features are the 17th-century Gallery, the Hall dominated by a Cupid staircase, and a room decorated in the Arts and Crafts style. The splendid grounds include a beautiful walled garden built in the 1730s, topiary terraces that were originally laid out in the 17th century, and fine specimen trees and a 17th-century dovecote that form part of the Woodland Walk.

STAINTON

2 miles W of Penrith off the A66 or A592

At Stainton, off the A592, **The Alpaca Centre** was set up in 1997 and has become a focal point for the development and expanding knowledge of the alpaca. The Centre is a working farm: breeding, rearing and selling alpacas, and welcomes visits at any time of the year. Visitors can see the alpacas in their paddocks and browse through the goods in the Spirit of the Andes shop, mostly made from the exceptional alpaca fibre. Also at the centre are a tea room and a gallery with a collection of furniture and ornamental pieces in wood.

GREYSTOKE

5 miles W of Penrith on the B5288

According to Edgar Rice Burroughs, **Greystoke Castle** was the ancestral home of Tarzan, Lord of the Apes, a fiction which was perpetuated in the 1984 film *Greystoke*. Tarzan's aristocratic credentials would have come as something of a surprise to the dignified Barons of Greystoke, whose effigies are preserved in **St Andrew's Church**. As imposing and spacious as a cathedral, St Andrew's boasts a wonderful east window with much 13th-century glass and, in the Lady Chapel, a figure of the Madonna and Child carved by a German prisoner-of-war. About 100 yards from the church stands the plague stone where during medieval times coins were left in vinegar in exchange for food for the plague victims. An

121 THE SUN INN

Newton Reigny, nr Penrith

The **Sun Inn** is a renowned hostelry setting the highest standards of hospitality in scenic surroundings.

see page 216

122 BRATHEN

Greystoke, Penrith

Brathen is a comfortable, characterful rural base for both B&B and self-catering guests.

see page 217

Penrith

A family home, Dalemain
dates back in part to
Norman times and contains
a wealth of paintings,
ceramics and furniture.
Delightful gardens surround
the house.

 see page 217

ancient sanctuary stone, now
concealed behind a grille, marks the
point beyond which fugitives could
claim sanctuary.

Around the time of the
American War of Independence,
Greystoke Castle was bought by the
11th Duke of Norfolk, a staunch
Whig who delighted in annoying his
dyed-in-the-wool Tory neighbour,
the Duke of Portland. Portland of
course detested the American
rebels, so Norfolk built two curious
castle/farmhouses close to
Portland's estate, and named them
Fort Putnam and Bunkers Hill after
the two battles in which the British
had been trounced. Norfolk
displayed a similarly elegant disdain
for one of his tenants, a religious
bore who maintained that church
buildings were an abomination. The
Duke built a medieval-looking
farmhouse for him and crowned it
with a very ecclesiastical spire.

Greystoke village itself is a
gem, its attractive houses grouped
around a trimly maintained village
green. Nearby are the stables where
Gordon Richards trained his two
Grand National winners, Lucius
and Hello Dandy.

TIRRIL

2 miles SW of Penrith on the B5320

Like its neighbour, Yanwath, Tirril
has connections with the Quaker
Movement. At Tirril there is an old
Quaker Meeting House (now in
private ownership), while **Yanwath
Hall**, reputed to be the finest
manorial hall in England, was the
birthplace of the Quaker Thomas
Wilkinson. Modern Yanwath also
boasts an interesting gallery, located
in a cottage garden setting.

DALEMAIN

3 miles SW of Penrith off the A592

Dalemain House is one of the
area's most popular attractions – an
impressive house with a medieval
and Tudor core fronted by an
imposing Georgian façade. The
house has been home to the same
family since 1679 – Sir Edward
Hasell bought the property in that
year – and over the years they have
accumulated fine collections of
china, furniture and family portraits.
The grand drawing rooms boast
some very fine oak panelling and in
the Chinese Room is some
beautifully preserved 18th-century
Chinese wallpaper and a rococo
chimneypiece by Nathaniel Hedges
in Chinese Chippendale style;
visitors also have access to the
Nursery (furnished with toys from
all ages) and Housekeeper's Room.

The Norman pele tower at
Dalemain House displays the
regimental collection of the
Westmorland and Cumberland
Yeomanry, a troop of mounted
infantry usually led by the Hasell
family itself.

The 16th-century Great Barn
contains an interesting assortment
of agricultural bygones. The
extensive grounds include a walled
orchard with ancient apple trees, a
medieval herb garden, a Tudor-
walled knot garden with a fine early
Roman fountain, a Tudor gazebo, a
wild garden alongside Dacre Beck,
a deer park, Fell Pony Museum and
woodland and riverside walks.

DACRE

4 miles SW of Penrith off the A66

There is much of historic interest in this village. The **Church** occupies a site of a former monastery which was mentioned by the Venerable Bede in his accounts of Cumberland in the 8th century. A later reference shows that in AD 926 the Peace of Dacre was signed between Athelstan of England and Constantine of Scotland. Fragments of masonry are reputed to have come from the monastery and the four weather-beaten carvings of bears in the churchyard are probably of Anglo-Viking origin. The bears are shown, respectively, sleeping, being attacked by a cat, shaking off the cat and eating the cat.

POOLEY BRIDGE

5 miles SW of Penrith on the B5320

Wordsworth noted the curious fact that the lake creates a sextuple echo, a natural phenomenon that the Duke of Portland exploited in the mid-1700s by keeping a boat on the lake equipped 'with brass guns, for the purpose of exciting echoes'. In Wordsworth's opinion Ullswater provides 'the happiest combination of beauty and grandeur, which any of the Lakes affords' – a view with which most visitors concur.

The charming village of Pooley Bridge stands at the northern tip of **Ullswater**, and there are regular cruise departures from here during the season, stopping at Glenridding and Howton. Rowing and powered boats are available for hire, and since Ullswater is in effect a public highway, private boats can also be launched. A speed limit of 10mph applies over the whole of the 8-mile-long serpentine lake. Also, the greater part of the shoreline is privately owned and landing is not permitted.

The oldest building in Pooley Bridge is part of **Holly House**,

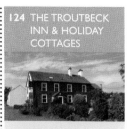

124 THE TROUTBECK INN & HOLIDAY COTTAGES

Troutbeck, Penrith

The assets of the **Troutbeck Inn** include excellent food and drink, top-notch B&B and self-catering accommodation and glorious views.

🍴 🛏 see page 218

125 THE ROYAL HOTEL AT DOCKRAY

Dockray, Matterdale, nr Penrith

The **Royal Hotel at Dockray** offers traditional hospitality, comfortable accommodation, Cask Marque ales and excellent food.

🍴 🛏 see page 219

Pooley Bridge, Ullswater

95

126 GREYSTONES COFFEE HOUSE, ART GALLERY & SELF CATERING

Greystones, Glenridding, nr Penrith

The owners of **Greystones** run a top-quality coffee shop, a fine art gallery and a separate house for a self-catering holiday.

 see page 220

127 THE WHITE LION INN

Patterdale, nr Cumbria

The **White Lion Inn** is a delightful 200-year-old hostelry with an all-day menu of home-cooked food and 7 dog friendly rooms for B&B.

 see page 219

128 DEEPDALE HALL

Patterdale, nr Penrith

Deepdale Hall offers excellent B&B or self-catering accommodation on a working farm in the lovely Deepdale Valley.

 see page 221

which dates back to 1691, while the Bridge of the village's name dates from 1763 when the elegant structure over the River Eamont was built at a cost of £400. At that time a regular fresh fish market was held in the village square. Before Bridge was added, the name Pooley meant 'pool by the hill' and was derived from the pond which existed behind **Dunmallard**, the cone-shaped hill on the other side of the River Eamont. Above the village, on the summit of Dunmallard, are the remains of an Iron Age fort and, of course, splendid views southwards over Ullswater.

WATERMILLOCK

7 miles SW of Penrith on the A592

This small village, perfectly situated on the shores of Ullswater, is hidden amongst the woodland which occupies much of the lake's western shores. About 4 miles southwest of the village, there are a series of waterfalls which tumble down through a wooded gorge and then into Ullswater. The name of the largest fall is **Aira Force** (70 feet high) and the second largest is **High Force**. They can easily be reached on foot through the woodlands of **Gowbarrow Estate**, which is owned by the National Trust. This famous waterfall, which can be viewed from stone bridges at top and bottom, was the setting for the romantic and tragic story of Emma, who fell in love with a renowned knight called Sir Eglamore. He had to leave her to follow the Crusades. As the months

lengthened into years and he had not returned, Emma became so distraught that she started to sleepwalk to Aira Force, where she eventually met her tragic death. On his return, the grief-stricken Sir Eglamore became a hermit and lived by the waterfall for the rest of his days.

GLENRIDDING

14 miles SW of Penrith on the A592

A popular base for walkers about to tackle the daunting challenge of **Helvellyn** (3,115 feet), Glenridding is the largest and busiest of Ullswater's lakeside villages. Lake cruises depart from here, rowing boats are available for hire and there's plenty of room for waterside picnics.

PATTERDALE

15 miles SW of Penrith on the A592

It is this village's magnificent setting that makes it such a popular tourist destination. Close to the head of Ullswater and with a series of fells framing the views, the scenery is indeed splendid. On the north side of the village is **St Patrick's Well**, which was thought to have healing properties. The medieval chapel dedicated to the saint was rebuilt in the 1850s.

CLIFTON

3 miles S of Penrith on the A6

One of the last battles to be fought on English soil took place at nearby **Clifton Moor** in December 1745. Bonnie Prince Charlie was in retreat and his exhausted troops were easily routed by the English forces. Eleven soldiers were killed and are buried in Clifton churchyard, but some of the wounded Highlanders were hanged from the Rebels' Tree on the outskirts of the village. The tree is a sorry sight nowadays with its gaunt, dead branches, but it is still a place of pilgrimage for the Scots.

To the southeast of the village is **Wetheriggs Country Pottery**, which was founded in 1855. Visitors can try their hand at the often messy business of throwing a pot, or they can paint a pot, paint on glass and make a candle, and also take a conducted tour of the steam-powered pottery, the only one of its kind in the UK. The pottery was designated an Industrial Monument in 1973, and has a tearoom, several shops and a pond that is home to three types of newt.

The steam engine at Wetheriggs Country Pottery was restored by none other than Fred Dibnah, the steeplejack who found fame as a broadcaster.

ASKHAM

3 miles S of Penrith off the A6

Askham is a pleasant village set around two greens. In the centre of the village is one of its most interesting shops, the **Toy Works**, which combines a traditional toy shop with a toymaker's workshop. Special services include advice on restoring rocking horses and a repair service 'for ailing and worn old teddy bears'. **Askham Fell**, which rises to the west, is dotted with prehistoric monuments

including one known as the Copt (or Cop) Stone, said to mark the burial site of a Celtic chieftain. On the edge of the village is **Askham Hall** (private), now the home of the head of the Lonsdale family, who abandoned Lowther Castle in 1936 and moved here.

LOWTHER

4 miles S of Penrith off the A6

Lowther Castle is now only a shell, most of it having been demolished in 1957, but it was clearly once a grand place: after one visit Queen Victoria is reputed to have said that she would not return to the castle as it was too grand for her. The ancestral owners of the castle were the illustrious Earls of Lonsdale, a family of statesmen and sportsmen. The most famous is perhaps the 5th Earl (1857-1944), known as the Yellow Earl because of the colour of the livery used on his private carriage. He was the first President of the Automobile Association and permitted his family colours to be used by that organisation. The yellow flag of the Lonsdales can be seen in Lowther Church. The grounds include the **Lakeland Bird of Prey Centre**, whose aim is to conserve birds of prey through education, breeding and caring for injured or orphaned birds before releasing them back into the wild.

The 5th Earl was a patron of amateur boxing; the famous Lonsdale Belt attests to his patronage and interest.

Lowther village itself was built in the 1680s by Sir John Lowther,

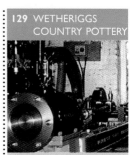

129 WETHERIGGS COUNTRY POTTERY

Clifton Dykes, Penrith

The only steam powered country pottery in the UK, Wetheriggs started life in 1855. Guided tours available.

🏛 *see page 221*

130 THE MARDALE INN
AT ST PATRICK'S
WELL

Bampton

The **Mardale Inn** combines
the best qualities of a much-
loved local with a
comfortable B&B base for
walking holidays or touring
the region.

 see page 222

131 THE HERMITAGE

Shap

The **Hermitage** is a superb
B&B with family owners,
traditional charm and high
standards of comfort and
hospitality.

 see page 223

who moved his tenants here to
improve the view from the new
house he was building. He also built
St Michael's Church where
several generations of the Lowthers
are buried in a series of magnificent
tombs beginning with a medieval
style alabaster monument to Sir
Richard, who died in 1608.
Fashions in funerary sculpture
continue through the obligatory
skull of the late 17th century to the
grandiose representation of the 1st
Viscount Lonsdale, who sits
nonchalantly with his viscount's
coronet. Later monuments show a
moustachioed Henry, Earl of
Lonsdale, in military garb, and a
charming Pre-Raphaelite plaque to
Emily, wife of the 3rd Earl, who is
depicted with her favourite dog at
her feet.

BAMPTON

8 miles S of Penrith off the A6

For several hundred years this small
village was well known for its
Grammar School, two of whose
pupils rose swiftly in the church
hierarchy. One was Hugh Curwen,
who as a Protestant became
Chaplain to Henry VIII, as a
Catholic under Queen Mary was
elevated to the Archbishopric of
Dublin, and then prudently re-
embraced Protestantism when
Elizabeth took the throne. Another
Bampton boy was less pliable:
Edmund Gibson was baptised in
the church here in 1669 and later
became a fiery Bishop of London
who repeatedly denounced the
degenerate morals of the age –
with little apparent effect.

A couple of miles south of
Bampton, **Haweswater** is the most
easterly of the lakes. It is actually a
reservoir, created in the late 1930s
to supply the growing needs of
industrial Manchester. Beneath the
water lies the village of **Mardale**
and several dairy farms for which
Haweswater Valley was once
famous. By 1940 Haweswater had
reached its present extent of 4
miles, and Manchester Corporation
set about planting its shores with
conifers. Today the area is managed
as a nature reserve and walkers
have a good chance of seeing
woodpeckers and sparrowhawks,
buzzards and peregrine falcons, and
with luck may even catch sight of
golden eagles gliding on the
thermals rising above Riggindale.
An observation is manned
throughout the breeding season if
the eagles are nesting.

Above Haweswater runs the
High Street, actually a Roman
road, which is now one of the most
popular fell walks in the Lake
District. It overlooks the remote
and lovely Blea Tarn and the lonely
valley of Martindale, a cul-de-sac
valley to the south of Ullswater,
where England's last remaining
herd of wild red deer can often be
seen.

SHAP

10 miles S of Penrith on the A6

This small village on the once-
congested A6 enjoys some grand
views of the hills. In coaching days
Shap was an important staging post
for the coaches before they tackled
the daunting climb up **Shap Fell** to

Shap Abbey

its summit some 850 feet above sea level. Much earlier, in medieval times, the village was even more significant because of nearby **Shap Abbey**, constructed in the local Shap granite which has been used in many well-known buildings, St Pancras Station and the Albert Memorial in London among them.

The Abbey stands about a mile to the west of the village, just inside the National Park, and it's well worth seeking it out to see the imposing remains of the only abbey founded in Westmorland. It was also the only one in the Lake District mountains, the last abbey to be consecrated in England (around 1199) and the last to be dissolved, in 1540. Henry VIII's Commissioners seem to have been especially thorough in their

99

Keld Chapel

132 THE NEW VILLAGE TEA ROOMS

Orton, nr Tebay

Award-winning home baking and home cooking guarantee a meal to remember at the **New Village Tea Rooms**.

see page 223

demolition of the Abbey, and local builders continued the depredations. But the mighty west tower and some of the walls remain, and they enjoy a lovely setting – secluded, tranquil and timeless.

From the Abbey there's a pleasant walk of well under a mile to **Keld**, a tiny village of just 17 houses. So quiet today, in medieval times Keld was a busy little place servicing the monks of Shap Abbey nearby. It was the monks of Shap Abbey who built the village's oldest building, the early 16th-century **Keld Chapel** (National Trust). After the closure of the Abbey, the chapel fell on hard times and for 200 years was used as a dwelling house – that's when the incongruous chimney was added. In 1860 it was 'serving as a cow-house' but was saved from this ignominious role in 1918 by the National Trust. A service is held in the tiny chapel once a year in

August; at other times, a notice on the chapel door tells you where you can obtain the key.

ORTON

15 miles S of Penrith on the B6260

By far the best approach to Orton is along the B6290 from Appleby to Tebay. This scenic route climbs up onto the moors, passing **Thunder Stone**, some mighty limestone bluffs and the pavements of **Great Asby Scar**, the setting for BBC-TV's *The Tenant of Wildfell Hall*. As motorists descend the side of Orton Scar, grand views open up of the Howgills and the Lune Gorge with the Shap Fells looming on the horizon.

A village now ('one of the prettiest in Westmorland' according to one writer), for centuries Orton was a market town of some consequence. There are reminders of Orton's former importance in the noble church tower, completed in 1504, in the attractive proportions of **Petty Hall**, an Elizabethan house at the lower end of the village (a private residence) and the grandeur of **Orton Hall**, built in 1662 and now converted into holiday apartments.

Orton's most famous visitor was Bonnie Prince Charlie, on his way northwards after the crushing defeat of his troops at Derby. He was followed soon afterwards by the Duke of Cumberland, 'Butcher' Cumberland, the victor of the

Battle of Culloden. The Duke may have stayed in the village at an inn that was later re-named the Cumberland Hotel. The Inn, dating from 1632, still stands in the centre of the village, although it is now a private house.

The village church, in common with many in the Eden Valley, has a massive 16th-century tower built for defensive purposes and, presumably, was one place that the villagers sought shelter. Its features include an ancient oak parish chest and a stained glass window by Beatrice Whistler, wife of the American artist James McNeill Whistler. Orton was the birthplace of George Whitehead (1636-1723) who, along with George Fox, was one of the founders of the Quaker Movement.

TEBAY

17 miles S of Penrith, by Exit 38 of the M6

At one time a sheep-farming area and a railway settlement, this long rambling village now owes its importance to the arrival of the M6 motorway, Cumbria's main thoroughfare. The village was the home of Mary Baynes, the **Witch of Tebay**, who died in 1811 at the age of 90. She is said to have foretold the coming of fiery horseless carriages speeding across Loups Fell where, today, the London-to-Glasgow railway line runs. Greatly feared by the people of Tebay, she is said to have withered and died at the same time as some eggs on which she had placed a curse were fried in boiling fat.

133 THE OLD SCHOOL

Tebay

The **Old School** is warmly recommended for its comfortable B&B accommodation and unbeatable hospitality.

🛏 *see page 225*

134 THE CROSS KEYS INN

Tebay

The **Cross Keys** is a comfortable roadside inn with well-kept real ales, goods wholesome food and good-value B&B accommodation.

🍴 🛏 *see page 224*

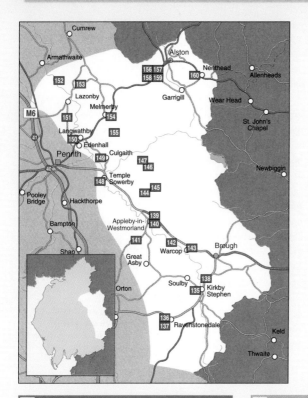

The Eden Valley & East Cumbria

The River Eden is entirely Cumbrian and is one of the few large rivers in England that flows northwards. The source of the river is on the high limestone fells above Mallerstang Common, near the North Yorkshire border, and it runs to the outskirts of Carlisle where it turns sharply east and flows into the Solway Firth. For much of its course, the river is accompanied by the famous Settle-Carlisle Railway, a spectacularly scenic route saved from extinction in the 1960s by the efforts of local enthusiasts.

Carved through boulder clay and red sandstone and sandwiched between the Lakeland fells and the northern Pennines, the Eden Valley is green and fertile – in every sense another Eden. But the valley was vulnerable to Scottish raids in medieval times and the number of pele towers and castles in the area are testament to a turbulent and often violent past.

This, too, is farming country and many of the ancient towns and villages have a market place. Appleby-in-Westmorland, the old county town of Westmorland, had an important market and also an annual horse fair that continues today and has gained a large following.

An attractive man-made feature of the valley is the collection of specially commissioned stone sculptures known as Eden Benchmarks dotted along its length. Each created by a different sculptor, they have been located beside public paths and, since they also function as seats, provide the perfect setting in which to enjoy the valley's unspoilt scenery. There are 10 of them in all, beginning with Mary Bourne's *Water Cut*, an intriguing limestone sculpture, shaped rather like a tombstone riven from top to bottom by a serpentine space representing the river. It stands on Lady Anne's Way, a public path along the eastern ridge of the Mallerstang Fells.

Pendragon Castle Ruins, Outhgill

103

KIRKBY STEPHEN

Surrounded by spectacular scenery, the old market town of Kirkby Stephen lies at the head of the beautiful Eden Valley. It was the Vikings who first established a village here and they named it 'Kirke and Bye'. Although essentially part of the Eden Valley, Kirkby Stephen has a strong Yorkshire Dales feel about it. Indeed, the church, with its long, elegant nave, has been called the Cathedral of the Dales.

Dating from Saxon times,

rebuilt in 1220 and with a 16th-century tower, the **Parish Church** is one of the finest in the eastern fells, dominating the northern end of the town from its elevated position. Until the last century the **Trupp Stone** in the churchyard received money from local people every Easter Monday in payment of church tithes and, at 8 o'clock, the curfew is sounded by the **Taggy Bell**, once regarded by local children as a demon. Inside the church are a number of pre-Conquest stones, some of which show Norse influence. The most remarkable is the 10th-century

River Eden, Kirkby Stephen

Loki Stone, one of only two such carvings in Europe to have survived. Loki was a Norse God; presumably the Viking settlers brought their belief in Loki to Kirkby Stephen. The carving of Loki shows a figure resembling the Devil with sheep's horns, whose legs and arms are bound by heavy irons, an image symbolising the overpowering of paganism by Christian beliefs. For many years the stone lay undiscovered, reused as a building stone. The church also boasts some interesting memorials, among them the Elizabethan tomb of Thomas, Lord Wharton and his two wives, and the earlier memorial to Sir Richard de Musgrave of Hartley Castle, who died in the early 1400s. Sir Richard was the man reputed to have killed that last boar upon Wild Boar Fell, and the story was given credence when, some years ago, the tomb was opened to reveal the bones of a man and woman alongside two tusks from a boar. The splendid pulpit, given by the town in memory of a much-loved vicar, is made of Shap granite and Italian marble.

Between the church and the market square stand the cloisters, which served for a long time as a butter market. The **Market Square** is surrounded by an ancient collar of cobblestones which marked out an area used for bull-baiting – a 'sport' that ceased here in 1820 after a disaster when a bull broke loose. The market, still held every Monday, has existed since 1351 and has always been a commercial focus

for the surrounding countryside. In the 18th century, knitting – mostly of stockings – was the most important product of the town. A restored spinning gallery reflects the importance of the woollen industry.

Close to Kirkby Stephen are three spectacular railway viaducts. Merrygill, with 9 arches, and Podgill, 11 arches, were on the long-forgotten Stainmore Railway that linked Darlington with Tebay and Penrith. Smardale Gill viaduct, 90 feet high with 14 arches, is on the gloriously scenic Seattle-Carlisle line. All three viaducts are in the care of the Northern Viaduct Trust.

AROUND KIRKBY STEPHEN

OUTHGILL

5 miles S of Kirkby Stephen on the B6259

This remote village has close links with the Clifford family of Skipton Castle, North Yorkshire. The village **Church of St Mary**, first built in 1311, was repaired by Lady Anne Clifford who, from 1643 when she finally obtained possession of the Clifford estates, devoted her life to restoring her many properties and lived in each of them for varying periods of time. Her estates included six castles – Skipton and Barden in Yorkshire, and Appleby, Brough, Brougham and Pendragon in Westmorland. Lady Anne's zeal for restoration didn't stop at castles: she also repaired the Roman road

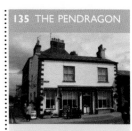

135 THE PENDRAGON

Kirkby Stephen

The **Pendragon** has won many friends, both locals and visitors, with its tasty home cooking.

see page 225

136 WESTVIEW & OAKLEA

Ravenstonedale

Westview and Oaklea offer luxurious B&B and self-catering accommodation in an idyllic setting.

see page 226

137 STOUPHILL GATE

Ravenstonedale

A friendly and homely retreat for B&B and self-catering guests in a glorious setting.

see page 226

between Wensleydale and the Eden Valley, a route she often travelled (along with a huge retinue) between her castles and her birthplace at Skipton. The route is now known as Lady Anne's Way but in times past it was aptly called the **High Way** since it was a regular place of employment for highwaymen such as Dick Turpin and William 'Swift' Nevison.

To the south is **Wild Boar Fell**, a brooding, flat-topped peak where the last wild boar in England was reputedly killed, while tucked down in the valley are the romantic ruins of Lammerside and Pendragon Castles.

Pendragon Castle, about a mile north of the village, is shrouded in legend but there are claims that it was the fortress of Uther Pendragon, father of King Arthur. If so, nothing remains of that 6th-century wooden castle. The present structure dates from the 1100s and was built by Hugh de Morville, one of the four knights who murdered Thomas à Becket, to guard the narrow pass of **Mallerstang**. Twice it was burned by the Scots and twice restored, on the latter occasion by the formidable Lady Anne Clifford in 1660. Another mile or so downstream, **Lammerside Castle** dates from the 12th century, though only the remains of the keep survive. They can be found along a bridle path between Pendragon and Wharton Hall.

RAVENSTONEDALE
5 miles SW of Kirkby Stephen on the A685

Known locally as Rissendale, this pretty village of stone-built cottages clustered along the banks of **Scandal Beck** lies on the edge of the Howgill Fells. The parish **Church of St Oswald** dates to 1738 and is especially interesting. An earlier church, built on the same site, had a separate bell tower that rested on pillars; at its centre hung a refuge bell. Anyone guilty of a capital offence who managed to escape to Ravenstonedale and sound the bell was free from arrest by the King's officials. This custom was finally abolished during the reign of James I.

Ravenstondale's Church of St Oswald is one of the few Georgian churches in Cumbria. The present church, surrounded by yew trees, is well worth a visit. It features bow pews facing one another, a three-decker pulpit complete with a sounding board and, at the back of the third deck, a seat for the parson's wife. The window at the east end of the Church of St Oswald commemorates the last woman in England to be put to death for her Protestant faith. Elizabeth Gaunt was sentenced in 1685 by the notorious Judge Jeffreys to be burnt at the stake for sheltering a fugitive rebel. She met her end at Tyburn in London.

NATEBY
2 miles S of Kirkby Stephen on the B6269

Now a quiet hamlet of houses standing alongside a beck, for

centuries Nateby was dominated by **Hartley Castle**. Believed to have been built in the 13th century, the castle was the home of Sir Andrew de Harcala, a renowned soldier during the reign of Edward II. Harcala was one of the first men to fight on a pony and he was made Earl of Carlisle in recognition of his services to the Crown. However, his failure to prevent Robert the Bruce invading the north of England led him to be accused of treason and he was executed in 1325. His castle was finally demolished by the Musgrave family, who used the stone to build their manor house at Edenhall near Penrith.

CROSBY GARRETT

4 miles W of Kirkby Stephen off the A685

Local legend has it that the Devil, seeing all the stones lying ready to build **Crosby Garrett Church**, carried them in his leather apron to the top of a nearby hill. He reasoned that, as people grew old, they would be unable to climb the hill and attend church and thus would come to him rather than go to Heaven. Such tales apart, the church itself is said to be of Anglo-Saxon origin though the visible fabric is 12th century. Inside there are some superb carvings, particularly near the font. The church is also famous for its hagioscope, cut through the wall to allow people in the north aisle to see the altar. Near the church gates is a tithe barn, built in the 18th century to store farm produce

given to the church as a religious tax. To the west of the village a splendid viaduct on the Carlisle-Settle Railway dominates the landscape.

WINTON

3 miles N of Kirkby Stephen off the A685

This is a quiet and picturesque hamlet whose name, in old English, means 'pasture farmland'. It is built on a spring line and, like many other Cumbrian villages of medieval origin, once followed the runrig, or two-field system of agriculture. The evidence is still visible in long, thin fields to the north of the village. These would have been individual strips in medieval times: the open fields were enclosed in the 17th and 18th centuries.

In the centre of the village is the manor house, built in 1726. It was formerly a boys' school where, apparently, the boys were treated like prisoners and not allowed to return home until the end of their education in case they told of their life at the school. The oldest building is **Winton Hall**, built of stone and dated 1665, but looking older with its stone buttresses and mullion windows with iron bars.

Those taking a walk on **Winton Fell** are likely to see red grouse lifting off from the large tracts of heather on the fellside. Indeed, the wildlife is much more prolific around this area where the limestone provides more plentiful food than on the fells around the lakes.

138 THE BAY HORSE INN

Winton

The **Bay Horse** is a warm and welcoming traditional village inn with fine food and drink and two rooms for B&B guests.

see page 227

139 THE LEMON GROVE

Appleby-in-Westmorland

The **Lemon Grove** is a delightful little café/ sandwich bar open all day for tasty home cooking.

see page 229

140 THE GOLDEN BALL

Appleby-in-Westmorland

The **Golden Ball** is a cosy, friendly town centre hostelry open all day for well-kept ales and great food – also rooms for B&B.

see page 228

KABER

4 miles N of Kirkby Stephen off the A685

In 1663, this small village was the improbable focus of the **Kaber Rigg Plot**, a rebellion against Charles II led by Captain Robert Atkinson of Watergate Farm in Mallerstang. The rising failed and Atkinson was hanged, drawn, and quartered at Appleby; tragically, a messenger carrying his reprieve was delayed on Stainmore and arrived too late to save Atkinson from his gruesome fate.

APPLEBY-IN-WESTMORLAND

The old county town of Westmorland, Appleby is one of the most delightful small towns in England. It was originally built by the Norman Ranulph de Meschines, who set it within a broad loop of the River Eden which protects it on three sides. The town's uniquely attractive main street, **Boroughgate**, has been described as the finest in England. A broad, tree-lined avenue, its sides are lined with a pleasing variety of buildings, some dating back to the 17th century. At either end, High Cross and Low Cross mark the original boundaries of the market. At its foot stands the 16th-century **Moot Hall**; at its head rises the great Norman Keep of **Appleby Castle** which is protected by one of the most impressive curtain walls in northern England. Now in private hands, the Castle is not currently

open to the public. During the mid-1600s, Appleby Castle was the home of Lady Anne Clifford, the remarkable woman who has already been mentioned several times and to whom Appleby has good cause to be grateful. The last of the Clifford line, the diminutive Lady Anne (she was just 4 ft 10 inches tall) inherited vast wealth and estates, among them no fewer than six northern castles. She lavished her fortune on rebuilding or restoring them all. Churches and chapels in the area also benefited from her munificence and at Appleby, in 1651, she also founded the almshouses known as the Hospital of St Anne, for '12 sisters and a Mother'. Set around a cobbled square, the picturesque cottages and minuscule chapel still serve their original function, maintained by the trust endowed by Lady Anne; visitors are welcome.

Lady Anne died in 1676 and was buried with her mother, Margaret Countess of Cumberland, in **St Lawrence's Church**. The church is well worth visiting to see their magnificent tombs and also the historic organ, purchased from Carlisle Cathedral in 1684, which is said to be oldest still in use in Britain.

Just a few years after Lady Anne's death, James II granted the town the right to hold a Fair during the week leading to the second Wednesday in June. More than 300 years later, the **Gypsy Horse Fair** is still thriving, with hundreds flooding into the little

Moot Hall, Appleby-in-Westmorland

141 THE NEW INN

Hoff, nr Appleby-in-Westmorland

Connoisseurs of real ales and lovers of good food will be happy on both counts at the **New Inn**.

see *page 229*

town (population 2,700) with caravans and horse-drawn carts. The trade, principally in horses, and the trotting races provide a picturesque and colourful spectacle.

AROUND APPLEBY-IN-WESTMORLAND

GREAT ASBY

4 miles S of Appleby-in-Westmorland off the B6260

This pretty village is set in a wooded hollow, its houses separated by **Hoff Beck**. Alongside the beck is **St Helen's Well**, and nearby are the splendid almshouses of St Helen's, built between 1811 and 1820. Across a footbridge is **Asby Hall** (in private hands), built in 1670. It was once the home of the Musgrave family of Edenhall, whose crest and coat of arms can still be seen above the door.

BROUGH

8 miles SE of Appleby-in-Westmorland on the A66/A685

This small town, standing at the point where the **Stainmore Pass** opens into the Vale of Eden, is, in fact, two settlements: **Church Brough** and **Market Brough**. Church Brough is a group of neat houses and cottages clustered around a little market square in which a maypole stands on the site of the former market cross. **Brough Castle**, built within the ramparts of the Roman camp of *Verterae*, was constructed to protect the Roman road over Stainmore Pass. The building of this Norman castle was begun by William Rufus in 1095 but it was largely destroyed in 1174 by William the Lion of Scotland. Many times Scottish raiders laid siege to Brough Castle and fierce battles were fought. An ancient ballad tells of the legendary

Gypsy Horse Fair, Appleby-in-Westmorland

142 THE SANDFORD ARMS

Sandford, nr Appleby-in-Westmorland

The **Sandford Arms** offers traditional ales, fine food and en suite accommodation in a delightful village location.

see page 229

bravery of one knight from the town who defended the tower alone after his comrades had fallen. He was finally vanquished when the Scottish army set fire to his hiding place but the incident was so dramatic that it became a part of local folklore and was remembered in the ballad of the Valiant Knight of Brough. Another fortification restored by the remarkable Lady Anne Clifford, the castle, with its tall keep 60 feet high is well worth visiting, if only for the superb panorama of the surrounding fells seen from the battlements.

Market Brough is also an ancient settlement and was particularly important in the 18th and 19th centuries when it became a major coaching town on the stagecoach routes between England and Scotland. It was on the

junction of several routes and boasted more than 10 inns. The width and breadth of its High Street also indicates its importance as a market town. Brough was granted a charter in 1330 enabling it to hold a weekly market as well as four cattle markets and an annual fair. A custom celebrated in Brough is the Twelfth Night Holly Burning, a unique festival with pagan origins.

The distinctive, low hills that lie to the west of Brough are drumlins – heaps of material deposited by Ice Age glaciers. In this area many drumlins are marked by broad, grassy ridges, remains of ancient lynchets or ploughing strips.

NORTH STAINMORE

10 miles SE of Appleby-in-Westmorland on the A66

The village lies on the Stainmore Pass which carries the old Roman road, now the A66, through a remote area of the North Pennines which David Bellamy has described as 'England's last wilderness'. Near Stainmore summit are the foundations of **Maiden Castle**, a Roman fort built to guard the pass against marauders. A few yards over the Cumbrian border, into County Durham, is the stump of the ancient **Rey Cross** which was erected before AD 946 and which, until 1092, marked the boundary between England and Scotland. It is thought to be the site of the battle at which the last Viking King of

York and North England, Eric Bloodaxe, was killed following his expulsion from the city.

WARCOP

5 miles SE of Appleby-in-Westmorland on the B6259

The largest village in this part of the Eden Valley, Warcop grew up as a crossing point of the river. The bridge, the oldest to cross the river, dates from the 16th century and the red sandstone buildings surrounding the village green, with its central maypole, make this a charming place to visit.

The **Church of St Columba** is built outside Warcop on the site of a Roman camp. An interesting building in its own right, it is particularly famous for the rush-bearing ceremony which takes place in late June each year. Warcop is surrounded by Ministry of Defence tank-firing ranges from which the public are understandably excluded, but on the hills above the village are stones, cairns and the remains of what is claimed to be a **Druid Temple**.

GREAT ORMSIDE

2 miles SE of Appleby-in-Westmorland off the B6260

This was once an important fort guarded by a pele tower, and the ancient **Church of St James**, which dates from the 11th century, occupies a site on the steep-sided defence mound. Relics of pre-Christian burials have been found in the mound, as well as a Viking sword (now in the Tullie Museum in Carlisle). A silver gilt and enamel bowl from the 8th century has also been found and is regarded as one of the most important pieces of Anglo-Saxon metalware to survive. A particularly beautiful piece, richly decorated with vine scrolls, birds and animals, it is now on permanent display in the Yorkshire Museum in York.

From the village a path leads across fields to the village of **Little Ormside**, with its large cedar tree said to have been brought back from Lebanon as a sapling by General Whitehead. On the voyage home he grew it in his hat, and shared with it his daily ration of one pint of water.

BRAMPTON

2 miles N of Appleby-in-Westmorland off the A66

This village, along with the surrounding area, was said to be haunted by the ghost of Elizabeth Sleddall, the wife of a 17th-century owner of nearby Crackenthorpe Hall. Elizabeth died believing that she had been cheated out of her share of the estate, so to shame the false inheritors her spirit was seen being driven around the countryside in a coach drawn by four black horses. Her ghost became so troublesome that the local people exhumed her body and reburied the remains under a larger boulder. Her ghost, while no longer troubling the local people, is said still to visit the Hall.

DUFTON

3 miles N of Appleby-in-Westmorland off the A66

Behind this delightful hamlet lies

143 THE HAYBERGILL CENTRE

Warcop, nr Appleby-in-Westmorland

The **Haybergill Centre** offers a unique venue for groups on courses, conferences, retreats or holidays in a spacious and environmentally timber building.

see page 230

144 THE NEW INN

Brampton, nr Appleby

The **New Inn** is an atmospheric 18th century hostelry serving local brews and an exceptional variety of excellent home cooking.

see page 231

145 MIDTOWN FARM

Dufton, nr Appleby

Midtown Farm offers luxurious, well equipped self-catering in picturesque surroundings.

see page 233

146 MILBURN GRANGE HOLIDAYS

Knock, nr Appleby-in-Westmorland

Milburn Grange Holidays are based in superb self-catering cottages in the beautiful, tranquil Eden Valley.

 see page 232

147 SLAKES FARM

Milburn, nr Appleby-in-Westmorland

Slakes Farm offers top farmhouse accommodation in a lovely quiet countryside setting.

see page 233

Dufton Gill, a beautiful, secluded wooded valley through which runs a footpath. Also from Dufton there is a track carrying the Pennine Way up to High Cup Nick, a great horseshoe precipice at the edge of the northern Pennine escarpment that was formed by a glacial lake during the Ice Age. Dufton was once a lead-mining centre under the management of the London Lead Company, who built cottages, a school and a library and supplied pipes for a reliable water supply.

LONG MARTON

3 miles N of Appleby-in-Westmorland off the A66

Visitors to this village can experience two very different forms of architecture, both of them equally impressive. The Norman village church, with its carvings of knights and monsters over the doorway, is remarkably unspoilt, while nearby the Settle-Carlisle Railway sweeps across a grand viaduct.

TEMPLE SOWERBY

7 miles NW of Appleby-in-Westmorland on the A66

Temple Sowerby prides itself on the title 'Queen of Westmorland villages', an accolade justified by its lovely setting in the Eden valley. (Here's a bonus: the average rainfall here is half that recorded in the Lake District National Park to the west.) To the north, the massive bulk of **Cross Fell**, the highest point in the Pennines, swells skywards to provide a spectacular backdrop. The village of Temple Sowerby, picturesquely grouped around a sloping green and an 18th-century red sandstone church, takes its name from the medieval Knights Templar who owned the manor of Sowerby until their Order was suppressed in 1308.

From Temple Sowerby there are delightful walks through the Eden valley or, if you prefer a gentle stroll, it's only a mile to the National Trust gardens at **Acorn**

Great Asby

Bank where **Crowdundle Beck** splashes beneath an elegant 18th-century bridge. The 16th-century manor house is now a Sue Ryder Home and not open to the public, but visitors are welcome to explore the attractive gardens planted with a collection of some 250 medicinal and culinary herbs. A circular woodland walk runs along the beck to a watermill that was first mentioned on the site as far back as the 14th century. At different times it has been a saw mill, a corn mill and a source of power for the local gypsum mines; now restored, it is open for visits. The 'Acorn Bank' itself is a stretch of of ancient oak wood sloping down to the beck.

NORTH AND EAST OF PENRITH

ARMATHWAITE

10 miles N of Penrith off the A6

Set on the western bank of the River Eden, the village has a particularly fine sandstone bridge from which there is a lovely view of **Armathwaite Castle** (private), the home of the Skelton family, one of whose forebears was Poet Laureate to Henry VIII. Close by, visitors to the **Eden Valley Woollen Mill** can see traditional looms rattling away and browse through a huge range of knitwear produced from the finest wools and mohair. The Mill offers an inexpensive making-up service and accepts commissions for pile and rag rugs. It is open daily during the season but times vary during the

winter months. Also worth seeking out in **Coombs Wood** to the south is another of the Eden Benchmarks. Entitled *Vista* and created by Graeme Mitchison, this remarkable sculpture seems to make the Lazenby Sandstone flow into liquid shapes. North of Armathwaite, the River Eden approaches Carlisle and the Solway Firth; these lower stretches of the river are surveyed in the next chapter.

EDENHALL

3 miles NE of Penrith off the A686

An old tradition asserts that in the 8th century the monks of Jarrow, fleeing from Viking invaders with the body of St Cuthbert, stopped here briefly. As a result the village church is dedicated to the saint. Part of the **Church of St Cuthbert** appears to be pre-Norman but most of the structure dates from the 1100s.

Close to the church is the **Plague Cross** which stands where there was once a basin filled with vinegar. This acted as a disinfectant into which plague victims put their money to pay for food from the people of Penrith. The plague of the 16th century killed a quarter of the village's inhabitants.

Edenhall is particularly famous for the story of the 'Luck of Eden Hall', a priceless glass cup which, according to legend, was stolen from some fairies dancing round the garden wall by a butler in the service of the Musgrave family back in the 15th century. Despite

148 THE KINGS ARMS HOTEL

Temple Sowerby, nr Penrith

The **Kings Arms Hotel** is a roomy, traditional hostelry with a relaxed atmosphere, real ales, bar and restaurant menus and ten guest bedrooms.

see page 234

149 THE BLACK SWAN INN

Culgaith, nr Penrith

The **Black Swan** is a marvellous 17th century inn providing its customers with outstanding hospitality, food, real ales and accommodation.

see page 235

150 BRIEF ENCOUNTER

Langwathby Station

An atmospheric café-
restaurant in the elegantly
restored Langwathby Station
on the Settle-Carlisle line.

see page 237

the fairies' entreaties, the butler refused to return the 6-inch high glass to them. As he departed with the precious goblet, the fairies laid a curse upon it: 'If ever this cup shall break or fall, Farewell the luck of Eden Hall.' On inspection, the glass was identified as a 13th-century chalice of enamelled and gilded glass that is thought to have come from Syria and may well have been brought back by a Crusader. It was a treasured heirloom of the Musgraves for many generations and is now in the Victoria & Albert Museum in London. The goblet is still intact, but Eden Hall has long since disappeared.

LANGWATHBY

4 miles NE of Penrith on the A686

Located on the opposite bank of the River Eden from Edenhall, Langwathby's name means 'the settlement by the long ford' and, though there are two prehistoric pathways crossing here, the name of the village and of its neighbouring settlements suggests a Viking past. Langwathby has a huge village green that still hosts maypole dancing on the third Saturday in May. The green is medieval in origin and would once have been surrounded by wood and mud houses, perhaps to protect cattle but also for defence against border raids. After the Civil War and the growth in prosperity in the late 17th century, these wattle-and-daub cottages were replaced by stone buildings. The drovers from Scotland passed through here to the market towns of England. West of

the village of Langwathby Hall Farm, Eden Ostrich World offers the chance to see these splendid birds in a farm setting in the heart of the Eden Valley. The farm is also home to rare-breed sheep, cattle and pigs, donkeys, deer, wallabies, alpacas and many other creatures from around the world. A giant maze was opened in 2001, and the farm has a tea room, gift shop, picnic areas and adventure play areas.

LITTLE SALKELD

6 miles NE of Penrith off the A686

A lane from the village leads to **Long Meg** and her Daughters, a most impressive prehistoric site and second only to Stonehenge in size. Local legend claims that Long Meg was a witch who, with her daughters, was turned to stone for profaning the Sabbath, as they danced wildly on the moor. The circle is supposedly endowed with magic so that it is impossible to count the same number of stones twice. Another superstition is that Long Meg will bleed if the stone is chipped or broken. The actual name, Long Meg, has been the subject of debate. It has been suggested that Meg may be a corruption of the word 'magus' meaning a magician.

There are more than 60 stones in the Circle (actually an oval), which is approximately 300 feet across. The tallest, Long Meg, is a 15 feet column of Penrith sandstone, the corners of which face the four points of the compass. Cup and ring symbols and spirals are carved on this stone, which is over 3,500 years old. The circle is now known to belong to the Bronze Age, but no one is certain of its purpose. It may have been used for rituals connected with the changing seasons, since the midwinter sun sets in alignment with the centre of the circle and Long Meg herself. The brooding majesty of the site was perfectly evoked by Wordsworth:

A weight of awe, not easy to be borne,
Fell suddenly upon my spirit – cast
From the dread bosom of the unknown
past,
When first I saw that family forlorn.

In 1725 an attempt was made by Colonel Samuel Lacy of Salkeld Hall to use the stones for mileposts. However, as work began, a great storm blew up and the workmen fled in terror, believing that the Druids were angry at the desecration of their temple.

It was the same Colonel Lacy who gave his name to the **Lacy Caves**, a mile or so downstream from Little Salkeld. The Colonel had the five chambers carved out of the soft red sandstone, possibly as a copy of St Constantine's Caves further down the river at Wetheral, as at that time it was fashionable to have romantic ruins and grottoes on large estates. Colonel Lacy is said to have employed a man to live in his caves, acting the part of a hermit.

Alternatively, the caves may have been intended to provide a wine store: Colonel Lacy used to entertain his guests here, and there were probably gardens around the caves. The rhododendrons and laburnums still flower every spring.

GREAT SALKELD
6 miles NE of Penrith on the B6412

The River Eden formed the boundary between the two old counties of Westmorland and Cumberland, so while Little Salkeld was in Westmorland, its larger namesake stood in Cumberland. The village is a picturesque collection of 18th-century cottages and farmhouses built in red sandstone which are typical of this area. Great Salkeld is best known for the impressive **Church** with its massive, battlemented pele tower built in the 14th century and complete with a dungeon. The Norman doorway in the porch is less than a yard wide and its arch has three rows of deeply cut zig-zags with five heads, one with a crown.

KIRKOSWALD
8 miles NE of Penrith on the B6413

The village derives its name from the **Church of St Oswald**: Oswald was the King of Northumbria who, according to legend, toured the pagan north with St Aidan in the 7th century. The church is unusual in having a detached bell tower standing on top of a grassy hill some 200 yards from the main building (this is in a valley, so the bells could not be heard by the villagers).

This once thriving market town still retains its small cobbled market place and some very fine Georgian buildings. There's also a striking ruined 12th-century **Castle**,

151 THE HIGHLAND DROVE INN

Great Salkeld, nr Penrith

The **Highland Drove Inn** is a superb place to pause for a drink, to relax over a superb meal or to stay while touring the region.

see page 236

152 CROSSFIELD COTTAGES

Staffield, nr Kirkoswald

Peace and tranquillity reign supreme at **Crossfield Cottages**, whose owners provide exceptional self-catering accommodation and exclusive fishing opportunities. Pets are welcome.

see page 237

153 HOWSCALES COTTAGES

Howscales, nr Kirkoswald

Howscales: converted farm buildings provide superb self-catering accommodation in tranquil rural surroundings.

see page 238

(formerly the home of the Featherstonehaugh family) which, although not open to the public, can be seen from the road and footpath. In 1210 a licence was received from King John to fortify the original structure and enclose the extensive park. The castle was later destroyed by Robert the Bruce in 1314 but was rebuilt and extended in the late 15th century. The whole site covered 3 acres, with the courtyard surrounded by a massive wall and a main gate with a drawbridge over the moat. The castle's splendour was due to the efforts of Thomas, Lord Dacre but, after his death in 1525, the panelling, stained glass and beamed ceilings were transferred to Naworth and the castle became a quarry. Today it is still protected by a wide moat, and the great turreted tower rises 65 feet above the remains of the vaulted dungeons.

One of Kirkoswald's most splendid buildings is the **College**, its name recalling the days when St Oswald's was a collegiate church. The two-storey house with its sloping-ended roof was originally built as a pele tower and converted into the college for priests in the 1520s. The manor house opposite has a particularly attractive entrance front in sandstone, which was added in 1696.

Just to the northwest of Kirkoswald are the **Nunnery Walks**, which start at a Georgian house built on the site a Benedictine Nunnery dating back to the time of William Rufus. Narrow footpaths have been cut into the sandstone cliffs along the

Kirkoswald Church

deep gorge of Croglin Beck, passing through beautiful woodland to reveal exciting waterfalls.

MELMERBY

9 miles NE of Penrith on the A686

Melmerby nestles at the foot of **Hartside Pass**, its spacious village green dissected by three becks. Even today, every householder in Melmerby has grazing rights on the green. Horses are grazed more commonly now, but in the past it would have been more usual to see flocks of geese – indeed, there was once a cottage industry here making pillows and mattresses from goose feathers. Overlooking the 13-acre village green is **Melmerby Hall**, a defensive tower that was extended in the 17th and 18th centuries. The village church, with its tower, is a Victorian building, but the first known rector of the church on the site came here in 1332.

From Melmerby the main road climbs out of the Eden Valley to the east and the landscape changes suddenly. The road passes Fiend's Fell, close to the highest point in the Pennine Chain, the summit of Cross Fell. Early Christians erected a cross on the highest point of the fell to protect travellers from the demons who haunted the moors. Today, a cairn marks the spot where the cross once stood.

ALSTON

18 miles NE of Penrith on the A689/A686

For a few weeks in 1999 the small town of Alston, 1,000 feet up in the Pennines, became transformed

into Bruntmarsh, the fishing village in which the fictional Oliver Twist spent his early years. To re-create the squalid conditions of the poor in early 19th-century England, production designers 'dressed down' the town, so much so that anxious visitors noticing the soot-blackened buildings enquired whether there had been a major fire.

One of the many strengths of Alan Bleasdale's re-working of the Dickens classic was the authenticity of the locations. Alston proved to be ideal, since the town centre has changed little since the late 1700s and there are many buildings even older than this.

The town has a cobbled main street and, from the picturesque **Market Cross**, narrow lanes radiating out with courtyards enclosing old houses. Many of the older buildings still have the outside staircase leading to the first floor – a relic from the days when animals were kept below while the family's living accommodation was upstairs. This ancient part of Alston is known as **The Butts**, a title acquired by the need of the townspeople to be proficient in archery during the times of the border raids.

The tall spire of **St Augustine's Church** is a well-known local landmark and its churchyard contains a number of interesting epitaphs, as well as affording wonderful views of the South Tyne Valley.

Considering its small population, Alston supports an

154 THE VILLAGE BAKERY

Melmerby

For more than 30 years the **Village Bakery** has earned worldwide acclaim for its healthy, wholesome and imaginative organic food.

see page 239

155 THE FOX INN

Ousby, nr Penrith

The **Fox Inn** is a friendly free house open every evening and Sunday lunch; it has a caravan and camping site.

see page 240

156 HARBUT LAW

Alston

Harbut Law gives guests the choice of B&B in the Victorian main house and self-catering in converted outbuildings.

see page 241

117

157 LOWBYER MANOR COUNTRY HOUSE

Alston

Lowbyer Manor is a superb country house with 9 luxurious bedrooms, superb breakfasts and lovely gardens.

 see page 241

158 THE CUMBRIAN PANTRY

Alston

A top-quality family business serving a day-long selection of cakes, pastries and hot and cold snacks.

 see page 242

159 THE CUMBERLAND HOTEL

Alston

A friendly family-run hotel at the foot of the main street, offering high standards of food, drink and accommodation.

 see page 242

Alston

astonishing diversity of shops and pubs. In addition, the town is home to a wide variety of craftspeople, ranging from blacksmiths to candlemakers, wood-turners to potters, and also boasts an outstanding art and crafts centre in the **Gossipgate Gallery**. Housed in a converted congregational church built 200 years ago and with its original gaslights still intact, this gallery is the premier centre in the North Pennines for contemporary art and craft. A programme of exhibitions runs non-stop from February to December, and in the gallery shop a huge range of artefacts is for sale, including original watercolours and prints, jewellery, glass, ceramics, sculpture

and striking turned wooden bowls made from native woods.

Another popular attraction in Alston is the **South Tynedale Railway**. This narrow-gauge (2 feet) steam railway runs regular services during the summer months and at the northern terminus of the 2½-mile long track travellers can join a stretch of the Pennine Way that runs alongside the River South Tyne. In between the station and the A686, is the **HUB Exhibition** of historic vehicles, a wealth of local images and the stories that bring them alive.

Alston Moor, to the south of the town, was once the centre of an extremely important lead mining region, one of the richest in

Britain. Lead and silver were probably mined on the moor by the Romans, but the industry reached its peak in the early 19th century when vast quantities of iron, silver, copper and zinc were extracted by the London Lead Company. A Quaker company, it was a pioneer of industrial welfare and also built the model village of Nenthead to house the miners. Here, not only were the workers and their families provided with a home, but education was compulsory and there were some public baths. **Nenthead Mines Heritage Centre** is a 200-acre site high in the hills that tells the story of the lead and zinc mining industry. One of the main visitor attractions is 'The Power of Water', an impressive interactive area that looks at the technology used, including three working water wheels that drive model machinery. Another is the Brewery Shaft with its 328 feet drop and amazing virtual stone feature.

160 NENTHEAD MINES

Nenthead, nr Alston

The largest lead mining complex in Britain, authentically preserved to provide a unique visitor attraction.

 see page 243

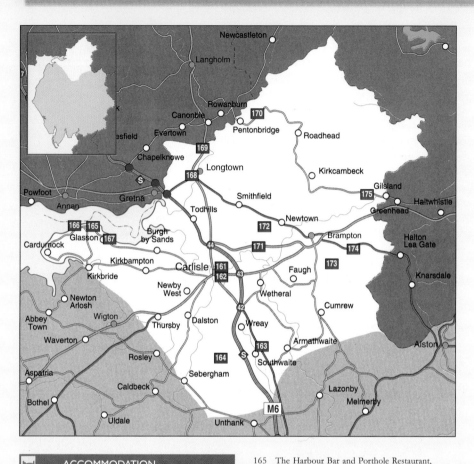

Carlisle & The Scottish Borders

For more than 350 years the area around Carlisle was known as the Debatable Lands, a lawless region where the feared Border Reivers sacked and plundered at will. Every winter, when their own food stocks were almost depleted, armed gangs from across the border would ride southwards to seize the cattle and sheep of their more prosperous neighbours. Stealing and murdering, they wreaked havoc in this area and almost every village would have had a fortified structure, usually a pele tower, where the inhabitants and their animals could hide safely. There are some 77 names on record as belonging to these disreputable Reiver families – among them the names Trotter and Maxwell – and anyone who wishes to find out if their family was involved should go to Carlisle's Tullie House Museum.

This is, too, the country of Hadrian's Wall, the most important monument built in Britain by the Romans; many stretches of the wall are still visible, and Birdoswald and other centres give an excellent insight into Roman border life. The wall was built as a great military barrier across the narrowest part of Britain, from the mouth of the River Tyne, in the east, to Bowness-on-Solway, in the west.

Guarded by forts at regular intervals, it was built between AD 122 and AD 128 following a visit by the Emperor Hadrian, who saw the then military infrastructure as insufficient to withstand the combined attacks of northern barbarians. Originally, much of the western side was built from turf, but by AD 163 this had been replaced by stone. The wall was finally abandoned in the late 4th century, and in later centuries many of the stones were used for local buildings and field walls.

There are many ways of exploring the Wall (including the bus number AD 122!), and for those with the energy to walk from end to end the newly opened Hadrian's Wall National Trail passes some of the country's greatest archaeological monuments.

Irthing Valley, Near Gilsland

CARLISLE

Carlisle's castle, cathedral, many other historic buildings, parks, thriving traditional market, shopping centres and leisure facilities all combine to endow Carlisle with the true feel of a major city. Carlisle is the largest settlement in Cumbria, with a population of around 130,000, and is also its county town. The city stands at the junction of three rivers, the Eden, the Caldew and the Petteril, and was already fortified in Celtic times when it was named Caer Lue, the 'hill fort'. It became a major Roman centre: it was the military base for the Petriana regiment, *Luguvallum*, guarding the western end of Hadrian's Wall, and also an important civilian settlement with fountains, mosaics, statues and centrally-heated homes.

According to a recent survey, if you are born in Carlisle you are more likely to stay here than the inhabitants of any other place in England.

Today, the squat outline of **Carlisle Castle** (English Heritage) dominates the skyline of this fascinating city. There has been a castle at Carlisle since 1092 when William Rufus first built a palisaded fort. The Norman Castle was originally built of wood, but, during the Scottish occupation in the 12th century, King David I laid out a new castle with stones taken from Hadrian's Wall. The 12th-century keep can still be seen enclosed by massive inner and outer walls. Entry is through a great 14th-century gatehouse, complete with portcullis, and with a maze of vaulted passages, chambers, staircases, towers and dismal dungeons. Children, especially, enjoy the legendary 'licking stones' from which parched Jacobite prisoners tried to find enough moisture to stay alive. Archaeologists working outside the castle walls unearthed the remains of three Roman forts, and many of the finds are on display in a special exhibition at the castle. Carlisle Castle is everything a real castle should be and is still the headquarters of the King's Own Royal Border Regiment, whose **Regimental Museum** is located within the castle walls. Two floors of displays include uniforms, weapons, medals, pictures, photographs and archives.

Carlisle Castle

During the Civil War the castle was besieged for eight months by the Parliamentarians under General Leslie. When the Royalists finally capitulated, Leslie began repairing the castle and the city walls. The Puritans were no respecters of Britain's ecclesiastical heritage: stones from six of the eight bays of the cathedral were used for the repairs and the building of block-houses for the Puritan troops.

Partly for this reason, **Carlisle Cathedral** is now one of the smallest cathedrals in England – yet it retains many interesting features, including an exquisite east window that is considered to be one of the finest in Europe. Below the beautifully painted wooden ceiling of the choir, with its gold star shimmering against deep blue, are the carved, canopied choir-stalls with their medieval misericords. These wonderful carved beasts and birds include two dragons joined by the ears, a fox killing a goose, pelicans feeding their young, and a mermaid with a looking glass. In St Wilfrid's Chapel is the superb 16th-century Flemish Brougham Triptych, which was originally in Cologne Cathedral. In the 19th century it was brought to Brougham Chapel near Penrith. The altar piece was later restored by the Victoria & Albert Museum in London and is now on permanent loan to Carlisle. It is a beautiful, intricate piece with delicately carved figures depicting scenes from the life of Christ.

It is hard to believe that it was here that Edward I solemnly used

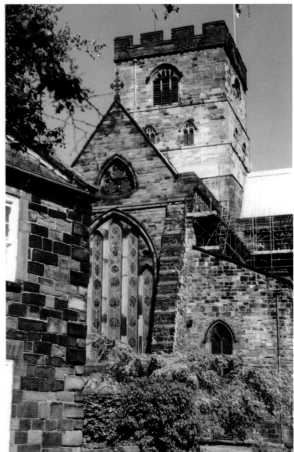

Carlisle Cathedral

bell, book and candle to excommunicate Robert the Bruce. It was here also that the church bells were rung to welcome Bonnie Prince Charlie in 1745. It is claimed that after the suppression of the Jacobite rebellion the bells were removed for their 'treason' and only replaced in the 19th century.

Carlisle Cathedral is one of the few where visitors can enjoy refreshments actually within the

161 TULLIE HOUSE MUSEUM & ART GALLERY

Carlisle

Tullie House and the nearby Guildhall are filled with fine collections covering fine and decorative arts, archaeology, local history and natural sciences.

 see page 244

precincts, in this case in the Prior's Kitchen Restaurant situated in the Fratry Undercroft. Seated beneath superb fan vaulting, customers have a good choice of home-made soups, cakes and pastries, as well as morning coffee, lunches and afternoon teas.

Although an appointment is usually necessary, a visit to the nearby **Prior's Tower** is a must. On the first floor of this 15th-century pele tower is a wonderful 45-panel ceiling incorporating the popinjay crest and arms of the Prior Senhouse. The 16th-century Prior's gatehouse leads to a narrow lane called Paternoster which is named after the prayer the monks would recite during their offices.

Like many great medieval cities, Carlisle was surrounded by walls. Guided walks and tours are available and the best view is to be found in a little street called **West**

Walls at the bottom of Sally Port Steps, near the Tithe Barn. The walls date from around the 11th century and they remained virtually intact until the 1800s.

When the castle was under siege, the **Sally Port** allowed an individual to 'sally forth'. It was later used for access to the **Tithe Barn** to avoid paying city tolls. It is unusual to find a Tithe Barn within a city wall, but this exception was probably made because of the Border raids. The barn dates from the 15th century and was used to collect and store taxes, or tithes, destined for the Priory.

Close by is **St Cuthbert's Church**, the official city church of Carlisle and where the Lord Mayor's pew can be found. Although the present building dates from 1778, there has been a church on this site since the 7th century. St Cuthbert was Bishop of Carlisle in AD 680. It is a charming Georgian building with several interesting features including a moveable pulpit on rails.

The award-winning **Tullie House Museum & Art Gallery**, in the centre of the city close to the cathedral, is certainly another place not to be missed. Through skilful and interpretive techniques the fascinating, and often dark, history of the Debatable Lands, as this border region was called, is told (see panel). One of the Museum's centrepieces is its

Tithe Barn, Carlisle

story of the Border Reivers who occupied the lands from the 14th to the 17th century. These lawless, unruly people raged interfamily warfare with each other, destroying or threatening the lives of the local people with their bloodthirsty raids. Their treacherous deeds have also added such words as 'bereave' and 'blackmail' to the English language. The horrific stories of the Reivers have been passed down through the generations in the Border Ballads, and many of the Reivers family names are still known – the museum even offers a genealogy service, so that visitors can find out if their ancestry includes any infamous forebears. What is perhaps the definitive Reiving story has been told in *The Steel Bonnets* by George MacDonald Fraser, author of the Flashman books.

The city of Carlisle dates back far beyond those desperate days, however, and Tullie House also has an extensive collection of Roman remains from both the city and the Cumbrian section of Hadrian's Wall. The Art Gallery features contemporary arts and crafts, and the spectacular underground Millennium Gallery has a stunning collection of local minerals, archaeological finds of wood and leather, artist-made glass and interactive exhibits. Old Tullie House showcases paintings and drawings by renowned Pre-Raphaelite artists, as well as other artworks and a selection of fine English porcelain.

A short walk from the Museum leads to the **Linton Visitor Centre**

in Shaddongate which provides an insight into the city's industrial heritage. Standing next to a 280 feet high chimney built in 1836 as part of what was once one of the largest cotton mills in Britain, the Centre has displays of hand-weaving on original looms, informative displays and a selection of world-famous fabrics and designer knitwear for sale.

The **Guildhall Museum**, a branch of Tullie House, is housed in an unspoilt medieval building constructed by Richard of Redeness in 1407. Originally a town house, it provides an ideal setting for illustrating the history of both the Guilds and the City. Several rooms are devoted to creating the atmosphere of trade Guilds such as the shoemakers, the butchers, the weavers and the glovers. There is a splendid early 19th-century banner of the Weavers Guild and an impressive collection of 17th and 18th century Guild silver. One of the silver bells on show is thought to be the earliest horse-racing trophy in the country. Displays also feature other items relating to the history of Carlisle and include medieval stocks and a magnificent ironbound Muniment Chest dating from the 14th century. Conducted tours of this remarkable Guildhall are available.

Not far from the Guildhall Museum is the Citadel, which is often mistaken for the Castle. In fact, this intimidating fortress with its well-preserved circular tower was built in 1543 on the orders of Henry VIII to strengthen the city's

Stanwix, Carlisle
One of the best eating places in the region, with a fine evening selection of dishes featuring the best local produce.

see page 243

defences. Much of it was demolished in the early 1800s to improve access to the city centre, but what remains is very impressive. Across the road from the Citadel is the railway station. The first railway to Carlisle opened in July 1836 and Citadel Station, which opened in 1850, was built to serve seven different railway companies whose coats of arms are still displayed on the façade. So elegant was its interior – and much of it remains – that Carlisle was known as the 'top hat' station. Today it is still an important centre of communications; InterCity trains from Glasgow and London now link with lines to Dumfries, Tyneside, West Cumbria and Yorkshire, and it is, of course, the northern terminus of the famous **Settle-Carlisle Railway** line.

One of the last great mainline railways to be built in Britain – it was completed in 1876 – the Settle-Carlisle line takes in some of the most dramatic scenery that the north of England has to offer. Scenic it may be, but the terrain caused the Victorian engineers many problems. It is only thanks to their ingenuity and skill that the line was ever finished. During the course of its 72 miles, the line crosses 20 viaducts and passes through 12 tunnels, each of which was constructed by an army of navvies who had little in the way of resources besides their strength and some dynamite to remove the rock.

Located on the northwestern edge of the city, **Kingmoor Nature Reserve** occupies an area

of moorland given to the city in 1352 by Edward III. Citizens enjoyed the right to graze sheep on the moors and to cut peat for fuel. Later, Carlisle's first racecourse was established here with annual Guild races being held up until 1850. A half-mile circular path wanders through the woodland with gentle gradients of 1 in 20 making it fully accessible to wheelchairs and pushchairs, and with seats every 100 yards or so providing plenty of resting places. Another path links the reserve to **Kingmoor Sidings**, which since the old railway sheds closed has been colonised by a wide variety of wildlife. In 1913 Kingmoor became one of the first bird sanctuaries in England, and today provides a peaceful retreat away from the bustle of the city centre.

AROUND CARLISLE

WREAY

5 miles S of Carlisle off the A6

This little village is known for its extraordinary **Church of St Mary**, designed by a local woman, Sarah Losh, in memory of her sister and her parents. It was built in 1835 and incorporates many Italian Romanesque features. The church is full of beautiful touches, including the carvings, mostly by Sarah herself, on the font.

DALSTON

4 miles SW of Carlisle on the B5299

Lying on the banks of the **River Caldew**, Dalston became a thriving centre of the cotton industry in the late 18th century, thanks to George Hodgson of Manchester, who used the river as a source of power for the flax mill and four cotton mills that were established here. The local economy was sustained still further by the creation of a forge and two corn mills.

At the eastern end of the village square stands **St Michael's Church**, believed to date back to Norman times, which can be approached via a memorial lychgate. One of the few red-brick buildings to be found in the village is the **Victorian Chapel**, which stands somewhat hidden between several Georgian houses along the village green.

There's a pleasant 2-mile circular walk along the banks of the River Caldew at Dalston.

BURGH BY SANDS

5 miles W of Carlisle off the B5307

On 7th July 1307, the body of King Edward I was laid out in the village church: he was already a dying man when he left Carlisle to march against his old enemy, Robert the Bruce. A monument to Edward was erected on the marshes and a later monument still marks the spot. At the time of the king's death, the **Church of St Michael** was already well over a century old and is possibly the earliest surviving example of a fortified church. Dating from 1181 and constructed entirely of stones from a fort on the Roman wall, the church was designed for protection against Border raids, which is why

its tower has walls seven feet thick. The tower can only be entered through a strong iron grille.

PORT CARLISLE

12 miles W of Carlisle off the B5307

At one time sailing boats could make their way by canal from Port Carlisle to the heart of the city of Carlisle. Boats were towed there, a journey that took about 1 hour 40 minutes, enabling Carlisle to be reached within a day by sea from Liverpool. The canal was later replaced by a railway which brought many Scandinavian emigrants through the village on their way to the United States and Canada. But the building of the Bowness railway viaduct altered the deep-water channels, causing Port Carlisle to silt up. The railway was eventually dismantled but its old course can still be traced and stretches of it form part of the Cumbrian Cycle Way. The stretch of the Solway coastline from Port Carlisle provided the setting for Sir Walter Scott's novel *Redgauntlet*, and the fortified farmhouse by the roadside at nearby Drumburgh is said to be the 'White Ladies' of the novel.

BOWNESS-ON-SOLWAY

14 miles W of Carlisle off the B5307

Hadrian's Wall continues along the Solway coast to Bowness, and many of the sandstone cottages around here contain stones from the Wall. Some of these stones can easily be identified, such as the small inscribed altar let into a barn near the King's Arms. The Roman fort of **Maia** once covered a 7-acre

165 THE HARBOUR BAR & PORTHOLE RESTAURANT AT THE HOPE & ANCHOR

Port Carlisle, nr Carlisle

Real ales and an across-the-board menu of home-cooked dishes in a friendly inn overlooking the Solway Firth.

see page 245

166 THE KINGS ARMS

Bowness-on-Solway

The **Kings Arms** is a delightful family-run inn at the western end of Hadrian's Wall: good food, great hospitality, B&B rooms.

see page 247

Glasson, Carlisle

In the little village of
Glasson, half a mile from
the rugged Solway coastline,
the **Highland Laddie Inn**
attracts with a good variety
of food and drink.

🍴 see page 248

site, but today there is only a plaque
explaining where it used to be.
Bowness is sometimes said to be
the end of the Wall, but in fact the
Wall just turned a corner here and
continued south along the coast for
another 40 miles.

One local story tells that, in
1626, some Scotsmen crossed the
Solway and stole the Bowness
church bells. The thieves were
spotted, chased and forced to
lighten their boats by throwing the
bells overboard. Later, the men of
Bowness crossed the Firth and, in

retaliation, seized the bells of
Middlebie, Dumfries. Two miles
south of the village lies **Glasson
Moss National Nature Reserve**,
a lowland raised mire extending to
93 hectares. Many species of
sphagnum moss are to be found
here, and the birdlife includes red
grouse, curlew, sparrowhawk and
snipe.

LONGTOWN

9 miles N of Carlisle on the A7

Situated on the north side of
Hadrian's Wall, only a couple of
miles from the Scottish border, this
is the last town in England. The
Romans occupied this land, and
they were followed by other
conquerors. The legendary King
Arthur attempted to organise the
Northern Britons against the pagan
hordes who tried to settle and
control this territory. In AD 573
the mighty battle of Ardderyd was
fought here and, according to
legend, 80,000 men were slain.

Longtown's position on the
River Esk, so close to the Scottish
border, has influenced its history
from earliest times.

Until 1750 Longtown was a
small hamlet of mud dwellings. Dr
Robert Graham, an 18th-century
clergyman, proposed the building
of the Esk bridge which was
completed in 1756, and it was this
venture that led to Longtown's
establishment as a bustling border
town. These days it has some fine
individual buildings and broad, tree-
lined terraces of colour-washed
houses.

On the outskirts of Longtown

Part of Hadrian's Wall

is **Arthuret Church**. The earliest records of the church date from 1150 and it was originally served by the monks of Jedburgh. But it is thought that the earliest church here may have been founded by St Kentigern in the 6th century; recent research has led some to believe that King Arthur was actually interred here after his last battle, Camboglanna, was fought a few miles east of Longtown at Gilsland. The present church, dedicated to **St Michael and All Angels**, was built in 1609, financed by a general collection throughout the realm which James I ordered after a report that the people of Arthuret Church were without faith or religion. The people that he referred to, of course, were the infamous Reivers, ungoverned by either English or Scottish laws.

Archie Armstrong, favourite Court Jester to James I and later to Charles I, is buried in the churchyard, which also contains an unusual stone cross. It consists of two parts of an early medieval wheel-head cross clamped together onto a tapering shaft with 19th-century decorations.

BEWCASTLE

14 miles NE of Carlisle off the B6318

Roman legionaries assigned to the fort at what is now Bewcastle must certainly have felt that they had drawn the short straw. The fort stood all on its own, about 9 miles north of Hadrian's Wall, guarding a crossing over the Kirk Beck. The site covered around 6 acres and most of it is now occupied by the ruins of a **Norman Castle**. Most of the south wall is still standing but little else remains and the castle is best admired for its setting rather than its architecture. An impressive survival in the village churchyard is the **Bewcastle Cross**, erected around AD670 and one of the oldest and finest stone crosses in Europe.

WETHERAL

4 miles E of Carlisle off the A69

Wetheral stands above the **River Eden**, over which runs an impressive railway viaduct, carrying the **Tyne Valley Line**, which was built by Francis Giles

Bewcastle Cross

168 THE SYCAMORE TREE CAFÉ

Longtown, nr Carlisle

The **Sycamore Tree Café** is open every day except Wednesday for breakfast, morning coffee, lunch and afternoon tea.

🍴 see page 247

169 MARCH BANK HOTEL & THE SPORTSMAN'S RESTAURANT

Scotch Dyke, north of Longtown (A7)

March Bank is a Victorian villa set in mature gardens, with comfortable rooms for B&B and an excellent restaurant.

🛏 🍴 see page 249

170 LIDDEL PARK

Catlowdy, Penton, Carlisle

Liddel Park offers excellent self-catering accommodation in a pleasant woodland setting.

🛏 see page 249

171 CROSBY LODGE COUNTRY HOUSE HOTEL & RESTAURANT

High Crosby, Crosby-on-Eden
Crosby Lodge ranks among the top country house hotels in the region, with outstanding service, food and accommodation.

⊨ ▯ see page 250

in 1830. Wetheral **Parish Church** lies below the village beside the river and contains a poignant sculpture by Joseph Nollekens of the dying Lady Mary Howard clasping her dead baby. Nearby, occupying a lovely riverside setting, is another of the **Eden Benchmarks**, a sculptured bench in St Bee's sandstone by Tim Shutter, entitled *Flight of Fancy*.

St Constantine was the local patron and the church is dedicated to the Holy Trinity, St Constantine and St Mary. Constantine is said to have lived in caves in what are now National Trust woodlands alongside the river, a location known as **Constantine's Caves**. (The caves were also used later by the nearby Priory to conceal their valuables during the Reiver raids.) Constantine died as a martyr in AD 657 and a life-sized statue of him can be seen in the grounds of **Corby Castle** to the south of the village. The castle also boasts an impressive 13th-century keep and terraced gardens overlooking the Eden. The Castle is no longer open to the public.

During the reign of William Rufus, one of his barons, Ranulph de Meschines, founded a priory for Benedictine monks at Wetheral above a red-rock gorge of the River Eden. It was a dependency of the Abbey of St Mary at York, and the prior and the monastery served the church and domestic chapel of Corby Castle. All that remains now is the imposing three-storey gatehouse.

WARWICK
4 miles E of Carlisle on the A69

It is well worth visiting the village's remarkable Norman **Church of St Leonard**, which consists of a restored nave and chancel with a curiously buttressed apse and a splendid arch leading into a modern vestibule. Warwick's other church, St Paul's, is reputed to have been commissioned by a wealthy Carlisle man who took umbrage at a sermon preached at St Leonard's.

CROSBY-ON-EDEN
4 miles NE of Carlisle off the A689

The tiny hamlet of **High Crosby** stands on the hillside overlooking the River Eden; the small village of **Low Crosby** sits beside the river, clustered around a Victorian sandstone church. Inside the church there's a modern square pulpit, intricately carved with pomegranates, wheat and vines. Apparently, it was carved from one half of a tree felled nearby; the other half was used to create a second pulpit which was installed in the newly-built Liverpool Cathedral.

A couple of miles east of Crosby, The **Solway Aviation Museum** is one of only a few museums located on a 'live' airfield, in this case Carlisle Airport. Opened in 1997, the museum is home to several British jet aircraft of the 1950s and 1960s, among them the mighty Vulcan and the Canberra. Other exhibits include a wartime air-raid shelter where a video presentation explains the story behind the museum, displays of the Blue Streak rocket programme, testing for which took place only a few miles from here, and a very impressive engine room which houses one of Frank Whittle's first development jet engines. Testing for the Blue Streak rocket programme took place just a few miles from Crosby-on-Eden.

BRAMPTON

Nestling in the heart of the lovely Irthing Valley, Brampton is a delightful little town where the Wednesday market has been held since 1252, authorised by a charter granted by Henry III. Overlooking the Market Place is the town's most striking building, the octagonal **Moot Hall** topped by a handsome clock tower. There has been a Moot Hall here since 1648, though the present Hall was built in 1817 by Lord Carlisle. The iron stocks at the foot of a double flight of external stairs were last used in 1836.

Just around the corner, in **High Cross Street**, is the house (now a shop) which once witnessed one of the high-points in Bonnie Prince Charles' rebellion of 1745. It was here that the Prince stayed during the siege of Carlisle and it was here, on November 17, 1745 that the Mayor and Aldermen presented him with the keys to the city as a token of surrender. A few months later, following the Prince's defeat, six of his supporters were captured, tried

and summarily hanged on the Capon Tree on the south side of the town and in sight of the Scottish hills. The tree survived until the last century; in its place there now stands a monument commemorating the event.

AROUND BRAMPTON

LOW ROW

3 miles E of Brampton off the A69

Within easy reach of the town is **Hadrian's Wall**, just 3 miles to the north. If you've ever wondered where the Wall's missing masonry went to, look no further than the fabric of **Lanercost Priory** (English Heritage). An impressive red sandstone ruin set in secluded woodland, the priory was founded in 1166 by Robert de Vaux. In 1306, Edward I spent six months at the Priory recuperating after his skirmishes with the Scots. Lanercost is well preserved, and its scale is a reminder that it was a grand complex in its heyday.

Just off Brampton's Market Place is St Martin's Church, which was built anew in 1874 and contains one of the undiscovered secrets of the area – some magnificent stained glass windows designed by one of the founder members of the pre-Raphaelite brotherhood, Edward Burne-Jones. It was his fellow-member of the brotherhood, Philip Webb, William Morris's associate, who designed the church and insisted that contemporary stained glass should be installed.

Iron Stocks, Brampton

Brampton Market Place

172 THE SPORTSMAN INN

Laversdale, nr Carlisle

The **Sportsman** is a picturesque village inn serving the best in food and drink.

see page 249

falling off his rocking horse. Now owned by the Howard family, Earls of Carlisle, the Castle is private but there are good views from the minor road off the A69 that passes in front of it – the scene is particularly attractive in spring when the lawns are ablaze with daffodils. Pre-booked parties are welcome all year round and the Castle has become a popular venue for weddings and corporate events.

Naworth Castle's supreme glory is the Great Hall, hung with French tapestries and guarded by four unique heraldic beasts holding aloft their family pennants. The Long Gallery extends for 116 feet and was used as a guardroom. It now houses an interesting collection of paintings, many brought together by the 9th Earl, George Howard. He entertained many pre-Raphaelite painters here, but the only surviving example of their work is Burne-Jones's *Battle of Flodden* – the rest were destroyed by a fire in 1844. In the courtyard there are some intriguing medieval latrines!

The area around Brampton had good reason to be grateful to the Dacres of Naworth, who as Wardens of the Northern Marches protected it against marauding Scots. However, the townspeople of Brampton in Victorian times must have had mixed feelings about a later descendant, Rosalind, wife of the 9th Earl of Carlisle. An enthusiastic supporter of total

However, the Priory suffered greatly in the border raids of the 13th and 14th centuries. One such raid is known to have been led by William Wallace, an early campaigner for Scottish independence. When the Priory was closed in 1536, the sandstone blocks were recycled once again for houses in the town. But much of the Priory's great north aisle remains intact, set in a romantic and hauntingly beautiful position in the valley of the River Irthing. The Priory is well signposted and lies only 3 miles off the A69 (leave at Brampton).

Also most impressive is **Naworth Castle**, built around 1335 in its present form by Lord Dacre as an important border stronghold. The castle passed through the female line to the Howard family after the last Lord Dacre was killed as a child – improbably as it might seem, by abstinence, she contrived to get most of the small town's 40 public houses and drinking rooms closed.

South of Brampton are **Gelt Woods**, lying in a deep sandstone ravine carved by the fast-flowing River Gelt. By the River Gelt is an inscribed rock called **Written Rock** which is thought to have been carved by a Roman standard-bearer in AD 207. Access is discouraged however, as the path can be dangerous.

TALKIN

2 miles S of Brampton off the B6413

Talkin Tarn, now the focus of a 120-acre country park, has been a popular place for watersports for over 100 years. Glacial in origin, the Tarn was formed some 10,000 years ago and is continually replenished by underground springs. Modern-day visitors can sail, windsurf, canoe or hire a rowing boat. Talkin Tarn Rowing Club has been rowing on the tarn for 130 years, and holds its annual regatta in July. Fishing licences are available, there's a nature trail and an orienteering course, a play area for children under 8, a tea room and a gift shop; guided walks with a warden are also available for organised groups. The park is a peaceful place but, according to legend, beneath the surface of the lake there is a submerged village destroyed by a wrathful god, the ruins of which can still be seen below the water's surface in a certain light.

GILSLAND

7 miles E of Brampton on the B6318

Located in one of the most picturesque settings along the whole length of Hadrian's Wall and overlooking the River Irthing, **Birdoswald Roman Fort** (English Heritage) is one of the best-preserved edifices along the Wall and unique in that all the components of the Roman frontier system can be found here. Set high on a plateau with magnificent views over the surrounding countryside, the early turf wall, built in AD 122, can be seen along with the fort. Originally, Birdoswald Roman Fort would have covered 5 acres and may have been the base for up to 500 cavalry and 1,000 foot soldiers. A few hundred yards to the east is the mile-castle of Harrow Scar.

Gilsland village is well known for its sulphur spring; there was once a convalescent home for miners and shipyard workers here. Now a hotel, it is owned by the Co-Operative Society and people still drink the waters as a cure for arthritis and rheumatism. Near the spring is the **Popping Stone**, traditionally the place where a man 'popped the question' to his lover. It was here that Sir Walter Scott successfully 'popped' to Charlotte Carpenter, daughter of a French refugee, after just three weeks' courtship. In spite of his family's early disquiet, the two were happily married for 30 years and had four children.

173 LONG BYRES AT TALKIN HEAD

Talkin Head, Brampton

Long Byres provides outstanding self-catering accommodation on a hill farm in an Area of Outstanding Natural Beauty.

⊨ see page 252

174 THE BELTED WILL INN

Hallbankgate, nr Brampton

Traditional home-cooked food, real ales and comfortable accommodation in a fine old country inn called the **Belted Will**.

❚ ⊨ see page 251

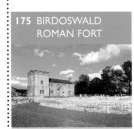

175 BIRDOSWALD ROMAN FORT

Gilsland

In a picturesque position, this is one of the best preserved wall forts, with a Visitor Centre providing an interesting insight into life at Birdoswald.

🏛 see page 252

Accommodation, Food & Drink and Places of Interest

The establishments featured in this section includes hotels, inns, guest houses, bed & breakfasts, restaurants, cafes, tea and coffee shops, tourist attractions and places to visit. Each establishment has an entry number which can be used to identify its location at the beginning of the relevant chapter or its position in this section.

In addition full details of all these establishments and many others can be found on the Travel Publishing website - www.travelpublishing.co.uk. This website has a comprehensive database covering the whole of Britain and Ireland.

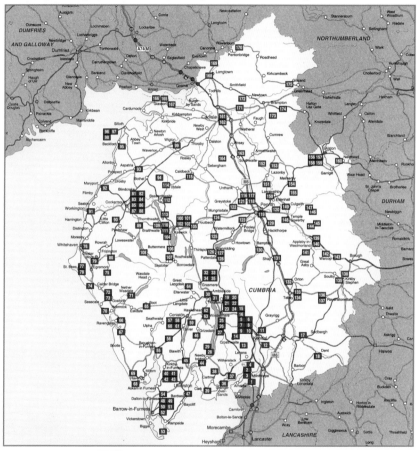

1   LAKELAND WILDLIFE OASIS

Hale, Milnthorpe, Cumbria LA7 7BW
☎ 015395 63027
e-mail: mail@wildlifeoasis.co.uk
⊕ www.wildlifeoasis.co.uk

Opened in 1991, **Lakeland Wildlife Oasis** quickly established itself as one of the Lake District's premier visitor attractions. "Half Zoo, half Museum, and totally fascinating" the Oasis takes visitors on an amazing journey through the world of wildlife using a unique combination of live animals and imaginative "hands-on" computer displays. Visitors can drape a snake around their neck, exchange inquisitive glances with a Ruffled Lemur or a beautifully poised Meerkat squatting on its haunches, and admire creatures rarely seen in captivity such as Flying Foxes and Poison Arrow Frogs. Or you can just relax in the tropical

hall, colourful with free-flying birds, bats and butterflies. Many rare species have found a secure home here, amongst them the fossa, of which there are only 44 in captivity. Friendly staff are always on hand to answer questions and let you meet some of the inhabitants face to face!

The Oasis was established by Dave and Jo Marsden, both of whom were animal keepers at Chester Zoo before setting up this popular family attraction. It is open every day of the year, (except for Christmas Day and Boxing Day), there is access throughout for the disabled, and other amenities include picnic areas, a snack bar and a gift shop. For parties of more than 30 people, it is advisable to book ahead and the Oasis will then provide a tour guide.

2   THE CROSS KEYS HOTEL

1 Park Road, Milnthorpe,
Cumbria LA7 7AB
☎ 01539 562115   Fax: 01539 562446
e-mail: stay@thecrosskeyshotel.co.uk
⊕ www.thecrosskeyshotel.co.uk

'Come and unwind at the **Cross Keys**'. That's the invitation extended by hosts Ian and Sandra Mills at their comfortably modernised traditional inn, which stands in the heart of Milnthorpe where the A6 meets the B5282. The inn is a Robinsons House serving a range of that brewery's ales throughout the day, and is a multiple winner of their Best-Kept Cellar awards.

Ian and Sandra both cook, and the printed menu and specials board propose a good selection of well-loved favourites such as cod & chips, steaks, steak & ale pie, lasagne, chilli , roast beef in a giant Yorkshire pudding and chicken and lamb curries. The Cross Keys is a great place to unwind, and a very comfortable, convenient base for touring a part of the country

with many scenic and historic attractions. Eight superbly appointed en suite bedrooms comprise 4 doubles, 2 four-poster rooms and 2 family rooms (children are very welcome and a cot can be provided), and a two-bedroom self-catering cottage is also available.

The Cross Keys can arrange guided tours in association with County Card, Milnthorpe's local taxi service. The inn has a large function room, two pleasant gardens and a large car park; all the major credit cards are accepted.

4   THE BLUE BELL HOTEL AT HEVERSHAM

Princes Way, Heversham, Milnthorpe,
Cumbria LA7 7EE
☎ 01539 562018 Fax: 01539 562455
e-mail: stay@bluebellhotel.co.uk
⊕ www.bluebellhotel.co.uk

The **Blue Bell Hotel at Heversham** offers old-world charm and up-to-date comfort and convenience for both leisure and business visitors. Frederick and Priscilla Adams, in the trade for 30 years, came here in 2006 and have lost no time in putting the hotel back on the map. They are the most attentive and friendly hosts, and their decision to do away with television and intrusive music enhances the civilised surroundings.

Originally a vicarage, with the oldest parts dating back to 1460, the hotel is now a Samuel Smith property, and that brewery's own real and other draught ales head the long list of drinks served inside, out on the terrace or in the rear garden.

The bar is open lunchtime and evening, all day at the weekend and all day every day in the summer. Food is served every session seven days a week, in the 60-cover main restaurant – also available for private parties and functions – and in the old beamed lounge bar, a cosy spot for a drink or something from the bar menu. The

chefs set great store by fresh seasonal produce, and the regular menu is supplemented by daily specials. Typical choices run from sandwiches and hot baguettes to potted shrimps, rainbow trout, classic haddock & chips, moules marinière, the curry and quiche of the day, beef stew, vegetarian lasagne, and roast chicken, beef and lamb. Booking is advisable at the weekend, and essential for the popular Sunday roasts.

Heversham lies in a rural location on the A6 between Milnthorpe and Levens. Access

to the main road network makes the Blue Bell an ideal base for exploring the beauty spots and places of interest in the region. Guest accommodation comprises 20 centrally heated upstairs rooms including two singles and two family rooms. They each have their own individual style, but all have en suite facilities, direct-dial phone, auto-call alarm, hairdryer, trouser press and hot beverage tray. The hotel can cater for meetings and conferences for up to 70.

3 THE BULLS HEAD

**Beetham Road, Milnthorpe,
Cumbria LA7 7QL**
☎ 01539 562133 Fax: 01539 564899
e-mail: the.bulls.head@hotmail.co.uk

Kerry and Mark Tipton are the hosts of the **Bulls Head**, a handsome, family-friendly inn on a corner site in the centre of Milnthorpe. It's a place to relax and unwind, to enjoy good ale, good food and good company. There's always a good choice of draught keg beers, and a board lists the day's home-cooked dishes,

served every lunchtime and evening seven days a week. Wednesday is quiz night, Thursday is gaming night and live bands perform on one or two Fridays each month.

HIDDEN PLACES GUIDES

Explore Britain and Ireland with *Hidden Places* guides - a fascinating series of national and local travel guides.

Packed with easy to read information on hundreds of places of interest as well as places to stay, eat and drink.

Available from both high street and internet booksellers

For more information on the full range of *Hidden Places* guides and other titles published by Travel Publishing visit our website on

www.travelpublishing.co.uk or ask for our leaflet by phoning **0118-981-7777** or emailing **info@travelpublishing.co.uk**

6 I LOVE ORGANICS

**Wainwrights Yard, Kendal,
Cumbria LA9 4DP**
☎ 01539 721100
e-mail: info@iloveorganics.co.uk
🌐 www.iloveorganics.co.uk

I Love Organics is a winning combination of café/coffee shop, health, beauty & organic products shop and health & beauty salon. The Organic Café is open from 9 to 5.30 Monday to Saturday and in summer also from 10 to 4 on Sunday for a fine selection of organic meals, from breakfasts (walnut & raisin toast with preserves, traditional Scotch whisky porridge, smoked salmon with scrambled eggs) to sandwiches with imaginative fillings, salads and soups, light main courses, desserts, cakes, fresh juices, speciality teas and a superb single-roast Columbian coffee. Snacks and drinks can also be ordered to take away.

The Health & Beauty Shop is Cumbria's largest stockist of organic, natural health and beauty products along with speciality foods, organic toiletries, books and home and

lifestyle goods and gifts. The Beauty Salon offers holistic facial and body treatments (including a 90-minute organic 'newskin' facial) and a range of therapies. Alexis and Ian Dixon's much acclaimed establishment is located off Stricklandgate, one of the main streets of Kendal. Turn into the Yard (alleyway) opposite the War Memorial and follow the signs.

**24 Finkle Street, Kendal,
Cumbria LA9 4AB**
☎ 01539 720547 Fax: 01539 738440
e-mail: infusionkendal@btconnect.com

Locals are buzzing over this new Italian restaurant situated 50 yards off Stricklandgate, one of the historic streets in the heart of Kendal. Visitors from outside the area are also quickly getting the news that **Infusion** is a restaurant that can hold its own with the best. Martin and Eliana took over in October 2006 and set about a top-to-toe refurbishment programme, opening in the Spring of 2007 in surroundings that could equal anything in London in terms of cool style.

Martin, a talented and experienced chef, lists seafood, veal and steaks among his specialities, but everything that comes out of his kitchen gets the best attention to detail in both preparation and presentation. The restaurant is open Tuesday to Saturday from 11 for tea, coffee and cakes. Lunch on set and à la carte menus is served from 12 to 2.30, followed by a selection of light bites before the full evening menu kicks in from 5.30. A special two-course Taster Menu is an alternative lunchtime and evening Tuesday to Thursday. Typical dishes on the lunchtime and light bite menus include a plate of antipasto, toasted panini, burgers, mussels, all kinds of pasta, grilled prawns with rocket, and butterflied chicken breast in garlic butter. From the Taster Menu come chicken livers with garlic and chilli, steamed fillet of sole with a saffron and asparagus sauce, and chicken in a flavour-packed Mediterranean tomato, olives, caper and anchovy sauce. The main menu tempts with the likes of seared scallops and king prawns with garlic, white wine, chilli, lemon juice and a pickled cucumber salad; pasta and risotto dishes; line-caught sea bass, Cumbrian lamb chops and chargrilled rump and fillet steaks. All the classic pizzas are available, along with less familiar variations such as del pescatore with tuna, mussels and prawns, or diavola with spicy Italian sausage. The dolci (sweets) ensure a fine ending to a memorable meal, and this excellent food is complemented by a well-chosen list of wines. It's best to book on Fridays and Saturdays. Infusion accepts all the major credit cards except Diners.

7 WATERSIDE WHOLEFOOD

Kent View, Kendal, Cumbria LA9 4DZ
☎ 01539 729743
e-mail: toni@watersidewholefood.co.uk
🌐 www.watersidewholefood.co.uk

Waterside Wholefood is a vegetarian and vegan restaurant, café and shop in a pleasant riverside setting a short walk from the centre of Kendal. Hands-on owner Toni Yates takes great pride in the range and quality of her product, and the superb food brings back locals and visitors for more of the same. Everything is made on the premises.

Virtually everything is organic, to enjoy on the spot or to take away, and the daily changing menu runs from soup and salad platters to quiche, filled jacket potatoes, tortillas and quesadillas, with fruit crumbles and sticky toffee pudding among the favourite desserts. Drinks include Fairtrade tea and coffee, dandelion coffee, barley cup, fruit juices and organic wines and beers. It's a very family-friendly place, with baby-changing facilities and is open from 8.30am to 4.30pm Monday to Saturday. There are seats for 36 inside and 32 outside overlooking the river. Waterside Wholefood also has a thriving outside catering business that can provide anything from canapés and finger or fork buffets to 3-course meals.

10 LYNDHURST GUEST HOUSE

8 South Road, Kendal, Cumbria LA9 5QH
☎ 01539 723819
e-mail: stay@lyndhurst-kendal.co.uk
🌐 www.lyndhurst-kendal.co.uk

Lyndhurst Guest House is a very friendly holiday base in a quiet riverside setting a short walk from all the amenities and attractions of Kendal. Local man Stuart and his partner Yvonne are the most welcoming of hosts, and the large number of repeat visitors is a tribute to their outstanding hospitality. The late-Victorian house has eight en suite letting rooms including singles, doubles and twins, all with high-quality decoration and furnishings, television and tea/coffee tray.

Breakfast offers the options of full English, vegetarian, or a low fat "weight watching" cooked breakfast as well as fruity porridge or fresh fruit salad. The hosts will provide packed

lunches and fill flasks and water bottles for guests and they also have a selection of walking maps to help guests plan their days in the fresh air. For golfers, '2 rounds for the price of 1' offers can be arranged at several local courses.

8   DICKIE DOODLES

Yard 2, Stricklandgate, Kendal,
Cumbria LA9 4ND
☎ 01539 738480
🌐 www.dickiedoodles.com

Open every evening from 8 till late, **Dickie Doodles** is a magnet for lovers of good music and well-kept ales. Shaun Bainbridge dreamed of a live music venue open seven nights a week and in 1999 he took over these premises, closed and empty at the time, and transformed them into what has become an unqualified success with a wide appeal. It is home to a multitude of musical talent covering many areas of the modern music spectrum and with performers ranging from talented amateurs to well-known professionals.

The week unfolds as follows:

- Monday: Acoustic jamming
- Tuesday: Electric jamming (there's a super in-house sound system)
- Wednesday: Traditional folk music
- Thursday: New and up-and-coming bands
- Friday and Saturday: Professional rock bands
- Sunday: Some or all the above!

Entrance (over-18s only) is free, and drinks (cash only) include a good choice of draught and bottled beers and lagers.

Dickie Doodles also shows arts and crafts exhibitions showcasing the work of talented local artists and makers. Shaun is a blacksmith by trade and some of his forgework is also on display.

Stricklandgate is one of the busy narrow streets at the heart of old Kendal, and the yards (alleyways) are a distinctive feature of the town. These were a line of defence against the constant threat of marauding Scots and could be sealed off by closing the single small entrance, keeping the families and their livestock safe inside. The Scottish threat has long since abated, and it's now tourists from around the world who come in peace to Kendal throughout the year. And for those who love their music, Dickie Doodles is definitely the place to head for.

9   THE RING O' BELLS

37 Kirkland, Kendal, Cumbria LA9 5AF
☎ 01539 720326

Standing by the church on the main road into Kendal, the **Ring o' Bells** is *the* place to enjoy the best of hospitality, good wholesome food and well-kept ales in traditional surroundings. Tenant Susan Dawson is ably assisted by her niece Heather, queen of the kitchen, and Jo, who does sterling work in the bar.

The interior is particularly homely and inviting, with an open fire to keep things cosy when there's a chill in the air. Black Sheep, Old Specked hen and Abbot Ale are the resident real ales, and the regulars are also partial to a drop of Theakston's Mild. The bar is open all day, every day, and food is served daily from noon to 7 o'clock. Heather produces tasty dishes served in generous helpings at very reasonable prices, and a choice of traditional roasts is added to the menu for Sunday lunch – best to book. Accommodation, available all year round, comprises three upstairs rooms including one that is suitable for a family. The tariff includes a hearty breakfast to set guests up for a day discovering the many places of interest in and around Kendal.

The building has a long and interesting history that starts in the 1740s when it was built with the consent of the vicar for the use of the church wardens. Reports suggest that the followers of Bonnie Prince Charlie performed their religious duties here when the rebels marched through Kendal in 1745. It is thus one of the very few pubs in the land that stand on consecrated ground. It is probable that Charles Dickens used to stay here when visiting his friend the Cumberland wrestler Thomas Longmire. The story goes that it was during one of those visits that the writer looked across to the baker's shop opposite and conceived the idea for a scene in *A Christmas Carol*, in which the poorer families are described as carrying their dough to the local baker to be made into loaves.

The area hereabouts is great walking country: the ruins of the Castle stand high on a hill overlooking the town, and Castle Hill is a splendid spot for walking, picnicking and taking in the spectacular views. And if energy flags, a bite or two of Kendal Mint Cake should do the trick!

11   THE GARDEN HOUSE HOTEL & RESTAURANT

Fowl Ing Lane, Kendal, Cumbria LA9 6PH
☎ 01539 731131 Fax: 01539 740064
e-mail: gardenhousekendal@yahoo.co.uk
🌐 www.gardenhousehotel.co.uk

The **Garden House Hotel** is a Grade II listed building dating from 1812 and designed by the architect who was also responsible for Kendal's distinguished Town Hall. He built it for a prominent doctor of the day, and for anyone looking for a place to relax and unwind it's just what the doctor ordered. Sympathetically modernised and refurbished to provide up-to-date amenities while retaining period appeal, it's a great base for a holiday spent walking, fishing, sightseeing or just sitting back and enjoying the quiet, civilised surroundings.

Open throughout the year, the hotel has 12 en suite bedrooms of individual appeal and various sizes, all beautifully decorated and furnished. The tariff includes a Continental breakfast, but a traditional English version is also available. The conservatory restaurant is open lunchtimes and Tuesday to Saturday evenings for a fine selection of home-cooked dishes, and the hotel has a full on-licence for residents and non-resident diners.

The Garden House is well named, as it stands in two acres of lovely gardens. It stands a 10-minute walk from the railway station and short distance from the centre of Kendal. At one point in its lifetime the house was the home of the famous naturalist, fell-walker and writer of guide books Afred Wainwright.

12 THE STATION INN

Oxenholme, nr Kendal, Cumbria LA9 7RF
☎ 01539 724094
e-mail: station.inn@btconnect.com
🌐 www.stationinnoxenholme.co.uk

The **Station Inn** is a splendid Victorian hostelry a five-minute walk from Oxenholme station and a 10-minute drive from Kendal. Business partners Andrew Hipwell and David Hughes took over the lease in August 2006, bringing almost 50 years joint experience in the catering and hospitality business. They have quickly earned a wide and growing reputation for serving high quality food and drink and providing excellent guest accommodation.

The inn is open all day, seven days a week, for drinks, which include Black Sheep and Blond Witch real ales (it's CAMRA-listed) and a good choice of foreign beers. Food is served in the carpeted bar and restaurant from 12 to 2 and 5.30 to 9 Monday to Friday and all day Saturday and Sunday. Dishes on the printed menu and specials board put as much emphasis as possible on seasonal local produce, and the choice really does offer plenty for all tastes and appetites, with up to 60 dishes on the main menu. Perennial favourites include Caesar salad, Cumberland sausage (very tasty, and even better with a spiced apple sauce), Lakeland lamb Henry,

breast of Cumberland chicken wrapped in smoked bacon, battered haddock, scampi and steaks. Sandwiches, jacket potatoes, burgers and salad platters are among the lighter alternatives, and Sunday brings three splendid roasts. The children's menu is one of the very best, teaching the little ones to appreciate what good food is all about. The kitchen can cater for all sorts of special occasions, including weddings and birthday parties.

This is excellent walking country, and for visitors with a love of the great outdoors the Station Inn has five en suite letting bedrooms, three on the ground floor, all with television,

hairdryer and tea/coffee making facilities. Rooms are let on a B&B basis, and a generous breakfast starts the day. Good food is not the only treat for children: there's an adventure playground, with a bouncy castle on Bank Holidays, in the large garden. As well as being a top place for both food and accommodation, the Station Inn also has a thriving social side. Darts teams play in the Milnthorpe & District Darts League, and the dominoes players are equally competitive.

13 THE WHEATSHEAF

Brigsteer, Cumbria LA8 8AN
☎ 015395 68254
e-mail: wheatsheaf@brigsteer.gb.com
🌐 www.brigsteer.gb.com

Brigsteer is a tiny village in the shadow of Scout Scar, 3 miles from Kendal and 5 from Junction 36 of the M6 (west off the A591 or north off the A590 via Levens). The building that houses the **Wheatsheaf** has been an integral part of the community for almost 250 years, starting life as three cottages and a shoeing room for horses; it then became an alehouse and was first licensed in the early 19th century. It was once the focal point for the local hunt, and hunt pictures recall those days on the walls.

Now handsomely and sympathetically modernised while retaining its traditional appeal, it is run in fine style by Gareth Webster and his family and is a lovely place to visit, whether it's for a drink on a break in a journey, a snack or a meal, or as a very comfortable base for touring the region. Gareth sources as much local produce as possible in his classic British cooking with a contemporary twist, using seasonal meat, game and poultry, and daily delivered fresh fish and seafood for his  à la carte menus. The bar is open from 12 to 3 and from 6 to 11, and food is served anywhere in the open-plan ground floor from 12 to 2 and from 6 to 9. Two locally brewed real ales are always on tap in the bar, along with other draught and bottle beers and lagers, a good selection of wines, cider, spirits and soft drinks.

For guests staying at this delightful inn there are 3 luxuriously appointed en suite bedrooms for Bed & Breakfast. In a village that is centrally located yet peaceful and relaxed, the Wheatsheaf is a perfect place to unwind and enjoy the surroundings, or to explore the many and varied attractions, both scenic and historic, that the region has to offer. These include Lake Windermere, Kendal, Latterbarrow Wildlife Reserve, Whitbarrow, Levens Hall and the National Trust's Sizergh Castle.

Mill Yard, Back Lane, Staveley, nr Kendal, Cumbria LA8 9LR
☎ 01539 822329 Fax: 01539 822969
e-mail: food@wilfs-cafe.co.uk
⊕ www.wilfs-cafe.co.uk

Overlooking the River Kent in the village of Staveley, a mile off the A591 Kendal to Windermere road, **Wilf's Café** has been serving fresh, wholesome snacks and meals to an appreciative public since 1997.

Wilf, Charlotte, chef Martin Lovett and his team produce an excellent range of everything from breakfasts (meat or vegetarian) to sandwiches, salads, jacket potatoes, rarebits and chilli to mouthwatering cakes and pastries, slices, shortbread and hot and cold puddings. Drinks include Fairtrade coffees and teas, hot chocolate, juices, soft drinks and milkshakes. Customers can eat in or take away, and the café can be hired for parties. The owners organise regular speciality evenings and slide & supper evenings with guest speakers, and they also offer a full buffet service away from the café.

Open all year round from 10 to 5, Wilf's has modern furnishings and some well-chosen artwork on the walls. It has recently expanded to seat up to 120, and the bigger it gets the more popular it becomes. The café is linked to its neighbour the Hawkshead Brewery, and customers at the café can take a tour and sample the ales, perhaps bringing a glass back to enjoy with their meal – or the other way round, taking food to the bar area of the brewery. Wilf originally opened a café in Ambleside where discussion about other catering avenues led Wilf and Charlotte taking a basic menu to Orienteering and Mountain biking events. It proved a great success. This side grew and the original café closed. When an opportunity arose to open another café on the Mill Yard site they jumped at it with the event catering business still playing an important part of 'Wilf's'.

The mill that once stood here was at the heart of the bobbin industry, and after the demise of that industry the yard has become home to a variety of enterprises – the tables in the Café were made in the yard, and so is the bread served in the Café.

14 CROSTHWAITE HOUSE

Crosthwaite, nr Kendal, Cumbria LA8 8BP
☎ 01539 568264
e-mail: bookings@crosthwaite.co.uk
🌐 www.crosthwaite.co.uk

Robin and Marnie Dawson invite guests to relax, unwind and enjoy the superb setting and civilised ambience of **Crosthwaite House**. Built in 1750, the handsome house, part creeper-clad, stands in its own grounds on the southern edge of the Lake

District National Park, and although off the beaten track is easily reached from the M6 (J36). Kendal and Bowness are both only five miles away, and it's a short walk past the Punch Bowl Inn into picturesque Crosthwaite.

The house has six superbly appointed guest bedrooms with en suite shower and toilet; the three at the front enjoy valley views, while the others overlook the village church. The owners also offer self-catering in two cottages

converted from 300-year-old barns; Top Bank sleeps 2, Middle Bank sleeps 4, and they share a pretty garden. In the attractive dining room residents and non-residents enjoy traditional home cooking by Marnie on her Aga, using local produce including fruit from their orchard. Guests can plan their day's activities in the roomy lounge – Robin has a wealth of information about local hill, woodland and riverside walks, local maps, even the day's weather forecast.

16 THE DUKE WILLIAM

63 Main Street, Staveley, nr Kendal,
Cumbria LA8 9LN
☎ 01539 821447
e-mail:
duke_william_staveley@yahoo.co.uk

The **Duke William** is a traditional village pub with a cosy, inviting atmosphere. It stands on the main street of the pleasant village of Staveley, set in delightful countryside half a mile off the A591 Windermere road and four miles northwest of Kendal. But this is much more than just a popular 'local'. Mark and Sarah Moore came here in March 2006 after managing another pub in the village, so they certainly know what the regulars look for in their pubs.

Mark has been a chef more than 20 years, and his super cooked-to-order dishes have quickly made this a sought-after destination for lovers of good food. Everything on the menus is worth trying, but the steak & Black Sheep ale pie and the Sunday roasts are particular favourites. Other options might include scampi and cod with lemon and tartare sauce, tuna pasta bake, vegetarian moussaka and generous salads, with hot

sandwiches and jacket potatoes for lighter lunches. Tuesday is steak night – rump, sirloin and gammon with all the traditional trimmings. They also offer a separate takeaway menu that includes burgers, pizzas, curries and pies. Pub hours: in summer lunchtimes and evenings and all day Friday, Saturday and Sunday; in winter noon to 2.30pm and 5.30pm until closing time. No food Wednesday.

17 THE GALLERY COFFEE HOUSE

32 Main Street, Sedbergh,
Cumbria LA10 5BL
☎ 01539 621083
e-mail: colinryan16@aol.com

The **Gallery Coffee House** is located in the centre of Sedbergh, a pleasant village on the edge of the Yorkshire Dales National Park. When Colin and Louise Ryan acquired the premises in February 2006 it was closed, and after a complete refurbishment they re-launched it as this superb coffee house in a Tudor-style building.

Everything on the tempting menus is prepared and cooked on the premises, with many dishes born of Colin's and his family's recipes. The choice runs from sandwiches, baps and warm filled rolls to soups, salads, quiches and penne pasta, along with superb baking: apple & honey bake, date & walnut slice, millionaire's

shortbread. Drinks include speciality teas, and customers can buy these and home-made chutneys and preserves to take home. The gallery is filled with paintings by local artists, some the work of Colin himself.

Always (and justifiably) busy, the coffee house is open from 10 to 5 seven days a week. Children are always welcome, and high chairs can be made available.

18 STONE CLOSE TEA ROOM & GUEST HOUSE

Main Street, Dent, Cumbria LA10 5QL
☎ 01539 625231
e-mail: stoneclose@btinternet.com
🌐 www.dentdale.com

Janet Browning and her lovely dog Maisie welcome visitors to **Stone Close Tea Room and Guest House**, tucked away in the village of Dent in one of Cumbria's finest dales. The building started life in the 17th century as two separate cottages, and it retains many original features including beams, flagstones and cast-iron ranges. The tea room is open from 12 to 5 (not Monday or Friday) for a selection of delicious, imaginative dishes based almost entirely on organic produce. Janet has three

rooms for B&B guests – a twin on the ground floor and a twin and a double upstairs.

Looking for:
- *Places to Visit?*
- *Places to Stay?*
- *Places to Eat & Drink?*
- *Places to Shop?*

4 Victoria Street, Windermere,
Cumbria LA23 1AB
☎ 015394 43318
e-mail: steve@thecook-house.com
🌐 www.thecook-house.com

Steve Marston is a cook and this is his home, so what better choice of name could there be for this splendid licensed café/bistro than **The Cook House**?

In August 2006 Steve and Louise took over what was at the time a tea room and curio shop. They ran it as a tea room until January 2007, when they closed it and created this super new eating place in the centre of Windermere.

Steve is in the kitchen and Louise in front of house have quickly made their mark here and are winning new friends every day.

The 22-seat café is open from 8 in the morning to 3 in the afternoon, seven days a week.. The choice runs from breakfasts and sandwiches to panini's, smoked haddock rarebit, Caesar salad, quiches, and burgers along with a mouth-watering selection of cakes, pastries and desserts. Other items are available on their specials board. Everything is homemade, and many items are available as gluten free if required. Most items are also available to take away.

The Bistro is open from 6.30 to 9.30 on Friday and Saturday, and with just 14 covers booking is strongly recommended. The evening menu changes every week (see the web site for the current menu) and examples include ham hock terrine, salmon and crab fishcakes, Cumberland sausage with black pudding gravy and Confit duck legs, with Toblerone cheese cake or panacotta with raspberry coulis to round things off in style. Many of the evening menu items are also available gluten free as everything is homemade.

20 THE LAKES HOTEL

I High Street, Windermere,
Cumbria LA23 1AF
☎ 01539 442751 Fax: 01539 446026
e-mail: admin@lakes-hotel.com
🌐 www.lakes-hotel.com

Two excellent enterprises based in one establishment, **The Lakes Hotel** and **Lakes Supertours**. Andrew and Marie Dobson's hotel occupies a handsome mid-Victorian building that was formerly a bank; it stands in the heart of Windermere close to the railway and bus stations. The guest accommodation comprises 10 rooms – doubles, twins and family rooms – all with en suite facilities and three located on the ground floor. Tariff is on a Bed & Breakfast basis.

Lakes Supertours is the best and most relaxing way to see and learn about Lakeland. They offer full- and half-day tours for small groups that take in all the major scenic,

cultural and historic attractions of the Lakes. Luxury high-topped mini-coaches have ample leg room and excellent visibility and are driven by

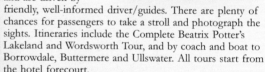

friendly, well-informed driver/guides. There are plenty of chances for passengers to take a stroll and photograph the sights. Itineraries include the Complete Beatrix Potter's Lakeland and Wordsworth Tour, and by coach and boat to Borrowdale, Buttermere and Ullswater. All tours start from the hotel forecourt.

22 THE ARCHWAY

College Road, Windermere,
Cumbria LA23 1BU
☎ 01539 445613
e-mail: stay@the-archway.co.uk
🌐 www.the-archway.co.uk

The **Archway** is a super B&B in a very pleasant, peaceful location. The late-Victorian property, with an attractive front garden and private parking to the rear, has four top-quality en suite rooms, all with comfortable beds, TV, DVD/CD player, beverage tray with home-made

biscuits and several thoughtful little touches. One room can accommodate an extra bed for a child. Jennifer and Stephen are welcoming of hosts, and Stephen's breakfasts, with home-made sausages and preserves among the many options, are well worth getting up for. Packed lunches can be provided for guests setting out for a day's sightseeing.

HIDDEN PLACES GUIDES

Explore Britain and Ireland with *Hidden Places* guides - a fascinating series of national and local travel guides.

Packed with easy to read information on hundreds of places of interest as well as places to stay, eat and drink.

Available from both high street and internet booksellers

For more information on the full range of *Hidden Places* guides and other titles published by Travel Publishing visit our website on

www.travelpublishing.co.uk
or ask for our leaflet by phoning
0118-981-7777 or emailing
info@travelpublishing.co.uk

21 THE GREY WALLS HOTEL

Elleray Road, Windermere,
Cumbria LA23 1AG
☎ 01539 443741 Fax: 01539 447546
e-mail: greywallshotel@totalise.co.uk
⊞ www.greywalls-hotel.co.uk

The **Grey Walls Hotel**, in a prime location in the heart of Windermere, offers excellent all-round facilities and an ideal base for touring the area. Behind the unique Cumbrian-stone exterior, the hotel has the friendly atmosphere of a large country house, and although they arrived only in January 2007, David and Laura Parry have already stamped their personalities on the place, attracting and welcoming both local residents and tourists.

The hotel incorporates a super traditional inn, The Greys, where seven Real Ales are headed by Cains from Liverpool. Busy, talented chefs prepare a varied selection of dishes to enjoy either in the bar or in the 24-cover restaurant (best to book in the latter, which is also available for private parties). The printed menu and the daily specials board offer plenty of choice, with steak & ale pie made with Cains Formidable Ale a firm favourite; Thursday is steak night, when various discounts are offered. Food is served from 12 to 2 and 6 to 9 Monday to Thursday and all day at the weekend. The pub has a games room, a children's room and a large-screen TV for major sports events, and when the sun shines the secluded beer garden comes into its own.

The upstairs guest bedrooms all have en suite facilities, television, hairdryer and tea/coffee tray; family rooms are available, and children of all ages are welcome. The tariff includes a traditional English breakfast, and last-minute mini-breaks of 2 or 3 nights are offered.

151

24 GLENVILLE HOUSE

Lake Road, Windermere,
Cumbria LA23 2EQ
☎ 015394 43371 Fax: 015394 48457
e-mail: mail@glenvillehouse.co.uk
🌐 www.glenvillehouse.co.ukk

Glenville House was built in traditional Lakeland stone in 1888 as a gentleman's residence. Now the most civilised of hotels, with many original features, it stands on the main road halfway between the centre of Windermere and the Lake at Bowness-on-Windermere. Rachel and Paul Wright, who came here in April 2006, have made this a very special place and are already attracting repeat visitors – and a look at the comments in the visitors' book shows why.

The guest accommodation consists of six superbly appointed bedrooms, one on the ground floor, all looking immaculate after a major refurbishment at the beginning of 2007. Four rooms are designated superior, two de luxe; all have television and welcome tray, and the top-of-the-range rooms also CD players. Thoughtful little extras complete the picture, helping to turn an enjoyable stay into a memorable one. This is a great part of the world for getting out and about, and if wet weather should arrive, the house has ample washing and drying facilities. Breakfast starts with a selection from the help-yourself buffet and follows with an excellent choice of cooked-to-order options.

There are not many parts of the country with more to offer the visitor, and among the almost endless of opportunities are walking, cycling, fishing, boating and steamer trips on the Lake, discovering the world of Beatrix Potter and taking a trip on a steam railway. And when complete relaxation is the order of the day Glanville has a quiet garden that's a perfect spot to unwind and think how delightful it is to be away from the hustle and bustle of life back in the city. The house, which is open all year round, has a large private car park. All the major cards are accepted.

23 DENEHURST GUEST HOUSE

Queens Drive, Windermere,
Cumbria LA23 2EL
☎ 015394 44710
e-mail: denehurst@btconnect.com
⊕ www.denehurst-guesthouse.co.uk

Denehurst Guest House stands in a quiet area away from the main road and a ten-minute walk from the town and the Lake. Ken and Cindy Ravenhall bought the guest house as a going concern in May 2006 and they provide outstanding hospitality and Bed & Breakfast accommodation for walkers, cyclists, holidaymakers and tourists from all over the world.

Most of the seven en suite bedrooms have four-posters or handsome wrought-iron beds. All have

television, video/ DVD, radio, refreshment tray, shortbread biscuits, hairdryer, books and magazines – and a teddy bear. The Superior and Four Poster rooms

have bathrobes, complimentary toiletries and bottled mineral water. One of the rooms is a ground-floor suite. Breakfast, served from 8.30 to 9.15, provides a fine start to the day, and packed lunches are available for guests planning a day discovering the many scenic delights of the region. Denehurst is open all year round.

25 AUNTY VAL'S TEA ROOMS

Church Street, Bowness-on-Windermere,
Cumbria LA23 3DG
☎ 015394 88211 Fax: 015395 61232
⊕ www.auntyvals.co.uk

Val and Paul Brook and their son Graham run **Aunty Val's Tea Rooms** one of the most popular places for visitors, as well as with the residents of Bowness. Eating here really is like having tea in your favourite aunt's house: cosy, civilised, with a special old-fashioned atmosphere – and super cooking to go with it. Val and Paul use local produce on a wide choice of quality dishes, from soups and omelettes, pies and quiches and Cumberland sausage to scones, chocolate fudge cake and ginger sponge. They also sell luxury preserves and other gifts to take home. Open 11 to 5 (closed Fridays in winter).

26 MAY COTTAGE

Kendal Road, Bowness-on-Windermere,
Cumbria LA23 3EW
☎ 01539 446478 mob: 07793 056322
e-mail: kc@may-cottage.com
⊕ www.lakeshospitality.co.uk

Victorian, **May Cottage** stands quiet, yet close to the Lake for boat rides, shops, restaurants, tapas bars and bistros. Personal welcome with hot drink on arrival. The light and airy rooms are all en-suite with fresh white cotton sheets. Cleanliness is of a high standard. Hearty traditional breakfast, lightly grilled by mine host former Great Britian & International Rugby Captain. Home area of famous poets, artists, sculptors, actors, playwrites and musicians with breathtaking scenic walks and drives. Car park, secure bike lock up and dry room. Access to sauna, steam, jacuzzi and swim areas with cafe/bar & lounge, Sky TV and billiards.

27 BLACKWELL 🏛

Bowness-on-Windermere,
Cumbria LA23 3JT
☎ 015394 46139
e-mail: info@blackwell.org.uk
🌐 www.blackwell.org.uk

Blackwell is one of Britain's finest houses from the turn of the last century and one of the country's most important examples of Arts and Crafts architecture. It has survived in a truly remarkable state of preservation and almost all of its original decorative features are intact. Since its restoration in 2001 the house has been filled with original furniture and artefacts from the period, which once again re-awaken its beautiful interiors and bring them to life.

The house was built as a spectacular holiday home for Sir Edward Holt, a wealthy Manchester brewer, and is situated in a stunning Lakeland setting, above Lake Windermere, looking across to the fells.

No Expense was spared in creating this romantic retreat from the smog and grime of Victorian industrial life. Everywhere you look inside there is beautiful craftwork, using motifs drawn from the surrounding nature outside. There are swaying flowers in the stained glass, leaves and berries in the woodwork and stone, and peacocks and wild flowers on the patterned wall coverings.

Blackwell houses an important and growing collection of both furniture and artefacts from the Arts & Crafts Movement, including pottery, metalwork and examples of carvings.

As well as being a perfect work of art in itself, Blackwell provides the perfect setting for changing exhibitions of the highest quality applied arts and crafts. Other attractions here include a tea room, serving a selection of freshly prepared meals and snacks, and a book and gift shop.

28 THE AQUARIUM OF THE LAKES 🏛

Lakeside, Newby Bridge,
Cumbria LA12 8AS
☎ 015395 30153

Naturally themed habitats of the Lake District feature in the UK's largest collection of freshwater fish. Discover the underwater tunnel featuring giant carp and amazing diving ducks. Learn about the mysterious life of a river after dark and encounter a variety of British mammals including harvest

mice, bank voles and brown rats! Also see playful otters, British sharks and rays. Enjoy browsing in the gift shops and experience breathtaking views across Lake Windermere from the coffee shop.

29 STOTT PARK BOBBIN MILL 🏛

Lowstott Park, Ulverston,
Cumbria LA12 8AX
☎ 01539 531087
🌐 www.english-heritage.org.uk

This extensive working mill was begun in 1835 to produce the wooden bobbins vital to the Lancashire spinning and weaving industries.

Although small compared to other mills, some 250 men and boys (some drafted in from workhouses) worked here in often arduous conditions to produce a quarter of a million bobbins a week.

Guided tours are included in the admission charge: the last tour begins ½ hour before closing. Please call for details of steam days.

30 MELROSE GUEST HOUSE

Church Street, Ambleside,
Cumbria LA22 0BT
☎ 01539 432500
e-mail: relax@melrose-guesthouse.co.uk
🌐 www.melrose-guesthouse.co.uk

Melrose Guest House is one of the most popular and most pleasant places to stay in Ambleside. The elegant Victorian house, which is conveniently placed for the town's many amenities and attractions, has been run since April 2006 by hardworking Alan and Lynn Salter. They have made many improvements since their arrival, and their hard work, high standards and enthusiasm are already attracting return guests.

The eight guest rooms (six en suite) spread over four floors consist of four doubles, two triples, a single and a family room with a double and two single beds. All have television, radio-alarm clock, hairdryer, refreshment tray & kettle, toiletries and good fresh towels. One room on the ground floor caters for those who find stairs a problem. Breakfast is served between 8.30 and 9.15 in the splendid breakfast room. There's a buffet-style choice of cereals, toast, preserves, juices, yoghurts, tea and coffee, and the option of a full English, lighter English or vegetarian meal. The owners can provide packed lunches with a little notice; they don't serve evening meals, but there are plenty of fine eating places nearby.

The guest house is popular with walkers and cyclists as well as tourists; guests have their own front door keys and there are ample drying facilities and safe storage for bikes. A garden bench at the front is a perfect spot for taking the sun and watching the world go by. The owners have four free passes into the nearby Low Wood Leisure Complex that are available to guests; its amenities include a swimming pool, gym, Jacuzzi, steam room and outdoor hot tub. Alan and Lynn ensure that every guest soon becomes a friend and if the visit is for a special celebration they'll go to the trouble of laying on a treat in the room on arrival.

31 STAGSHAW GARDEN

Ambleside, Cumbria LA22 0HE
☎ 015394 46027
e-mail: stagshaw@nationaltrust.org.uk
⊕ www.nationaltrust.org.uk

This steep woodland garden, noted for its flowering shrubs, was created by the late Cubby Acland, Regional Agent for the National Trust. It contains a fine collection of shrubs, including rhododendrons, azaleas and camellias. Adjacent to the garden are Skelghyll Woods, which offer delightful walks and access to the fells beyond.

Photo by Stephen Robson

32 THE ROWAN TREE

Church Bridge, Grasmere,
Cumbria LA22 9PX
☎ 015394 35528
e-mail: calveley@mac.com
⊕ www.rowantreegrasmere.co.uk

A tea garden was founded over two centuries ago in Grasmere for the refreshment of travellers on what was then an important coaching route. The **Rowan Tree**, founded in 1989, continues that tradition under Barry and Gill Calveley in a superb riverside location opposite St Oswald's Church. A superb variety of freshly baked cakes, pastries and hot and cold fish and vegetarian dishes is served on separate lunchtime and evening menus that use organic ingredients whenever possible.

The daytime menu offers sandwiches, panini, baked potatoes, chilli, nachos, macaroni cheese, pizzas, salads and cakes, accompanied by teas, coffees, organic soft drinks, beers and wines. In the evening the more formal menu is full of superb dishes such as crab cakes, sea bass with a parmesan and basil crust, salmon with asparagus and lemon sauce, and a Mediterranean herb pastry vegetable pie with spinach, tomatoes, basil, pine nuts, onions, garlic and feta cheese. The bright, airy inside room is furnished in light pine, while the terrace overlooking the river has wicker chairs set at wrought-iron tables.

Easedale, nr Grasmere,
Cumbria LA22 9QN
☎ 015394 35317 Fax: 015394 35058
e-mail: info@lancrigg.co.uk
🌐 www.lancrigg.co.uk

Lancrigg Vegetarian Country House Hotel
enjoys a setting of timeless tranquillity in 30 cares
of gardens and woodland overlooking peaceful
Easedale. Starting life in the 17th century as a
modest farmhouse, it was later renovated and
enlarged with the considerable encouragement of
William Wordsworth. The Lake Poets used regularly to meet here, and Charles Dickens and Wilkie
Collins stayed here on their trips to southern Scotland. It was
opened in 1985, by Robert and Janet Whittington, as an
elegant and civilised hotel, serving only vegetarian wholefood

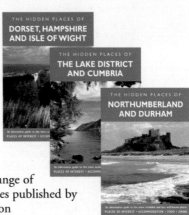

home cooking.

The 12 individually
designed guest bedrooms
are in the main house and a
nearby cottage; all have
private bathrooms (some
with whirlpool baths),
television, telephone and
beverage tray. The evening

meals, served in a gracious chandelier-lit room that commands fine
views across the valley, use the best and freshest natural
ingredients, often organic and always free of artificial additives,
and the interesting menus have delighted many a non-vegetarian.
The bread, cakes and croissants are made from organic stone-
ground flour by a local baker in a wood-fired brick oven.

HIDDEN PLACES GUIDES

Explore Britain and Ireland with
Hidden Places guides - a fascinating series of national and local
travel guides.

Packed with easy to read information on hundreds of places of
interest as well as places to stay,
eat and drink.

Available from both high street
and internet booksellers

For more information on the full range of
Hidden Places guides and other titles published by
Travel Publishing visit our website on

www.travelpublishing.co.uk
or ask for our leaflet by phoning **0118-981-7777** or
emailing **info@travelpublishing.co.uk**

THE HIDDEN PLACES OF
**DORSET, HAMPSHIRE
AND ISLE OF WIGHT**

THE HIDDEN PLACES OF
**THE LAKE DISTRICT
AND CUMBRIA**

THE HIDDEN PLACES OF
**NORTHUMBERLAND
AND DURHAM**

34 DALE LODGE HOTEL

Grasmere, Cumbria LA22 9SW
☎ 01539 435300 Fax: 01539 435570
e-mail: enquiries@dalelodgehotel.co.uk
🌐 www.dalelodgehotel.co.uk

Dale Lodge Hotel has established itself as one of the very best hotels in the region, with a big reputation and a large following for both accommodation and food. The building, which dates from 1840, stands in 3½ acres of beautiful grounds, and the setting, the stunning scenery, the service and the hospitality make it a perfect choice for a relaxing break or a base for exploring the many local attractions.

It's also an unbeatable venue for wedding or other celebrations. Each of the 14 graciously appointed bedrooms has its own individual style, and all have en suite facilities, television and hot beverage tray. Rooms can be booked on a B&B or Dinner B&B basis. Public areas include a residents' lounge with a library and open fires, a garden room, bar and restaurant.

Owners Brian and Gillian Roberts and their head chef James Goodall have created an exciting, ever-changing selection of dishes for both bar and restaurant menus. Traditional favourites like Cumberland sausage, fish & chips, braise lamb shanks and steak & ale pie share the menus with the likes of smoked salmon and haddock fishcakes; beef or chicken fajitas; pan-fried scallops with Jerusalem artichoke risotto; roast poussin with creamed leeks, baby root vegetables and a light ginger sauce; and red snapper with rocket, wild mushrooms, baby turnips, toasted walnuts and salsa verde. Everything tastes as good as it sounds, and scrumptious home-made desserts round off a meal in fine style.

The outstanding food is accompanied by an equally distinguished wine cellar. Tweedies Bar is a real gem, a magnet for lovers of good ale, with a menu of snacks, sandwiches and 9" pizzas. There are usually at least five real ales on tap, and in their time here the Roberts family have featured no fewer than 190 different brews – no wonder it was voted CAMRA's top pub for spring 2007! One section of the hotel is now the Tourist Information Centre, the one in Grasmere having closed.

35 OAK BANK HOTEL

Broadgate, Grasmere Village,
Cumbria LA22 9TA
☎ 015394 35217 Fax: 015394 35685
e-mail: info@lakedistricthotel.co.uk
🌐 www.lakedistricthotel.co.uk

Oak Bank Hotel is a classic Lakeland building in a prime location in the heart of Grasmere Village, just off the main A591 Windermere-Keswick road. Built as a private residence in 1872, it has been a hotel since the 1920s, and since Easter 2007 it has been in the capable hands of Simon and Glynis.

Open all year round except for three weeks in January, it's the perfect choice for a relaxing break, a romantic weekend or a Lakeland holiday, and is well placed for touring this marvellous part of the world.

The 15 high-quality bedrooms offer space, comfort and character; top of the range are the Acorn Suite with a separate lounge area and a Jacuzzi, and the Iris Room with a four-poster bed and a balcony looking out over the gardens, river and fells. Food gets equal billing with the accommodation, and the dining room and conservatory are open from 6.30 to 8.30 every evening for both residents and non-residents. The daily changing four-course menu tempts with such well-constructed, beautifully presented dishes such as lasagne of smoked trout topped with smoked salmon served with a chive and lemon sauce; pan-seared guinea fowl with roasted leeks and a grain mustard and redcurrant sauce; crispy tower of seafood; and lemon mousse with a raspberry coulis.

Fine food deserves fine wine, and the Oak Bank's list certainly succeeds. The bar is a cosy spot for a pre- or post-dinner drink, and guests can relax, meet and make friends or plan the next day's activities in the two lounges warmed in winter by cheerful open fires.

37 WOODLANDS HOTEL & PINE LODGES

Meathop Park, Grange-over-Sands,
Cumbria LA11 6RB
☎ 01539 534128
🌐 www.whpl.co.uk

Owner Peter Baker, General Manager Rosalind McTaff and Bar & Restaurant Manager Steven Sumner-Roberts make a fine team at the **Woodlands Hotel & Pine Lodges**, where they offer a choice of Bed & Breakfast or self-catering accommodation in beautiful, secluded surroundings. The garden setting, in the heart of a delightful five-acre wood, truly puts this hidden gem in a world of its own, and the prospect of spotting red squirrels and roe deer adds to the pleasure of a stay here.

The five quality guest rooms in the house, all overlooking the gardens and wood, can be booked on a B&B or Dinner, B&B basis, while the self-catering facility comprises seven Scandinavian-style pine lodges in the hotel grounds, each sleeping up to four guests. They are extremely well built, with log-clad walls, slate roofs and raised bases in local stone. Inside, they have spacious pine-clad living areas with TV and radio, fully-fitted kitchens, two comfortable bedrooms, luxury bathrooms with spa baths and walk-in power showers and a separate sauna or cloakroom. Patio doors open on to raised balconies and more of the glorious views.

The 40-cover restaurant is open from 6 to 9.30 every day and for Sunday lunch, and booking is recommended for non-residents. The hosts have a warm welcome for the whole family, and the friendly, relaxed surroundings quickly put everyone at ease. The bar is a pleasant spot to meet the other guests over a glass of cask ale or something from the well-chosen wine list.

The hotel, which is open throughout the year, is located just 15 minutes from J36 of the M6 – off the main A590 onto the B5277 signed Grange-over-Sands, then first left on the road marked Meathop.

36 BLACKROCK HOLIDAY FLATS

Morecambe Bank, Grange-over-Sands,
Cumbria LA11 6DX
☎ 01539 534107/532836

Blackrock Holiday Flats are located in the heart of Grange-over-Sands facing Morecambe Bay and a short walk from the shops, gardens and promenade. Three self-contained units, each sleeping two, are equipped with everything needed for an independent, go-as-you-please self-catering stay. Dolphin Cottage stands in a private cul-de-sac and commands fine views of the Bay from the lounge/dining room and the bedroom; it has its own private car park.

Blackrock Flat no 1, which also enjoys great views, is situated on the first floor, with access by a path by the side of the garages and up a few steps; one of the garages is

exclusively for the flat. Blackrock Flat no 2 is located partly below No 1; the lounge and bedroom are in open-plan layout and it, too, has its own garage. All are very cosy and comfortable and open all year round. Bookings are weekly in season, and shorter breaks are available outside peak periods. Grange-over-Sands is a very pleasant place for a holiday, with a generally mild climate, lots of shops, cafés and restaurants and some excellent walking.

View from Dolphin Cottage

38 THE BYRE

Broughton House Farm, Field Broughton,
Cumbria LA11 6HN
☎ 01539 536577
e-mail: p-crowe@talk21.com
🌐 www.cottageinthelakes.org

Penny and James Crowe welcome visitors from all over the world to their home in a picturesque hamlet in a rural setting close to Cartmel. They offer outstanding self-catering in **The Byre**, a self-catering holiday cottage next to their handsome farmhouse

on a 120-acre beef farm. The centrally heated two-bedroom cottage was renovated as part of a barn conversion and combines period charm and character with all the modern conveniences. The kitchen has everything needed for a carefree, independent stay, with fitted pine units, electric cooker and microwave, dishwasher, toaster, kettle and crockery. It has a separate dining area, and a small flight of stairs leads to a roomy lounge with a three-piece suite,

electric fire and TV/DVD player.

The cottage is open all year round and children over 5 are very welcome (but no pets). The Byre is close to many excellent walks and many other activities, including climbing, sailing, fishing, riding and golf. Nearby Cartmel, one of the prettiest villages in the Peninsula, has plenty to interest the visitor, including the gatehouse of the Priory, the marvellous Church of St Mary & St Michael, the summer National Hunt racing....and sticky toffee pudding.

39 THE ENGINE INN

Cark-in-Cartmel, nr Grange-over-Sands,
Cumbria LA11 7NZ
☎ 01539 558341 Fax: 01539 558986
e-mail: karen@engineinn.co.uk
🌐 www.engineinn.co.uk

The **Engine Inn** is a cheerful, convivial inn that's equally popular as a much-loved local, an excellent restaurant and a comfortable Bed & Breakfast hotel. Run if fine style by Chris and Karen, the 17th century inn was formerly called the Fire Engine and took its name from the steam engines

that used to service the local mills of Cark. It stands on the southern edge of the Lake District on the Cumbria Way, just 2 minutes from Holker Hall with its 125-acre deer park and motor museum.

A log fire keeps things cosy in the bar, where customers can relax over a game of pool, a glass of real aleor something from the good wine list before their meal or while planning the next day's activities. The Inn holds a 'Cask Marque' for its real ales which include Old Speckled Hen and Black Sheep. Drinks are served all day and food from 12 to 3 and from 6 to 9 (all day Saturdays and School Holidays and all day until 8 on Sunday).

The chalkboard lists the day's specials, which run from soup and super sandwiches (hot beef & onion, bacon & brie, Cumberland sausage, prawn & smoked salmon) to haddock in beer batter, the day's roast which may be locally reared lamb, beef burger, steak & kidney pie, steak & ale cobbler, chilli and lasagne. Food is available to take away in mid-afternoon and after 9.30 (but call first). For guests staying overnight, the inn has five en suite upstairs rooms, one suitable for a family; the tariff includes a hearty English breakfast.

Chris and Karen are happy to discuss any special dietary requirements and can cater for birthday and other celebrations, buffet suppers and steam gatherings.

40 THE STAN LAUREL INN ‖ ⊨

31 The Ellers, Ulverston,
Cumbria LA12 0AB
☎ 01229 582814
e-mail: thestanlaurel@aol.com
⊕ www.thestanlaurel.co.uk

Starting life as a row of cottages, the **Stan Laurel Inn** is a delightful hostelry named after Ulverston's most famous son. Trudi and Paul Dewar only took over in April 2007, but they have already stamped their personalities on the place and are winning a growing following among both the good folk of Ulverston and visitors to this lovely part of the world. A minimum of three real ales, including the regular Thwaites Original, is always on tap in the cheerful bar, and wholesome, unpretentious food is served in generous helpings every lunchtime and evening (book for Sunday lunch).

The choice spans made-to-order baguettes and sandwiches, soups, daily roasts, lasagne, gammon steak, chilli tortilla stacks and liver & bacon, and boards outside list bargains for each day of the week, such as Pie & a Pint, Soup & a Sarnie and Friday's Fish for a Fiver. If you get in a fine mess about what to order, don't scratch your head and look silly – order anything, it's all fresh, good and tasty! The Stan Laurel is also a good base for touring the area, with three guest rooms – a double and a triple en suite, and a single with a private facilities.

41 THE DEVONSHIRE ARMS ‖

1 Bradyll Terrace, Victoria Road, Ulverston,
Cumbria LA12 0DH
☎ 01229 582537

A short walk from the centre of Ulverston, the **Devonshire Arms** is a friendly, convivial pub open lunchtime and evening and all day on Saturday and Sunday. Manager Jenette and Bar Manager Tony keep a good selection of real ales and keg beers, and the home-cooked food choice includes all-time favourites like fish & chips, Cumberland sausages, meat & potato pie and lasagne. All-comers are invited to cast inhibitions aside for the Friday and Saturday karaoke nights.

42 THE KINGS ARMS HOTEL

King Street, Ulverston,
Cumbria LA12 7DZ
☎ 01229 582850 Fax: 01229 236803
e-mail: lynnekingsarms@aol.com

Ulverston, with its fascinating alleys and cobbled streets, its ancient church, Laurel & Hardy Museum, Glass Centre and Canal, is a place that needs plenty of time to explore, and visitors looking for a comfortable, well-appointed base need look no further than the **Kings Arms Hotel**.

Stuart and Lynne Ward, who took over here in 2006, keep the welcome mat out for all who pass through the door, whether they've come for a drink, a meal or a holiday, and they have earned a fine reputation for the quality of the hotel's facilities in every department. They have really given the handsome Victorian building in the heart of town a new lease of life, and their 25 years in the trade have helped them turn the place round, not just as a regular meeting place for local residents but also as a place where visitors can pause for refreshment or enjoy a stay in the comfortable bedrooms.

The bar is open all day, seven days a week for drinks, which include Hartleys XB and a good selection of draught keg ales including Robinsons Smooth and Dark Mild. Children are welcome up to 8.30 in the evening. Quality home cooking is another plus, served from 12 to 5 every day on the printed menu and specials board; among the favourite dishes are fish specials and the ever-popular steak & ale pie.

The accommodation comprises six upstairs rooms which can be booked on a room only or Bed & Breakfast basis. One minute's walk away, Stuart and Lynne also have a holiday cottage sleeping up to 5 guests and available to let all year round. There is a function room catering for up to 100 and available for all kinds of occasions.

Market Place, Ulverston,
Cumbria CA12 7BA
☎ 01229 582546

Leaseholders Stephen and Vanessa have brought a breath of fresh air to the **Braddylls Arms**, which stands on the Market Place in the delightful town of Ulverston. The inn is open for drinks all day Monday to Saturday and at lunchtime on Sunday, and the bar choice includes two real ales, one of them always from the local Ulverston Brewery. Tables and chairs are set out at the front for alfresco sipping, and there's more outside seating in a landscaped area at the back with heaters and a canopy. A variety of snacks, including sandwiches, filled baguettes, panini and burgers, is served between 11.30 and 6 every day except Sunday.

For guests staying overnight, the inn has four excellent upstairs rooms – two doubles (one en suite), a double/twin and a single. The very reasonable tariff includes a generous cooked breakfast. Thursdays and Fridays bring live entertainment to the inn – open mike night on Thursday, karaoke on Friday. There's always plenty to see and do in Ulverston, including the Laurel & Hardy Museum, the Lakes Glass centre, the Church of St Mary and walks along the canal towpath or up Hoad Hill for a panoramic view of the town. And there's no more delightful starting point for a day's exploring than the Braddylls Arms.

Haverthwaite, nr Ulverston,
Cumbria LA12 8AJ
☎ 01539 531216 Fax: 01539 530695
e-mail: anglersarms@ktdbroadband.com

Ten real ales and great food served in a convivial atmosphere brings customers from near and far to the **Anglers Arms**, which stands in the heart of Haverthwaite, 200 yards off the A590 and a short distance from Ulverston. When Michael and Linda Cairns took over in 2003 they brought many years of knowledge and experience in the business, and their warm, genuine welcome extends to young and old alike – and their dogs.

The real ales come from a variety of breweries, including Moorhouses, Hawkshead, Copper Dragon, Black Sheep, Tom Woods and Everards, and the number rises to about 40 during the Beer Festivals hosted by the pub every March and August. Food is an equally important part of the business, served every lunchtime and evening, and such is the popularity of the place that booking is advisable at all times, and essential at the weekend. Appetites large and small are admirably catered for on menus that range from light bites, sandwiches, burgers and jacket potatoes at lunchtime to seasonal fish and game, mince & onion pie, steak & ale pie (made with Hawkshead ale), roast chicken, lamb Henry (braise shoulder with herbs, garlic, red wine and redcurrant jus) and a mighty 24oz gammon steak served with all the trimmings.

The pub stands in a quiet rural community surrounded by quaint villages and the outstanding beauty of the Lake District National Park. Across the road from the pub is the Lakeside & Haverthwaite Railway, which originally carried passengers and freight to the steamers on Lake Windermere. Closed in 1967 but later preserved by an enthusiastic band of workers, it now runs a regular steam-hauled service throughout the summer season.

Spark Bridge, nr Ulverston,
Cumbria LA12 8BS
☎ 01229 861006
e-mail: sparkbridgeinn@aol.com
🌐 www.royaloaksparkbridge.co.uk

The **Royal Oak** enjoys a superb, picturesque location at Spark Bridge, half a mile off the A5092, at the foot of the Furness fells in the Lake District National Park. The building dates from the mid-17th century and was once an alehouse on a drovers' road, when it was known as The Foresters.

Leaseholders John and Tony took over only in May 2007, but already the place is buzzing. The hosts have plenty of experience in looking after their clientele, and the reward for that experience is a rapidly growing band of regulars. The bar is open all day, every day, for drinks, which include a minimum of three real ales – Black Sheep is the resident, accompanied by frequently changing guests. The chef prepares a fine selection of dishes for the printed menu and specials board, served from 12 to 2 and 6 to 9 daily. The choice really does cater for all tastes and appetites, with sandwiches and baguettes for quicker snacks, and other options ranging from the wonderful Morecambe Bay shrimps and Bantry

Bay mussels to cod with chips and mushy peas; penne pasta with smoked salmon and cream; steaks; steak & mushroom pie; BBQ-sauced chicken breast with bacon and cheese; braised lamb shank; and vegetable kiev. Super puds round things off in style, and the food is complemented by a well-chosen list of wines, mainly from the New World.

The Royal Oak is also a lovely place to take a break from the daily routine and an ideal base for touring this beautiful part of the world. The three superior letting rooms all

have en suite facilities, luxury toiletries and a beverage tray with bottled water and biscuits: Coniston has a four-poster, Hawkshead a double and a single bed, and Ullswater a double bed and two singles, making it perfect for families. A full English breakfast is served from 8.30 to 10 – and if that's too early, they'll even serve breakfast in bed!

The inn has a pleasant beer garden at the back and ample off-road parking.

Satterthwaite, nr Ulverston,
Cumbria LA12 8LN
☎ 01229 860237
e-mail: rnbbruce@aol.com

Rob and Rebecca Bruce, son Daniel and their chef Peter England have a real success on their hands at the **Eagles Head**, which stands in the heart of Grizedale Forest a short drive west of Lake Windermere. It started life in the 16th century as a farmhouse with an attached barn, and has been refurbished and modernised down the years while retaining its traditional charm and warmth.

Exposed stone walls, local prints and pictures, brass and copper set the scene in the welcoming bar, where local brews always feature among the real ales on tap. These include two brewed specially for the pub by the Moorhouses Brewery: Eagles Head (4% abv) and Grizedale Ale (4.8%). The Eagles Head is open all day every day in the high season (May - Oct) and Bank Holidays throughout the year, otherwise it opens lunch time and every evening session (closing Monday lunch time). Peter uses meats and other produce from local suppliers, and all his dishes are cooked to order. Portions are generous, prices very reasonable, and true, fresh flavours are always to the fore; local trout, game pies and the Sunday roasts are particular favourites, but everything is well worth trying.

Food hours are 12 to 2.30 and 7 to 8.30; no food Mondays except Bank Holidays and School Holidays. Special dietary needs can be accommodated with a little notice. There are seats for 40 inside and 40 more in the newly created outside seating area. The owners plan to add another string to their bow by adding guest accommodation, but meanwhile nearby Bowkerstead Farm (Tel: 01229 860208) is a camping site for tents, caravans and motor homes, and a riding centre with stabling for horses.

47 THE BRADDYLLS ARMS

Main Street, Bardsea, Cumbria LA12 9QT
☎ 01229 869707

Tenants Karen and Tom, chef Neil and manager Michele make a great team at the **Braddylls Arms**, which stands on the main street of Bardsea, 2 miles south of Ulverston. It's very near the coast, and the patio commands stunning views of the Bay. The bar is open every session and all day at the weekend for a good range of drinks, and an excellent selection of Neil's dishes is served every session except Monday lunchtime. The inn also has 3 en suite bedrooms for Bed & Breakfast guests.

48 THE COFFEE BEAN

224 Dalton Road, Barrow-in-Furness, Cumbria LA14 1PN
☎ 01229 433665

The **Coffee Bean** is a very popular destination for locals and visitors alike, on one of the town's pedestrian main thoroughfares. Anthony and Mary Goulding took over in 2004, refurbishing the place and adding their own brand of style and hospitality. Both cook, producing a tempting variety of tasty snacks and meals, from jacket potatoes to quiches and all-day breakfasts. Children

are always welcome, and a high chair is available. The Coffee Bean is open from 9 to 5 Monday to Saturday. Cash only.

49 THE RAMS HEAD HOTEL

110 Rawlinson Street, Barrow-in-Furness, Cumbria LA14 2DG
☎ 01229 821728 Fax: 01229 877844

The **Rams Head Hotel** is a handsome Victorian building on a corner site, an easy walk from the centre of Barrow. Its prime site and its outstanding hospitality make it a great favourite with both locals and visitors, and hosts Malcolm and Helen Barker and their family, here since 2004, have an equally warm welcome for familiar faces and first-timers. The hotel is open all day, from noon to midnight, serving a fine selection of drinks that include wines, spirits, soft drinks and the occasional guest real ale; Worthington Bitter and Carling are favourites with the regulars.

Hot and cold snacks are available all day, and for guests staying awhile the pub has seven comfortable bedrooms ranging from singles to family size, let on a room only basis. The beer garden really comes into its own in the summer, and

the hosts have plans to build a gazebo. The Rams Head is always friendly and relaxing, and inhibitions are well and truly cast aside for the karaoke sessions on Wednesday, Friday and Saturday nights. Live acts perform on Sundays, and sports fans can watch the big events on a big TV screen.

50 THE DUKE OF EDINBURGH HOTEL & BAR

Abbey Road, Barrow-in-Furness,
Cumbria LA14 5QR
☎ 01229 821039 Fax: 01229 833352
e-mail: theduke1871@googlemail.com
⊕ www.thedukehotelandbar.co.uk

In the heart of Barrow, the **Duke of Edinburgh Hotel & Bar** has been transformed by licensee Barry Ellis from a sad state of disrepair into the toast of the town. The bar area opened after refurbishment in October 2006 and 18 guest bedrooms came on stream in August 2007. This number will shortly be increased to 30, all with super kingsize beds, luxury en suite bathrooms and flat-screen TV. The bar stocks an impressive eight real ales, and a good selection of home-cooked food is served at lunchtime Tuesday to Thursday, from 12 to 9 Friday and Saturday and from 12 to 5 on Sunday.

53 PIEL CASTLE

Barrow in Furness, Cumbria
⊕ www.english-heritage.org.uk

The impressive ruins of a 14th century castle with a massive keep, inner and outer baileys, and towered curtain walls are still standing. It was built by the Abbot of Furness on the southeastern point of Piel Island, to guard the deep-water harbour of Barrow-in-Furness against pirates and Scots raiders. Piel Island, 3 ¼ miles SE of Barrow-in-Furness can be reached by smallboat from 11am, from Roa Island, summer only; subject to tides and weather. There is a small charge for this service; for details, call John Cleasby on 01229 475770 or 07798 794550

51 THE COFFEE SHOP

In the Dock Museum, North Road, Barrow-in-Furness, Cumbria LA14 2PW
☎ 01229 876331
e-mail: val.morley@sodexho.uk.com

The Dock Museum is one of the leading attractions in the North of England, and visitors to this superb modern museum can take a break in the **Coffee Shop**. Val Morley, who has managed the coffee shop since 2003, provides a tempting variety of home baking, snacks and made-to-order hot dishes. There are seats for 50 inside, and 24 more at picnic tables outside on the terrace. The Museum and the Coffee Shop are open from 10 to 4.30 in season (closed Monday) and from 10.30 to 3.30 out of season (closed Monday and Tuesday). Admission to the Museum is free.

52 THE DOCK MUSEUM

North Road, Barrow-in-Furness,
Cumbria LA14 2PW
☎ 01229 894444
e-mail: dockmuseum@barrowbc.gov.uk
⊕ www.dockmuseum.org.uk

One of the very best attractions in the North of England, the **Dock Museum** tells in fascinating detail the story of Barrow and its rapid growth from a small fishing village in the early-19th century to a town famed throughout the world for its industrial production and innovation. It was once the biggest iron and steel centre in the world and a major shipbuilder. Its first iron steamship was launched here in 1873, and in 1901 the Barrow shipyard built Britain's first submarine – and in 2007 it is once again building state-of-the-art subs.

The spectacular modern museum was built over an original Victorian dock, occupying a landscaped waterfront site with walkways linked to the Cumbria Coastal way, a picnic area and an adventure playground. Inside are exciting interactive

displays, a range of model ships, film shows, photographs and access to many images from the nationally important collection of glass negatives. It also hosts a vibrant programme of exhibitions and events throughout the year. Visitors can enjoy a wide range of snacks and hot meals in the coffee shop. Parking and admission are free at the Museum, which is open daily except Monday in season (10 to 4.30) and Monday and Tuesday out of season (10.30 to 4).

54 THE RED LION INN

5 Market Street, Dalton-in-Furness,
Cumbria LA15 8AE
☎ 01229 467914
⊕ www.redliondalton.co.uk

Dating from the early part of the 17th century, the **Red Lion Inn** is an immaculately kept hostelry with many traditional features and a friendly greeting from leaseholder Gary Thompson and his staff. It excels in all aspects – as a much-loved local, as a place to seek out for good food and as a base for touring the Furness Peninsula. The inn is open from 4 to 11 Monday to Thursday, from noon to midnight Friday and Saturday and from noon to 10.30 on Sunday. Well-kept ales, including Black Sheep Bitter and Ruddles County, have earned the inn a Cask Marque recommendation, and the food produced in the kitchens bring appreciative diners from near and far.

The menu offers something for everyone: classics like

fish & chips, superb steaks from Coopers Farm in Leece; almost forgotten favourites such as corned beef hash patties; seafood specials; modern classics such as chargrilled tuna or sizzling Chinese-style duck; and the likes of lemon thyme and asparagus risotto for vegetarians. Booking is advisable on Friday and Saturday evenings. For guests staying awhile the Red Lion has seven excellent bedrooms – four en suite, two on the ground floor, two in a purpose-built extension. All are welcome to join in the Thursday night quiz.

55 THE BLACK COCK INN

Princes Street, Broughton-in-Furness,
Cumbria LA20 6HQ
☎ 01229 716529
e-mail: dpike91556@aol.com
🌐 www.blackcockinncumbria.com

The **Black Cock** is a top-of-the-range inn offering the very best in hospitality, food and accommodation. The 16th century building stands in the heart of the attractive little town of Broughton-in-Furness with glorious Lakeland scenery close at hand. This much-loved inn is full of history, charm and atmosphere, and in summer window boxes and hanging baskets make a lovely colourful show. Behind the immaculate black-and-white frontage is just as inviting, whatever the season: the lounge bar with roaring log fires and low-beamed ceiling has a wonderful traditional ambience, and changes made by go-ahead landlord David Pike since his arrival in October 2005, including a very smart and stylish extension, have been carefully planned to retain all the period appeal.

David's vigour and stock of ideas have contributed greatly to the popularity of the old place, and the chef has won a strong and loyal following with his mouthwatering menu that combine pub classics with more exotic options. Typical dishes – the choice changes frequently – might include meat & potato pie with mushy

peas, lamb cutlets with all the trimmings, medallions of pork with a wholegrain mustard sauce, Cajun chicken breast, vegetable curry and Thai and Indian specials. Food is served in the spacious dining area from 12 to 2 and 5 to 9, with extended hours in high season, and such is the demand that booking is recommended for all meals to be sure of getting a table at the time you want. Children are made very welcome, and they can even choose from their own special menu.

The bar is open all day, seven days a week for drinks, which include a selection of five real ales – Theakston's Best and Marston's Pedigree are the regulars. The Black Cock is very much part of the social scene in Broughton, and it's also a great place to stay when touring the Furness and Cartmel Peninsulas, with five en suite guest bedrooms that include a family suite. There's excellent walking hereabouts, and many of the Lake District's finest scenery lies within easy reach, along with many historic features to discover. Broughton itself is well worth taking time to explore, and it's good to know that when the day's activities are over the Black Cock beckons with its special brand of hospitality.

The inn has a lovely secluded beer garden, tables and chairs at the front and plenty of off-road parking.

56 BRACELET HALL

Woodland, Broughton-in-Furness, Cumbria
LA20 6AQ
☎ 01229 716276
07745903725
e-mail: bracelet-hall@hotmail.com
🌐 www.bracelethall.co.uk

Bracelet Hall is a late-17th century farmhouse in a picture postcard setting looking down towards Coniston Water and miles of scenic countryside. Elizabeth and John Kirkbride (John was born here) invite guests all year round into their home, which has three en

suite letting bedrooms with four-poster beds; one room has a Jacuzzi and sauna. A real farmhouse breakfast sets guests up for a day exploring the lovely surrounding countryside. Cash and cheque only.

57 THE BLACK BULL INN, HOTEL & BREWERY

Coniston, Cumbria LA21 8DU
☎ 01539 441335 Fax: 01539 441168
🌐 www.conistonbrewery.com

The Bradley family – Susan, Ron and son Ian – have held the reins at the **Black Bull** for more than 30 years. The inn, which dates back to the 16th century, enjoys a glorious setting at the foot of the 800-metre Old Man of Coniston (the 'big toe' of the mountain is a large piece of stone set in the wall of the lounge). The inn has long been a favourite with walkers and climbers, and in the convivial bar they can quench their thirsts with the real ales produced by Ian and his team in the brewery behind the pub. Since 1995 the Coniston Brewing Company's brews have won numerous awards, the ultimate accolade coming in 1998 when Bluebird Bitter was crowned Supreme Champion Beer of Britain.

Food is also big business at The Black Bull, and local specialities such as Lakeland lamb, Esthwaite trout and

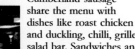

Cumberland sausage share the menu with dishes like roast chicken and duckling, chilli, grilled gammon and the choice from the salad bar. Sandwiches and snacks are added at lunchtime, and there's always a good choice for vegetarians. Food is served every day from noon to 9 o'clock. The painter Turner, the poets Coleridge and de Quincy and the speedboat ace Donald Campbell have all enjoyed the inn's hospitality, and for today's visitors touring this glorious part of the world there are 15 well-appointed en suite bedrooms.

58 THE CROWN INN

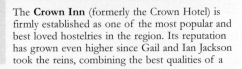

Coniston, Cumbria LA21 8ED
☎ 01539 441243 Fax: 01539 441801
e-mail: info@crowninnconiston.com
⊕ www.crowninnconiston.com

The **Crown Inn** (formerly the Crown Hotel) is firmly established as one of the most popular and best loved hostelries in the region. Its reputation has grown even higher since Gail and Ian Jackson took the reins, combining the best qualities of a comfortable Bed & Breakfast base with an equally appealing spot for a drink and a meal. It stands in the picturesque village of Coniston, the venue for the exploits of Donald Campbell and his boat Bluebird and his tragic death on the lake.

The hotel has been completely refurbished to a very high standard, providing comfort and service in the most civilised of surroundings. The accommodation comprises 12 well-appointed bedrooms including doubles, twins, triples and a family room; single bookings are available at quieter times. All the rooms have en suite bath or shower, central heating, television, direct-dial phone, hairdryer and hot drinks tray. Bookings are on a Bed & Breakfast basis, with two-day and five-day breaks available at certain times of the year. Alternative accommodation is offered in Holly Cottage, a lovely detached whitewashed house two minutes' walk from the inn, providing self-catering facilities for up to five guests.

Hartleys XB, Cunbria Way and seasonal guests head the list of drinks served in the convivial bar, and snacks and meals can be ordered throughout the day in the public lounge bar and dining room. The chefs use the best and freshest of seasonal ingredients in their dishes, which include home-made pies and local favourites like trout, Cumberland sausage and sticky toffee pudding on menus that cater for a wide range of tastes and appetites. The inn is on the path of the Cumbrian Way, and the hosts always make walkers very welcome.

The opportunities for walking and climbing are almost endless, including several ways up the Old Man of Coniston; a lakeshore walk to Torver and some of the best rock climbing in the land on Dow Crag. The Ruskin Museum is just round the corner, and the man himself is buried in the churchyard of St Andrew's (he preferred this resting place to Westminster Abbey). The elegant Victorian steam yacht Gondola and the traditional timber-built Coniston launch offer trips on the Lake.

60 THE SUN HOTEL

Coniston, Cumbria LA21 8HQ
☎ 01539 441248 Fax: 01539 441219
e-mail: thesun@hotelconiston.com
⊕ www.thesunconiston.com

The **Sun Hotel** is one of the favourite destinations in Cumbria, whether it's for a drink, a meal or a holiday in the most delightful surroundings. It was built in 1902 by the local brewery on the Walna Scar Road leading up to the Old Man of Coniston, on the old packhorse trail to the west. The brewery already owned a 16th century pub on the site, so it made sense to build the hotel next to it.

The whole place is warm, comfortable and very friendly, a tribute to the interest and effort invested by the family owners. Families with children (and pets!) are very welcome at The Sun, and the ten letting bedrooms, all with en suite or private bathroom, include three family rooms. Five cooked breakfast options get the day off to the best of starts, preparing guests for a day's walking or exploring the many and various attractions in the vicinity of the hotel. Alternative accommodation is provided in a holiday flat at the back of

the hotel, with two bedrooms, two bathrooms, a lounge and a mini-kitchen.

The owners are always making improvements, one of the most striking being the revealing of handsome wood panelling in the drawing room. The chefs expect their guests to work up good appetites on their excursions, and they make excellent use of locally sourced produce, including fell-bred traditional English and Scottish beef cattle, on menus that take their inspiration from both traditional English and foreign cuisines. A lovely conservatory was

added in 2001, and this and the lounge look out over the terrace to the garden that runs down the hill towards the lake and the village.

The superbly restored pub is a real gem, with exposed stone walls, flagstones, beams and a splendid old range in the fireplace. It's the perfect setting for meeting or making friends over a drink – 5 real ales and 35 wines available – or enjoying something from the bar menu.

59 BRANTWOOD

Coniston, Cumbria LA21 8AD
☎ 015394 41396 Fax: 015394 41263
e-mail: enquiries@brantwood.org.uk
🌐 www.brantwood.org.uk

Brantwood is the most beautifully situated house in the Lake District. It enjoys the finest lake and mountain views in England and there is no other house in the district with such a diversity of cultural associations. The home of John Ruskin from 1872 until his death in 1900, Brantwood became an intellectual powerhouse and one of the greatest literary and artistic centres in Europe. Tolstoy, Mahatma Gandhi, Marcel Proust and Frank Lloyd Wright can all be numbered amongst Ruskin's disciples.

The house is filled with Ruskin's drawings and watercolours, together with much of his original furniture, books and personal items. The video presentation and special displays provide a fascinating insight into the work of this great man and his life in a Victorian country house. Every

Thursday during the season there'll be lace making demonstrations and readings from Ruskin's writings are performed regularly in the study. An excellent bookshop specialises in Ruskin and related art and literature.

Brantwood's Estate comprises of 250 acres of gardens, pastures, ancient woods and high moors. Experience Ruskin's legacy and inspiration among eight distinctive gardens, which have been lovingly restored. Walk among beautifully scented azaleas and bluebells or marvel at magnificent views.

61 THE SHIP INN

Bowmanstead, nr Coniston,
Cumbria LA21 8HB
☎ 01539 441224

The Ship is a traditional country inn standing half a mile south of Coniston, overlooking Coniston Water on the A593 road to Torver. Built in the late 17th century, it was once a popular venue for drovers, and hosts Graham and Nicola Belcher have retained a fine period appeal while providing all the comforts demanded by today's visitors. The floral displays that deck the exterior in spring and summer have won many awards, and the bar is a delightfully relaxed and civilised spot for meeting or making friends over a glass or two of Hartleys XB or Cumbria Way real ale.

Bar meals, served from 12 to 2 and 6 to 8.45 (from 5.30 in high season) range from familiar favourites such as scampi, chilli con carne, steak & ale pie and sticky toffee

pudding to daily changing specials like mushroom & red pepper stroganoff, salmon with hollandaise sauce and strawberry & kiwi pavlova. The Ship is an ideal base for touring the region or just relaxing and enjoying the beautiful surroundings; the accommodation comprises three double rooms and a single, let on a B&B basis. The inn is closed Monday and Tuesday between November and March except during Christmas week, otherwise open lunchtime and evening, and all day on Bank Holidays and School Holiday weekends.

62 THE QUEEN'S HEAD HOTEL

Main Street, Hawkshead,
Cumbria LA22 0NS
☎ 015394 36271 Fax: 015394 36722
e-mail: enquiries@queensheadhotel.co.uk
🌐 www.queensheadhotel.co.uk

The **Queens Head** is a striking black-and-white timbered building standing in the heart of pretty Hawkshead. Owners Mr & Mrs Merrick provide everything a guest could want for an enjoyable visit, from the open-arms welcome and genuine hospitality to the comfortable accommodation and the super food. One look at the menu tells you that local produce means just that, with exceptional dishes featuring, among other ingredients, trout from Esthwaite Water, pheasant from the Graythwaite Estate, the Woodall family's traditionally cured hams, Herdwick lamb and the famous damsons from the Lyth Valley.

The ten guest bedrooms, all with private bathrooms and some with splendid four-posters, can be booked on a Bed & Breakfast or Dinner, Bed & Breakfast basis, and the owners

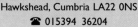

also offer self-catering accommodation in two nearby cottages and a studio apartment; the largest sleeps four, and all are beautifully appointed and fully equipped for a carefree stay – and guests in those units can order food from the hotel. Both options provide an ideal opportunity to relax and unwind, to soak up the scenery and culture of Lakeland, to walk, climb, cycle, fish, sail or take a boat trip....or to do nothing and enjoy the warm, friendly ambience of the hotel.

63 IVY HOUSE HOTEL & RESTAURANT

Hawkshead, Cumbria LA22 0NS
☎ 015394 36204
e-mail: ivyhousehotel@btinternet.com
🌐 www.ivyhousehotel.com

The **Ivy House Hotel & Restaurant** occupies a Grade II listed early-18th century building in a central position in the charming village of Hawkshead. Run by Rob (an ex-Rugby Union professional) and Julia Treeby with the valued assistance of Bradley and Jessica, it is well known throughout the region and is highly recommended for quality in everything it offers. Many visitors have become loyal regulars, either to eat or to stay.

The chef makes excellent of the best and freshest produce, as much of it as possible from local sources, in his tempting menus, which are served every evening from 6.30 to last orders at 9 o'clock. The restaurant ahs a warm,

intimate feel that makes it an ideal choice for a romantic meal or a special treat; non-residents must

book. Six beautifully appointed bedrooms (5 en suite, the other with an adjacent private bathroom) are in the main house, with five more in Mere Lodge just across the drive. All have televisions, hairdryers and hot drinks trays.

64   THE OLD DUNGEON GHYLL HOTEL

Great Langdale, Ambleside,
Cumbria LA22 9JY
☎ 01539 437272
e-mail: neil.odg@lineone.net
🌐 www.odg.co.uk

The **Old Dungeon Ghyll Hotel** enjoys a breathtaking, isolated location at the head of the Great Langdale Valley in the heart of the Lake District. For 300 years it has been attracting walkers, climbers and tourists, and since 1984 it has been run in fine style by Neil Walmsley, himself a keen fell-runner, and his wife Jane. It takes its name from one of the most dramatic of the Lake District waterfalls, tumbling 60 feet down the nearby fell.

Guest accommodation comprises 14 warm, comfortable bedrooms, some with en suite showers, some with four-posters. The residents' lounge is a great place to relax, meet the other guests and plan the day's activities, and the hotel has a drying room for wet clothes. This marvellous place was originally an inn with a farmhouse, and the oldest part is the middle section. Other bits were added down the years and the stables were made into a dining room. At the other end, the shippon was made into what is now the Climbers Bar, incorporating the old cow stalls. In the Hikers Bar, real ales (usually at least four) are served in an ambience of real charm and character. Neil and Jane both

cook, serving hearty home-made dishes on both bar and restaurant menus (non-residents should book).

In the days when charabancs brought visitors from Little Langdale over Blea Tarn Pass, they would stop at the top and blow the horn – one toot for each passenger needing a meal! The hotel became very popular with climbing clubs and a favourite venue for club dinners; great names of successive generations in the world of climbing, including Sir John Hunt, Joe Brown and Don Whillans. Clubs are still very welcome, and the hotel is the start point of several walks and climbs, including the famous peaks of Crinkle Crags, Bowfell and the Langdale Pikes.

65 DALE VIEW

Boot, Eskdale, Cumbria CA19 1TG
☎ 01946 723236
e-mail: daleview@booteskdale.fsnet.co.uk
🌐 www.booteskdale.co.uk

For more than 20 years John and Leigh Gray have been welcoming guests – many of them repeat visitors – to their lovely home **Dale View**. Built in 1881 as the mine managers house, it is now a first-class B&B in the picturesque

village of Boot in unspoilt Eskdale. The house has four beautifully appointed letting rooms, two on the

first floor and two on the second floor, and guests start the day with a splendid breakfast served in the flagstone-floored breakfast room.

66 MUNCASTER CASTLE

Ravenglass, Cumbria CA18 1RQ
☎ 01229 717614 Fax: 01229 717010

Muncaster Castle has been the Pennington home for 800 years. Tour the great hall, octagonal library and elegant dining room using the free audio tour, describing the unique treasures within.

Himalayan Gardens, described by John Ruskin as the "Gateway to Paradise", comprise over 70 acres of glorious gardens featuring plants and trees from all over the world. Spectacular rhododendron, camellia and azalea collections are set against the dramatic backdrop of the Lake District fells.

Join Max MeadowVole in the indoor MeadowVole Maze. Shrink to 5cm small and try to reach the other side without being eaten! Discover fascinating facts as you progress and you may win a prize.

Muncaster Interactive computers allow visitors to interact with Muncaster as never before! Enjoyable and fun, you can learn fascinating facts, watch the webcams or just play games!

The World Owl Centre is also based at Muncaster and features one of the largest collections of owls in the world. Over 50 species of owls, from the tiny Pygmy Owl to the huge European Eagle Owl. Delight in the daily displays. Meet the Birds at 2.30pm and Heron Happy Hour at 4.30pm (March to Nov)

Darkest Muncaster – a winter of evening magic! Stimulating, enchanting and thoroughly enlightening, Muncaster's famous gardens come alive with a visual feast which will tingle your senses and entertain the entire family.

179

67 THE BROWN COW INN

Waberthwaite, Cumbria LA19 5YJ
☎ 01229 717243

Owner Les Gott and chef Clare Fell are building a great reputation for good food and hospitality at the **Brown Cow**, a delightful inn located on the A595 3 miles south of Ravenglass. Les ran a pub in Coniston for 5 years, so he knows what his customers want, and his reward is a growing band of contented regulars. The bar is open all day for a wide selection of drinks, headed by Theakstons Best and Cumberland Ale.

The dining room opens at 10.30 Monday to Saturday for a full English or Continental breakfast and light bites, with the bar menu taking over at 11.30 (noon on Sunday); then come afternoon tea, high tea and the main evening menu served until 8.30. Dishes on this menu include all-time classics like cod & chips, steaks, Cumberland sausage and a very popular steak, onion and ale pie, and new classics like chicken, lamb, prawn and vegetables curries. Smaller portions can be served on request, and a takeaway service is available. Children are welcome, and the inn accepts all the major credit cards. Les plans to add another string to his bow with Bed & Breakfast accommodation.

68 QUIET COTTAGE

2 Poolside, Haverigg, nr Millom,
Cumbria LA18 4HW
☎ 01229 772974
e-mail: quietcottage@tiscali.co.uk
🌐 www.quietcottagegolakes.co.uk

Quiet Cottage is a superb self-contained self-catering unit set in 1½ peaceful acres and open all year round. It's owned and run by Mr and Mrs Haston, who have a warm welcome for their guests, including children but not pets. The cottage, in the village of Haverigg, lies close to the beach and an RSPB sanctuary at Hodbarrow. The RAF Museum in the village is a popular visitor attraction, and other places to visit nearby include Millom Folk Museum and Black Combe Fell.

69 BANKFIELD HOUSE COUNTRY HOTEL & RESTAURANT

Kirkstanton, nr Millom, Cumbria LA18 5LL
☎ 01229 772276 Fax: 01229 771017
e-mail: info@bankfieldhouse.com
🌐 www.bankfieldhouse.com

Idyllically located in five acres of beautiful countryside just off the A5093, **Bankfield House Country Hotel & Restaurant** is a real hidden gem. The building dates from 1710 and in almost 300 years has had only five owners. Since April 2006 it has been owned and personally run by Paul and Alyson Rhind; they have really put it back on the map with their hard work, personal service and attention to detail and they are attracting a clientele from outside the vicinity as news of the excellent ale, food and hospitality spreads.

The inn is open all year round from 10 o'clock for morning coffee, followed by the bar menu from 11.30, sandwiches, snacks and pastries until 6 and the main evening menu served until last orders at 8.30. The bar menu offers a wide choice of familiar favourites such as Cumberland sausage, lasagne, curries, home-made tarts and quiches, pizzas, steaks, beef & ale pie and salad platters. The evening menu extends the chefs' repertoire with tempting choices such as black pudding with whisky or pepper sauce; duck breast on a bed of red onion marmalade; sea bass with a dill and white wine sauce; and crunchy-style sweet & sour pork. Locally sourced meat, game and fish are the basis of the dishes, and both preparation and presentation are priorities. Booking is recommended on summer Saturdays and all year for the traditional Sunday lunch – the latter so popular that many of the regulars come every week.

Bankfield is also a popular choice for private parties and functions. It's a lovely spot to relax and unwind, and an ideal base for exploring the many attractions of coast and countryside close by. The five upstairs letting rooms, including a splendid bridal suite with a four-poster bed, walk-in shower and Jacuzzi, can be booked on a B&B or Dinner, B&B basis.

Station Road, Drigg, Cumbria CA19 1XQ
☎ 01946 724231
e-mail: vicdrigg@btconnect.com
🌐 www.thevicatdrigg.co.uk

The **Victoria Hotel** was built around 1850, when the railway arrived here, so naturally it was called the Railway Hotel. It stands off the A595 coastal road beside the main West Coast line, and the occasional train still stops here on its way to Barrow or Carlisle. New tenants Dave and Karen brought 30 years' experience with them when they took over the lease in June 2007, and their expertise and enthusiasm is already winning the place many friends, as a

place to meet for a convivial drink, to relax over a meal or to provide a start point for exploring the region. The bar is open every lunchtime and evening and all day on Sunday, and Jennings Bitter is a favourite tipple, to quench a thirst or to accompany a snack or a meal. Karen makes fine use of local produce for her tasty, wholesome, well-priced food, which includes a good variety of classic pub dishes such as Cumberland sausages, steak & ale pie, lasagne, liver & bacon, chilli con carne, curries and the always-in-demand fish specials.

Pub hours are 12 to 2 and from 4.30 Monday to Friday, 12 to 2 and from 6 on Saturday and from 12 onwards on Sunday; food is served every lunchtime and evening. The guest accommodation at the Victoria, available throughout the year, consists of six excellent upstairs rooms, including some suitable for families. The nearby coast and the endless acres of countryside offer many visitor attractions. Among the closest is Drigg Dunes nature reserve on the dunes and salt marshes by the River Irt; the dunes command fine views across to the Lakeland mountains and fells, and the reserve itself is home to what is believed to be Europe's largest colony of black-headed gulls.

71 STRANDS HOTEL

Nether Wasdale, nr Santon Bridge,
Cumbria CA20 IET
☎ 01946 726237 Fax: 01946 726122
e-mail: info@strandshotel.com
🌐 www.strandshotel.com

Strands Hotel enjoys a scenic location in a picturesque village east of the A595 and close to Wast Water, in the heart of the Wasdale Valley. Since June 2006 it has been owned and run by Mark and Lesley Corr, who really have given the place a new lease of life. Their warm, genuine welcome is second to none, and as news of the grand hospitality and outstanding facilities spreads the owners are already receiving repeat bookings.

Open from 4 o'clock on Monday, then all day every day, the hotel has two bars where guests and their friends have the choice of a minimum of four real ales. Mark has created his own micro-brewery that supplies 2 or 3 of his own ales, including Errmmm Bitter and T'Errmmminator Bitter (ask Mark to explain this!). Food is a major part of the business, and the printed menu and daily specials board provides a mouthwatering choice both lunchtime and

evening. Typical dishes run from lamb's liver pâté, smoked salmon Benedict and air-dried ham salad to sea bream steamed with a lime, honey and chilli marinade, roast duckling with a classic orange sauce, braised oxtail and steak, mushroom & T'Errmmminator pie. Booking is advisable on Friday and Saturday evenings and all evenings in peak season.

Strands also offers excellent accommodation in 11 upstairs rooms, all but one with en suite facilities. Children and dogs are always welcome. A good traditional breakfast sets guests up for a day discovering the local attractions, which include lovely beaches (just 6 miles away), golf, Muncaster Castle and the Owl Centre, the Roman fort at Hardknott and the La-al Ratty Steam Railway. The hotel has a cosy little residents' lounge, a beer garden and plenty of off-road parking.

72 THE LION & LAMB HOTEL

The Square, Gosforth,
Cumbria CA20 1AL
☎ 01946 725242 Fax: 01946 725276
e-mail: lionandlamb@tiscali.co.uk
🌐 www.lionandlamb.co.uk

Gosforth is a superb start point for discovering the beautiful western part of the Lake District, with many attractions of coast and countryside more or less on the doorstep. On the Square in the centre of town, the **Lion & Lamb Hotel** provides a particularly friendly base for tourists, but hosts Stewart and Fiona Burgess, here since 2000, have much more to offer than a super place to stay. The hotel, in a building that dates from the 17th century, is very much at the social heart of the community, and the bar is a favourite meeting place for both locals and visitors from outside the area.

Open all day, every day, it serves up to six real ales, with Jennings Bitter and Moorhouses Bitter the regulars. Open fires keep the place cosy in the evenings or on chilly days, while tables outside catch the noonday summer sun. To the rear is an undercover area, heated and lit, where smokers can light up. A long and varied menu based as much as possible on local produce, is served every session except Sunday evening; giant fish & chips and surf 'n' turf are among the most popular dishes, and special deals are available on fish night (Tuesday) and steak night (Thursday). Children are welcome in the bar and restaurant up to 9 o'clock in the evening.

The accommodation at the Lion & Lamb comprises 11 rooms of various sizes, all with en suite facilities, and a hearty breakfast sets guests up for a day's sightseeing....and there's certainly no shortage of things to see and do: Wast Water, with Nether Wasdale at its base and Wasdale Head at its tip; Calder Bridge and Santon Bridge; the delightful seaside resort of Seascale; Ravengalls on the Esk Estuary; and the charming Ravenglass & Eskdale Railway, the first narrow-gauge railway in Britain.

73 GOSFORTH HALL HOTEL

Wasdale Road, Gosforth,
Cumbria CA20 1AZ
☎ 019467 25322
e-mail: enquiries@gosforthhallhotel.co.uk
www.gosforthhallhotel.co.uk

Gosforth Hall is located on the western edge of the Lake District National park, close to Wastwater (the deepest Lake in England) and Scafell Pike (the highest mountain in England). Built back in 1658, the year of Oliver Cromwell's death, the Grade II* listed building retains many of it's original features, including the Coat of Arms dated back to 1673, located in the bar which CAMRA recently voted West Cumbria Pub of the Season for Spring 2007 . The Hall stands next to St Mary's Church with

its famous Viking Cross and is an excellent base for visiting the Eskdale Valley, Ravenglass, Muncaster Castle and Whitehaven. Rod and Barbara Davies, who took over the Hall in 2002, greet every guest as a friend, and take great pride in the accommodation, food and drink they provide at this superb place.

Their well-kept real ales, wide range of drinks, including a fine wine cellar and choice of meals keep the guests coming back time-and-time again. The restaurant is open for evening meals seven nights a week, although diners have the option of eating in

the bar, lounge, restaurant or beer garden. The seasonally changing menu takes its inspiration from home and abroad with dishes ranging from creamy garlic mushrooms, devilled kidneys & black pudding, steaks and seasonal game to kleftiko, chicken fajitas and spinach & brie pancakes. Barbara's signature dish, the chicken melt is a great favourite.

The nine beautifully appointed guest bedrooms include the superb Suite, which boats a four-poster bed and a truly vast en suite bath.

The hotel is an ideal base for touring the unspoilt Western Lake area and discovering the many scenic and historic delights of coast and countryside. Walking can be anything from a stroll by the lake to tackling the 3-Peak challenge – or guests can just sit back and relax in a walled beer garden where they might even catch a glimpse of the resident Barn Owl.

74 THE WHITE MARE

Beckermet, nr Calder Bridge,
Cumbria CA21 2XS
☎ 01946 841246 Fax: 01946 841100
e-mail: phil@whitemare.co.uk
🌐 www.whitemare.co.uk

Philip Ward is the friendly, enterprising owner and manager of the **White Mare**, a country house hotel, pub and restaurant in the village of Beckermet, close to the coast between Calder Bridge and Egremont and just a mile off the main A595 coast road. Dating back to the early 19th century, it has considerable charm and character, and open fires in the main lounge make it a cosy, inviting spot for a drink. Here, and in the Sports Bar at least six real ales are always on tap; the bars are open lunchtime and evening and all day Saturday (noon to 1am) and Sunday (noon to midnight).

With the new Bistro now open food is big business here. The Bistro and Restaurant menus are available 7 day per week. The chefs are kept busy producing a wide selection of food, with daily specials, vegetarian meals, children's dishes and special Senior Citizens menus also being catered for: Monday is steak night; Tuesday is curry night; Wednesday Dining around the World followed by a quiz (with £50 jackpot), Friday is special fish night, live entertainment on Saturday and roasts and bar meals served all day on Sunday. Philip and his staff love parties at the White Mare and are happy to organise anything from hen and stag nights to weddings and wakes. The inn has two approved venues for civil marriage ceremonies and superbly appointed marquees can cater for up to 250 guests.

Pool, darts and dominoes matches are held throughout the year, and they're always on the lookout for new players. All the major sporting events are shown in the Sports Bar, and everyone is invited to join in the Wednesday night quiz. The restaurant is also a popular venue for local singers and groups. The White Mare is definitely a place to tarry awhile, and B&B accommodation in eight rooms, including a bridal suite and family rooms, is available seven days a week, with attractive special offers at the weekend.

75 THE RED LION HOTEL

2 Market Place, Egremont,
Cumbria CA22 1AE
☎ 01946 824050
e-mail: redlionhotel@btopenworld.com

The huge red lion plastered on the front leaves visitors in no doubt that they've arrived at the **Red Lion Hotel**. It began life in the early years of the 18th century as a coaching inn, when it was an important stopping place on what was then the main Whitehaven-Barrow road. John Walker, who took the reins here in 1998, has expended lots of time, effort and enthusiasm in a major refurbishment programme that has restored the old place to its pristine style and elegance, making it a splendid place to meet for a drink, to relax over a meal or to spend a few days discovering the many attractions in and around Egremont.

The bar is open all day, every day for drinks, which include a good selection of draught and bottle beers and lagers, cider, stout, wines, spirits and non-alcoholic drinks. John Smiths Bitter, Fosters, Carlsberg and Kronenbourg are among the favourites with the regular patrons. The drinks can be enjoyed on their own over a chat or to accompany the hearty home-cooked food that the Red Lion serves every lunchtime and evening.

For guests staying awhile, the hotel has 11 rooms for B&B, varying from simple and homely with shared facilities to top-of-the-range en suite rooms, and the tariff varies accordingly. Egremont, set among the low hills of the Ehen Valley, is a small town with a lot of history, and well worth spending time to explore at leisure. Chief among the nearby attractions are the Castle,

the Florence Mine Heritage Centre and the Lowes Court gallery with its changing fine art exhibitions. The town also hosts a number of unique annual events, including a medieval festival, Crab Fayre Day in September and the World Gurning Championships. As well as being a great place for a drink, a meal and a touring base, the Red Lion is also one of Egremont's social centres. Entertainment, usually in the from of discos, brings a young crowd at regular weekends, and at the back of the hotel is a spacious function suite that's a popular venue for private parties.

187

Main Street, St Bees, Cumbria CA27 0DE
☎ 01946 822425 Fax: 01946 824949
e-mail: manorhousemaz@aol.com
🌐 www.themanorhousestbees.com

A warm Lakeland welcome awaits visitors to the **Manor House Inn & Coast 2 Coast Bar**, along with comfortable accommodation, delicious home-cooked food, real ales, a summer café and a pleasant beer garden.

Dating from 1720, the Manor House is one of the oldest buildings in St Bees, full of charm and period character, and the next-door Coast 2 Coast Bar occupies the even older former Royal Oak Inn. The two premises have been run since September 2006 by Margaret (Maz) and Jim Fee, their daughters Rebecca and Claire and their son Ian, and they and their customers ensure that there's always a real buzz about the place.

The bar is open from 4pm on Monday (earlier if a Bank Holiday) then all day for the rest of the week. Rebecca is in charge of the bar, where Cumberland Ale is the regular among the 3 or 4 real ales on tap. Claire and Ian are the stars in the kitchen, producing a good selection of dishes including the very popular Sunday lunchtime carvery. Food is served from 12 to 4 (not Monday) and 6.30 to 9 (not Sunday).

Eight beautifully decorated and furnished en suite bedrooms provide a very comfortable base for exploring the Western Lakes and fells, or for venturing on to the 190-mile Coast 2 Coast walk from St Bees across the Pennines to Robin Hood's Bay on the North Yorkshire coast. Maz and Jim also run a B&B with 5 en suite rooms at Jasmine House in nearby Moor Row, a five-minute drive away. Jasmine House (Tel: 01946 815795) was voted the best B&B in Copeland for 2006.

Beach Road. St Bees, Cumbria CA27 0ES
☎ 01946 820175 Fax: 01946 820456
🌐 www.hartleys-ice-cream.co.uk

In an unbeatable location overlooking the foreshore at St Bees, **Hartleys Beach Shop & Tea Room** is one of the most popular places in the region for enjoying a snack. It's a long, single-storey building where locals, tourists, walkers and holidaymakers swarm like bees to a honeypot. It provides fuel for those setting out on the Coast- to-Coast Walk across the Pennines, and of course much-needed refreshment for those at the end of the walk.

The tea room is open daily from 9 to 5, with hot food served until 4 o'clock. The food choice runs from made-to-order sandwiches with generous fillings like tuna savoury, corned beef & onions and chicken mayo, to soup, beans on toast and home-made cakes, teacakes and scones. And very few summer visitors leave without trying one or more of the delicious ice creams, which are made by the firm established by the Hartley family in 1931 in Egremont, where they are still made. The business

was taken over in 1981 by the Richardson family, who run the beach shop with friendly, hardworking staff.

The ice creams come in more than 60 flavours, with some diabetic varieties and also eight flavours of sorbets. They are sold to the public and to the retail and catering trades in tubs from 125ml to 10 litres, and freezer packs are a speciality. They are made fresh every day in the Church Street creamery in Egremont, and new lines include semi-freddo desserts – a perfect way to end a meal. The tea room has seats for 48 inside, and when the weather is kind, tables and chairs are set outside. Hartleys at St Bees also has a gift shop and mini-mart selling walking and camping essentials.

79 GROVE COURT HOTEL

Cleator, Cumbria CA23 3DT
☎ 01946 810513 Fax: 01946 815412
e-mail: annebarwise@btconnect.com
⊕ www.grovecourt.com

Just off the A5086 in Cleator, surrounded by delightful countryside, the **Grove Court Hotel** was once the village's junior school. It closed around 20 years ago, when it became a hotel, and when Ian and Annie Barwise took over in December 2006 they completely refurbished the place. Anne was once a pupil at the school, and she can now give a lesson in how to be a charming, attentive host.

The superbly appointed interior, smartly and sympathetically modernised, has an eyecatching bar counter and plenty of comfortable seats in which to relax and enjoy a chat and a drink. The link with school food is well and truly broken by the talented chefs, who use mainly local produce in excellent dishes served from 11.45 to 1.45 and from 6.45 to 9. The wide choice runs from sandwiches and jacket potatoes to pub classics – steaks and steak pie,

roasts every day, lasagne, chilli con carne, battered cod and haddock, scampi, salmon, liver & onions, chicken or beef curry, oriental chicken stir-fry – and always a fine variety of vegetarian dishes. The head chef is Martyn Harding, the sous-chef Craig Andrew Brough. The Grove Court is a popular venue for wedding receptions and other special occasions, and the impressive function can hold up to 220 guests.

For guests taking a break, this delightful place has 15 ground-floor en suite bedrooms of various sizes, including three family rooms; some are located in the old classrooms. Ian and Anne can definitely chalk up a success at their splendid hotel, which is open throughout the year.

76 THE BEACON

West Strand, Whitehaven,
Cumbria, CA28 7LY
☎ 01946 592302
e-mail: thebeacon@copelandbc.gov.uk
🌐 www.copelandbc.gov.uk

Situated on Whitehaven's attractive
harbourside, **The Beacon** is home to the
town's museum collection. It traces the social,
industrial and maritime heritage of the area,
using local
characters, audio-
visual displays
and fascinating
museum pieces.
The Met Office
Weather Gallery,
where you can
monitor, forecast
and broadcast the weather, offers panoramic
views of the town and coast. Also, don't miss
the Harbour Gallery, which offers free entry
to the changing exhibitions, the gift shop and
café. Guided heritage walks are available
through town and over the headland to Haig
Colliery Mining Museum. Disabled access and
facilities.

HIDDEN PLACES GUIDES

Explore Britain and Ireland with
Hidden Places guides - a fascinating
series of national and local travel
guides.

Packed with easy to read information
on hundreds of places of interest as
well as places to stay, eat and drink.

Available from both high street and
internet booksellers

For more information on the full range
of *Hidden Places* guides and other
titles published by Travel Publishing
visit our website on

www.travelpublishing.co.uk
or ask for our leaflet by phoning
0118-981-7777 or emailing
info@travelpublishing.co.uk

80 THE SHEPHERDS ARMS HOTEL

Ennerdale Bridge, Cumbria CA23 3AR
☎ 01946 861249
e-mail: shepherdsarms@btconnect.com
🌐 www.shepherdsarmshotel.co.uk

In the centre of Ennerdale Bridge, on Wainwright's
famous Coast to Coast Walk, the **Shepherds Arms
Hotel** is an ideal base for discovering a lovely part
of the world. It's also a very pleasant spot for
enjoying a drink or a meal, in the bar, in the
panelled Georgian restaurant or in the newly refurbished outdoor at the back of the building. From
Easter to the end of September the bar is open all day,
every day, and out of season lunchtime and evening
Monday to Thursday and all day at the weekend.

Old beams and open fires create a cosy ambience in the
400-year-old building for a drink and a chat – Jennings
Bitter and Cumberland Ale are among the five real ales on
tap in the summer (three in the winter). Food is served

lunchtime and
evening, and the
printed menu and
daily specials
board provide
plenty of choice
for all tastes and appetites. Eight centrally heated upstairs
bedrooms – six en suite, two with private bathrooms –
are available throughout the year for B&B guests. The
Coast to Coast Walk runs the whole length of Ennerdale,
and there are some lovely walks around secluded
Ennerdale Water.

191

Crown Street, Cockermouth,
Cumbria CA13 0EX
☎ 01900 823449

Dating from the 18th century and once known as The Commercial, the **Kingfisher Inn** is located close to the centre of the wonderful town of Cockermouth. Ian and Julie Wright have been running this outstanding hostelry since 2004, before which they ran a nearby restaurant. They have retained many old friends and made many new friends in the subsequent three years, both among the locals who come here for the warm, inviting ambience and among visitors, who know that they can look forward to the warmest of welcomes and unbeatable hospitality. The inn is closed Monday lunchtimes then open from 6pm. Otherwise it is open lunchtimes and evenings Tuesday - Thursday and all day, Friday, Saturday and Sunday between Easter and October. Out of season it is open Monday evening and lunchtimes and evenings Tuesday to Sunday.

Hartleys XB is the regular real ale, and the bar stocks a good selection of keg beers. The Kingfisher is also an excellent place for a meal, and the menus provide a good choice of traditional home-cooked dishes – steaks, steak pies, chicken, fish specials, daily roasts – served between 11.30 and 2 Tuesday to Sunday and from 6 to 9 Tuesday to Saturday. There are seats for 22 in the dining room, or diners can eat in the bar, or on good days in the pub's delightful surprise, a secluded garden overlooking the river. Cockermouth is a gem of a town, with a broad main street and handsome Georgian houses, Children are welcome until 9 in the evening.

There's always plenty to see here, including the house where Wordsworth was born, the Castle, the Printing House Museum and Jennings Brewery. And it's good to know that when energy flags and a pause for refreshment is the order of the day Ian, Julie and the staff at the Kingfisher are ready to provide it.

Wellington Farm, Cockermouth,
Cumbria CA13 0QU
☎ 01900 822777
⊕ www.wellingtonjerseys.co.uk

In 1946, the Stamper family bought Wellington Farm, where they have lived and worked ever since. They have seen many changes, the most notable coming in 2004 when, faced with the growing financial pressure on dairy farming, they started a new project. **Wellington Jerseys Ice Cream** was opened in March 2005 and is managed by Gill and Susan Stamper.

Their 280-acre dairy farm has a Jersey herd that provides the milk for the superb ice creams made on the premises by Leigh Stamper. Leigh's repertoire runs to some 40 flavours, with 16 available at any one time, including the award-winning whisky & marmalade and a selection of seasonal varieties. The ice cream is what the farm is best known for, but visitors also come from miles around to enjoy the excellent food served in the **Old Stackyard Tea Rooms**. The choice runs from home-made cakes and

tray bakes to steak pies and other hot dishes served with super chips, accompanied by speciality teas, freshly ground coffee and other drinks. Food is served from 10 to 5 (hot dishes from 11.30 to 2.30) and when the weather is kind visitors can enjoy their food on the terrace accompanied by wonderful views of the Western fells. The ice creams and other dairy products, along with local preserves and crafts, are sold in the farm shop.

A short walk from the tea room, Dubbs Moss is an area of wetland and woodland, rich in wildlife, owned by the Cumbria Wildlife Trust. It's a lovely spot to work up an appetite, but it can be a bit soggy, so wellies are definitely a good idea. To get to the farm follow the signs off the Egremont roundabout on the A66 at Cockermouth; take the exit for Mitchells Agricultural Market and follow the signs for the farm. There's plenty of parking at the farm, with disabled parking and access, and other services include baby-changing facilities.

83 ROOK GUEST HOUSE

9 Castlegate, Cockermouth,
Cumbria CA13 9EU
☎ 01900 828496
⊕ www.therookguesthouse.gbr.cc/

Rook Guest House provides comfortable, high-quality B&B accommodation close to the Castle and just a short drive from the A66. Three stylish bedrooms in the early-18th century house are all en suite, and owner Vicky Waters, here for more than 10 years, is on hand to see that her guests are enjoying their stay. Children are welcome, and Vicky makes sure that the day starts with a good breakfast for everyone. Cockermouth has a wealth of history to discover, and Rook Guest house is an ideal base for tourists.

84 NORHAM COFFEE HOUSE & RESTAURANT

73 Main Street, Cockermouth,
Cumbria CA13 9JS
☎ 01900 824330

Susan Black and Andrea Nawrockyj are the joint proprietors of **Norham Coffee House & Restaurant**, tucked away off Main Street in the heart of the fine old market town of Cockermouth. This is their first venture into the catering business, but since they came here in April 2006 they have made it a popular spot for customers of all ages, whether they be local residents or visitors who come to Cockermouth throughout the year. The printed menu makes excellent use of local produce to provide plenty of choice for all tastes and appetites; among the favourites are lasagne, steak pie, the Wednesday roasts, the home baking and the scrumptious desserts.

There are seats for 50 inside and a further 25 on the sheltered patio. Some come to Cockermouth to look at the ruined castle, some to admire the work of local artists in Castlegate House, others to sample the products of the long-established Jennings Brewery. But whatever their reason for visiting the town, they will be pleased that they dropped in at Norham Coffee House.....and Susan and Andrea will be pleased that they did. Opening times are 9 to 4 Monday to Saturday. Cash and cheque only.

85 THE BUSH HOTEL

Main Street, Cockermouth,
Cumbria CA13 9JS
☎ 01900 822064

Whatever brings visitors to Cockermouth – the Castle, the museums, Wordsworth's house, Castlegate Gallery – it's always well worth pausing awhile at the **Bush Hotel** to get a real flavour of the local brews, the local characters and the local atmosphere.

Leaseholders David and Tracy Bell and Bar Manager Jim Weldon, all with considerable local experience, have an equally warm and genuine welcome for familiar faces and first-time visitors at this appealing former coaching inn. The arched entrance to the courtyard used by the old stage coaches still stands, and behind the striking black and white frontage the inn has an inviting old-world atmosphere, with comfortable chairs and settees, upholstered stools, carpets and a handsome old brick hearth.

The inn is open all day, seven days a week for drinks on a long list that starts with a selection from the local Jennings Brewery, including Best Bitter, Mild, Cock a Hoop, Cumberland Ale and Snecklifter. There's also a good choice of other draught and bottle beers and lagers, stout and cider. This is definitely one of the best places in Cockermouth to socialise over a drink, with a convivial atmosphere created by the management, the staff and locals and visitors of all ages and from all walks of life who come here for the good beer and the good conversation. When the weather is kind, the beer garden, with heaters for cooler evenings, is a popular spot for alfresco sipping.

86 ALFIE'S CAFÉ

1 Old Kings Arms Lane, Cockermouth,
Cumbria CA13 9LS
☎ 01900 822256
⊕ www.alfiescafe.co.uk

Tucked away down the lane between Boots and a Travel Agent, **Alfie's Café** is a place to relax and enjoy a break with a range of hot and cold drinks and light meals. The long courtyard off Cockermouth's main street is away from the bustle of the town, but Alfie's has a cheerful, convivial atmosphere all of its own.

Owner Marty Hetherington crated the café in 2005, naming it after her dog, and she and her staff – Lucy, Danika, Marianne, Martha and Steph – have made it a really homely, inviting place, recommended by the residents of Cockermouth and many local guest houses.

The choice includes the excellent soups of the day,

perhaps pea & mint or roasted tomato & red pepper, sandwiches, burgers, lemon cake, chocolate cake, apple scones and Victoria sponge. Alfie's is open from 10 to 6 Monday to Saturday.

87 JUNIPERS RESTAURANT & CAFÉ BAR

11 South Street, Cockermouth,
Cumbria CA13 9RU
☎ 01900 822892
⊕ www.junipersrestaurant.co.uk

Junipers Restaurant & Café Bar is a magnet for all lovers of good food. Debbie and Lee refurbished the place when they took over in 2004, having previously owned another restaurant in Cockermouth. Lee is a chef with 30 years' experience, which he puts to excellent use in both the café bar and the restaurant. The former, softly lit, with plenty of comfortable seats, is a super place to meet friends for a speciality coffee or a glass of beer or wine, and from 6.30 the drinks can be accompanied by a selection of hot and cold tapas-style dishes.

The upstairs restaurant is open every day except Sunday lunch and all Tuesday for a menu of worldwide inspiration,

typified by spicy meatballs, chicken liver pâté with Cumberland sauce, tandoori chicken salad, Scottish salmon with a timbale of sweet chilli rice, steaks and beef bourguignon. The lunchtime menu offers lighter versions of the evening dishes, along with sandwiches, fishcakes, burgers and jacket potatoes.

88 GRAYSONSIDE

Lorton Road, Cockermouth,
Cumbria CA13 9TQ
☎ 01900 822351 Fax: 01900 821665
e-mail: stay@graysonside.co.uk
🌐 www.graysonside.co.uk

Set within 32 acres in the Lake District
National Park, **Graysonside** is a superb base
for touring a beautiful part of the country.
Former farmers Andrew and Janette
Likeman, who arrived here in 2000, offer
quality, comfort
and space in ten
rooms for B&B,
six on the
ground floor, all
with en suite
bathrooms.
Breakfast is
served in a
superb room in
the newly created extension – evening meals
are provided by arrangement, and this room
is available for small parties or meetings for
up to 30. The owners also offer self-catering
accommodation in a ground-floor apartment
for 2.

HIDDEN PLACES GUIDES

Explore Britain and Ireland with
Hidden Places guides - a fascinating
series of national and local travel
guides.

Packed with easy to read information
on hundreds of places of interest as
well as places to stay, eat and drink.

Available from both high street and
internet booksellers

For more information on the full range
of *Hidden Places* guides and other
titles published by Travel Publishing
visit our website on

www.travelpublishing.co.uk
or ask for our leaflet by phoning
0118-981-7777 or emailing
info@travelpublishing.co.uk

91 THE TRAVELLERS REST

63 High Street, Workington,
Cumbria CA14 4EU
☎ 01900 602064 Fax: 01900 66461

Every member of the family is made welcome at
the well-named **Travellers Rest**, which is handily
located in the heart of Workington. The delightful
Jacki Dawson, who took over as tenant in July
2006, has given the place a real sparkle, and the happy
atmosphere and the smiles on the faces of both
customers and staff are a tribute to her fine hospitality.
John Smiths Extra Smooth, Theakstons Mild and
Fosters Lager are the favourite tipples served all day in
the bar, and food is served from 12 to 2 and 6 to 8.30
every day.

Among the many popular dishes are liver & onions,

Lakeland
lamb, steak
pie, the
Sunday
roasts, *real*
chips and

the local speciality sticky toffee pudding. Children have
their own menu or can have half-portions from the
main menu; they can also dip into the toy box or romp
in the outside play area; they can also enjoy free refills
of drinks. All are welcome for the Monday quiz, which
starts at 9 and includes a free supper.

89 THE OLD VICARAGE

Church Lane, Low Lorton,
Cumbria CA13 9UN
☎ 01900 85656
e-mail: enquiries@oldvicarage.co.uk
🌐 www.oldvicarage.co.uk

The Old Vicarage is an elegant, traditional country house offering excellent accommodation in trim gardens and grounds surrounded by the unspoilt countryside of the Vale of Lorton. Hosts Jane and Peter Smith provide real home-from-home comfort and ambience, and relaxation comes easily in the guests' sitting room with a real fire, books, games and local newspapers.

Six en-suite rooms in the main house include one ground-floor room and one four-poster

room; two more rooms, a double and a twin in the former stables and coach house, are an ideal choice for a family. Rooms are booked on a Bed & Breakfast basis, with dinner available by arrangement.

The locally-sourced centrepiece of a meal might be roast rack of Lakeland lamb or rosemary and pepper-crusted Lakeland trout with sauce mousseline. Guests start the day with a super breakfast looking out onto the lawn (and perhaps spotting a red squirrel) and a quiet malt in front of the fire makes a lovely end to the day while planning the next day's outings.

"There is a yew tree, pride of Lorton Vale" wrote William Wordsworth in his poem Yew Trees. It's still there, behind the village hall in High Lorton. Stunning views and glorious scenery add to the pleasure of a stay in this outstanding place, with Grasmoor, Grisedale Pike and Whinlatter nearby, and walks can be as gentle or energetic as you like.

Deanscales, Cockermouth,
Cumbria CA13 0SL
☎ 01900 823278
e-mail: oldpostinghouse2@aol.com
⊕ www.oldpostinghouse.co.uk

Fine food and superb guest accommodation are two of the assets of the **Old Posting House**, which stands alongside the A5086 three miles south of the A66 and Cockermouth. Mike Peat, who previously ran a pub in Bradford, took over the reins here in 2003 and lost no time in making improvements at this grand old place. A major extension is providing a new dining area that brings the number of covers to 110 – and at busy times every one of them is needed, so popular has the inn become, not just with the local community but also

with the many tourists who flock to this part of the world, particularly in the summer; booking is recommended for all meals.

Local produce features prominently on the main printed menu, served every lunchtime and evening, and the specials board. Dishes on the latter might include variations on haddock (battered, poached or stuffed with tuna and prawns), ham shank with a BBQ sauce, chicken with bacon and leeks in a stilton sauce, grilled swordfish, roast pork or poached salmon with prawns and mushrooms in a white wine sauce. Mike has also brought on stream four upstairs guest bedrooms with walk-in showers and flat-screen TVs.

Built some 300 years ago as a stopping place in coaching days, this splendid hostelry was for many years called The Beehive. When alterations were in progress many years ago, the builders working on one of the walls found the ancient village posting boxes – large boxes for the wealthy, smaller ones for the ordinary folk. The find was authenticated by English Heritage, who insisted that the premises should return to their old name. Those old boxes take pride of place on display in the bar, which also features extensive collections of plates and teapots.

92 THE LAKE DISTRICT COAST AQUARIUM

South Quay, Maryport,
Cumbria CA15 8AB
☎ 01900 817760
e-mail: info@ld-coastaquarium.co.uk
🌐 www.lakedistrict-coastaquarium.co.uk

The Aquarium was built in 1997 using private funding with support from the European Regional Development Fund. It has a wonderful position on the South Quay of Maryport Harbour, affording views out across the Solway Firth to Scotland on most days. The harbour area has received substantial public investment from the mid 1980's onwards as part of a regeneration programme following the closure of local coal mining, steel making and shipbuilding, and tourism was seen as having a vital part in this.

The Aquarium is privately owned and not part of a national chain, and is the size of a typical modest Sea-Life Centre that most of the public are familiar with. The 45 displays that make up the live exhibition all contain local or Irish Sea species, as well as a wide variety of shellfish and invertebrates. It is rated as being one of the best places to go to see native sealife now that most other aquariums have diversified into being eclectic selections of world wide species.

In order to broaden the appeal of the attraction and make it possible to stay all day, there is a highly rated integral café overlooking the harbour, a well stocked gift shop, a 12 hole crazy golf course , a radio control boat pool and water cannon game, and an extensive adjacent free adventure play park run by the local authority.

It is open every day year round from 10-5 except on the 25th and 26th of December, and all admission tickets are valid for re-entry on the day of issue so that people can take advantage of the scheduled fish feeding demonstrations.

93 BRANDRAW HOUSE

2 West Street, Aspatria,
Cumbria CA7 3HG
☎ 016973 21207
e-mail: info@brandrawhouse.com
🌐 www.brandrawhouse.com

Robert and Joan Ahrens extend a home-from-home welcome for guests at their 19th century family home. Secluded in its own grounds in Aspatria, on the A596, **Brandraw House** has eight upstairs guest rooms, three of them en suite, all individually decorated and furnished. The tariff includes breakfast; packed lunches and

evening meals are available by prior arrangement. The house has many original features, and many of the rooms command superb views.

94 SNITTLEGARTH LODGES

Snittlegarth, Ireby, Wigton,
Cumbria CA7 1HE

☎ 016973 71235

e-mail: green_snittlegarth@hotmail.com

Country roads lead from the A591 and A595 to the quiet village of Snittlegarth, where Roddy and Ros Green provide superior self-catering accommodation in two luxurious pine lodges. **Snittlegarth Lodges** were created and opened as recently as January 2007 but have already won many friends. Open all year round, they have superbly appointed interiors that contain everything needed for a relaxing, come-as-you-please holiday.

Each lodge sleeps up to four guests, and short breaks are available at certain times of the year. The woodland setting is home to abundant wildlife, including red squirrels, and this whole area, at the top end of the Lake District national Park, is great walking country. The attractions hereabouts are many and varied: rambling and birdwatching around Bassenthwaite Lake, climbing on Skiddaw, spectacular scenery and Trotters World of Animals, providing a great day out for all the family.

95 THE GINCASE

Mawbray Hayrigg, nr Silloth, Wigton,
Cumbria CA7 4LL

☎ 016973 32020/31443

e-mail: val@gincase.co.uk

🌐 www.gincase.co.uk

Farmhouse Tearoom, Craft Barn, Gallery and Farm Park. **The Gincase** has all these on one site, making it one of the leading visitor attractions in the area. The hands-on owners are Val and John Nattrass, and in the tea room, where a cooking range dating from 1760 is among the period items on show, Val uses local produce and traditional recipes in her delicious home baking. Morning coffee, hot and cold lunches and afternoon tea can be enjoyed in the Gincase building or out in the lovely orchard garden.

The adjoining Craft Barn is filled with high-quality items made by hand in Cumbria, and the bright, airy Gallery exhibits work in many media and styles by Cumbrian artists, the displays changing every six weeks. The Rare Breed Farm and Animal Park is home to a wide variety of animals including cows and

calves, goats and kids, sheep and lambs, pigs and piglets, ponies, donkeys, chickens, ducks, geese, turkeys, rabbits and guinea pigs.

Also at this family attraction is a children's playground with ride-on toys and a sandpit. In a quiet location just a mile from the picturesque Solway Coast, The Gincase is open daily except Mondays out of season. The Farm Park is open from Easter to the end of October. Facilities include free parking, disabled access and toilets, and baby changing facilities.

97   NITH VIEW GUEST HOUSE

1 Pine Terrace, Silloth-on-Solway,
Cumbria CA7 4DT
☎ 016973 32860   mob: 07989 688452
e-mail: enquiries@nithview-
guesthouse.co.uk
🌐 www.nithview-guesthouse.co.uk

Location, hospitality, comfort and facilities all excel at **Nith View Guest House**, which stands on the seafront at Silloth, looking over the Solway Firth and across to the beautiful Scottish hills.

Hosts Garry and Louise Griffiths take justifiable pride in the lovely homely atmosphere they have created and in the excellent service and good food they provide. Smartly modernised behind its handsome exterior, the Victorian house is

fully centrally heated and has five guest bedrooms including a suite, all with private facilities shower and toilet, TV with Freeview and DVD, and tea/coffee tray.

Cots are available (or guests can bring their own) and the house has ample off-street parking and secure storage for bicycles, golf clubs and other items.

Rooms are booked on a Bed & Breakfast basis, and reductions are available for stays of more than 3 nights. Silloth is a delightful port and family seaside resort with low rainfall and a mild yet invigorating climate. It's a super place to explore at leisure, and the hearty Nith View breakfast will set guests up for discovering the many attractions, including the sandy beaches, the two-mile promenade and the sunken rose garden. It also has a renowned 18-hole championship golf course where the wonderful contralto Kathleen Ferrier learned to play the game.

96 SILLOTH CAFÉ

2 Station Road, Silloth, Cumbria CA7 4AE
☎ 016973 31319

Centrally located in the village from which it takes its name, the **Silloth Café** is equally popular with locals and visitors to this charming old port and seaside resort. In this substantial building on a corner site, Alison Henderson and her niece Amanda offer a warm, friendly welcome and a good selection of snacks and meals to enjoy in the café or to take away.

Fish & chips head the menu, and other choices run from filled rolls to Cumberland sausage, haggis and home-made pies and patties – something for everyone and most of it locally sourced. Gluten free dishes are available on request. Children are welcome – there's a special junior menu and high chairs are available. Opening hours are 11.30 to 1.30 and 4.30 to 8.30. Closed Wednesday. Cash and cheque only.

99 THE HARE & HOUNDS

West Street, Wigton, Cumbria CA7 9NP
☎ 016973 42879

Stephen and Judith Parker have breathed new life in to the **Hare & Hounds**, transforming it from a sad state of neglect into a thriving place recommended near and far for its well-kept ales and good food. Southwest of Carlisle between the main A595 and A596, it's open all day seven days a week for a good selection of keg ales, and tasty traditional food can be enjoyed daily from 11 to 3 and 6 to 8.30. Pub classics such as Cumberland sausage and steak pie are among the favourite dishes.

The energetic new tenants have made this one of the most popular places in Wigton, both with

the locals and with tourists pausing for refreshment during a walk round this pleasant market town, for long the centre of business and social life of the Solway Coast.

Stephen and Judith also run The Victoria, a popular drinking pub a short walk away.

98 TANGLEWOOD CARAVAN PARK

Causeway Head, Silloth,
Cumbria CA7 4PE
☎ 016973 31252
e-mail: tanglewoodcaravanpark@hotmail.com
🌐 www.tanglewoodcaravanpark.co.uk

Tanglewood is a family-run caravan park on the fringes of the Lake District National Park, in a tree-sheltered setting a mile inland from the pleasant small port and seaside resort of Silloth-on-Solway. Mike and Jen Bowman and Mike's parents Elaine and Norman have 11 modern static holiday homes with plenty of space (32' X 12') with car parking beside each home. They are fully equipped except for bed linen, with one latge end bedrooms and two singles, electric lighting, hot and cold water, toilet, shower, gas fire, cooker, fridge, TV and panel heating.

Tanglewood also has space for up to 30 touring caravans and motor homes, with electric hook-ups and water/drainage facilities provided, and campers are equally welcome. Modern tourist facilities comprise toilets, hot & cold water in washbasins, showers, shaver and hair-dryer points, chemical disposal points, dishwashing facilities and an automated laundry room. The Coach House has been converted into a licensed lounge bar open to Park clients and the public from 8pm daily and from lunchtime on Saturday and Sunday. A
children's games room adjoins the bar, and the site also has a play area with swings and a sandpit. Nearby Silloth is a delightful place with a sandy beach and many other attractions, and the caravan park is a perfect base for walking, touring and discovering the superb natural beauty of the region.

Tanglewood, which is open all year except the month of February, is one of the best of its kind, approved by the British Tourist Authority, the Automobile Association, the Caravan & Camping Club and the British Holiday & Home Parks Association.

204

100 LITTLEFIELD

32 Eskin Street, Keswick,
Cumbria CA12 4DG
☎ 01768 772949
e-mail: littlefield@keswick98.fsnet.co.uk
🌐 www.keswick98.fsnet.co.uk

The high percentage of returning visitors testifies to the excellent hospitality dispensed at **Littlefield**, which lies near the heart of Keswick close to numerous places of interest. Patrons love the warm welcome and the fact that nothing is too much trouble for hands-on owners Alison and Maureen.

The four en suite bedrooms – two on the first floor, two on the second – command

super views; all have showers, and one has a bath as well, and guests start the day with a superb breakfast that will fuel a day's sightseeing. The delightful owners invite guests to relax, enjoy, recharge their batteries and return soon to this little gem.

102 HONISTER HOUSE

1 Borrowdale Road, Keswick,
Cumbria CA12 5DD
☎ 017687 73181
e-mail: honisterhouse@btconnect.com
🌐 www.honisterhouse.co.uk

John and Susie Stakes came to **Honister House** in October 2006, their first venture into this type of business, and they have lost no time in building a reputation for outstanding hospitality and facilities here in the heart of Keswick. Their splendid B&B in one of the town's oldest buildings has three en suite bedrooms available throughout the year, decorated and furnished to a high standard and featuring Lakeland paintings and prints by local artists. Two of the rooms can be booked as a self-contained suite that's ideal for families.

The award-winning breakfasts are sourced locally

whenever possible using organic and Fairtrade produce – and it's a real treat to find

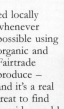

porridge and kedgeree among the options. Keswick is filled with interesting things to see and do, and John and Susie keep a range of guides, maps and books to help guests plan their day's activities. Children are welcome, but Honister cannot cater for pets.

I Penrith Road/Southey Street, Keswick,
Cumbria CA12 4HF
☎ 017687 71119   Fax: 017687 72341
e-mail: sewell5@aol.com

Shane and Joe Sewell and all the staff welcome visitors to **Rumours Bar & Restaurant** situated centrally in the busy and popular town of Keswick. Shane had worked here for several years before she and Joe took over the lease in 2003. To what was previously the County Hotel they have added adjacent properties, refurbished the whole place to a very high standard and created a top-of-the-range place to relax, dine and drink, meet and make

friends, enjoy a game of pool or watch the big match on sports TV. The bar stocks a good selection of draught keg ales and other draught and bottle beers and lagers – Fosters and John Smiths Smooth and Scotch Bitter are among the favourites.

Shane is a super cook and the regulars rave about her dishes, the generous portions and the very reasonable prices. The choice of good honest dishes freshly prepared to order is really impressive. Sandwiches, baguettes, hot rolls, sausage butties and toasted panini make tasty quick snacks, and burgers, single or double, come in no fewer than 18 varieties, including beef, chicken, venison, bison, kangaroo, ostrich, wild boar and vegetarian. Classic pub dishes – cod & chips, pasta, scampi, steaks, gammon, steak pie – are always in demand, along with roast beef, which is a popular fixture on the menu, and the weekly specials (one for each day of the week) of a main course and a drink. Home-made fruit crumble is a great way to end a meal. Smaller portions of many dishes are available for children or those with lighter appetites. Table service operates from 6 to 9 in the restaurant, while at lunchtime and after 9 food is ordered at the bar.

Rumours is open seven days a week: 11.30am to midnight Monday to Thursday, 11.30am to 2am Friday and Saturday and noon to 1am on Sunday. Food is served from 12 to 2.30 and from 6pm until an hour before closing. Children are welcome in the bar up to 9 o'clock.

103 LAKESIDE TEA GARDENS

Lake Road, Keswick, Cumbria CA12 5DJ
☎ 017687 72293

Stephen and Dina Goodwill are the proprietors of the **Lakeside Tea Gardens**. Equally popular with local residents and the many visitors to Keswick, it stands close to Derwent Water and is open every day from March to the first weekend in December, and at weekends at other times. The Tea Gardens can accommodate 50 inside and a further 180 outside this includes seating for 52 under cover.

Hot and cold dishes are available at the self-service counter between 10 and 5.30 (6 on Sunday), and local produce features prominently on the menus. Popular dishes include Cumberland sausage and pies supplied by the local butcher; they boil their own hams and roast their own turkeys, and the rolls with hot and cold fillings provide tasty lighter snacks. Cakes and pastries come fresh daily from a local baker – the cream scones are particularly hard to resist. The white self-playing piano (pianola) is a talking point in the main room. Cash and cheque only. Licensed for beer and wines.

104 THE SWINSIDE INN

Newlands Valley, Keswick,
Cumbria CA12 5UE
☎ 017687 78253
⊕ www.theswinsideinn.com

There are few finer places for a leisurely Lakeland holiday than the **Swinside Inn**, which stands in the lovely Newlands Valley, with stunning views from the terrace. This fine old drovers' inn is surrounded by endless acres of glorious countryside, looking one way towards Grisedale Pike and in the other down towards Derwent Water. The inn is a popular place for walkers and tourists, whether they've come for a refreshing drink, to settle down to a snack or a meal, or to spend a few days in the comfortable accommodation. The bar is open all day seven days a week for drinks, and the real ales – Cumberland Ale, Deuchars IPA and a rotating guest – are kept in fine fettle.

Meals are served from noon to 9pm from Easter to the end of October, and lunchtime and

evening out of season. All the food is sourced locally and freshly prepared, pub classics such as steaks, lasagne and curries share the menu with local specialities like Cumberland sausage and Borrowdale trout. The food is complemented by a well-chosen list of mainly New World wines. The six centrally heated bedrooms, all with en suite showers, TV and hot drinks tray, are available all year round.

105 THRELKELD MINING MUSEUM

Threlkeld Quarry, Keswick,
Cumbria CA12 4TT

☎ 017687 79747 / 01228 561883

⊕ www.threlkeldminingmuseum.co.uk

The Threlkeld Quarry & Mining Museum is situated three miles east of Keswick, in the heart of the breathtaking Lake District in Cumbria. The quarry and museum have been lovingly run by knowledgeable and dedicated staff for more than ten years, and the site continues to expand through the dedication of the staff and volunteers.

The quarry itself is a RIGS site and displays contacts between the "Skiddaw Slate" and the granite intrusion, as well as other fascinating features.

The museum now has a new mining section which has been developed with the help and cooperation of the Cumbria Amenity Trust Mining History Society and a number of individuals.

The Mining Room contains artefacts, plans and photographic records of explorations of many local mines, which, in this area, exploited copper, iron, lead, zinc, tungsten, graphite, barites and fluorite. A representative display of local minerals can be seen and there is a new section on lighting, drilling and explosives.

The museum offers activities for all the family, from budding geologists to hopeful prospectors, including an underground tour of a realistic mine, a quarry site with a unique collection of machinery and mineral panning.

There is ample free parking, a shop and refreshments available. Open 7 days a week from Easter to October.

106 THE GRANGE CAFÉ

Grange in Borrowdale, nr Keswick,
Cumbria CA12 5UQ
☎ 01768 777077

Shirley and John Harrison and their son Mike have made many friends in their long ownership of the **Grange Café**, which stands in the shadow of Catbells in the Jaws of Borrowdale (in the centre of Grange village). Locals, walkers and tourists all appreciate the family's excellent home cooking, offering daily specials and

vegetarian choices, with favourites that include hearty vegetable soup, fresh cakes and scones, and gingerbread made by John to his grandmother's farmhouse recipe. The Café is open from 10 to 5.30 daily from mid March to late November, also Christmas and February half term.

HIDDEN PLACES GUIDES

Explore Britain and Ireland with *Hidden Places* guides - a fascinating series of national and local travel guides.

Packed with easy to read information on hundreds of places of interest as well as places to stay, eat and drink.

Available from both high street and internet booksellers

For more information on the full range of *Hidden Places* guides and other titles published by Travel Publishing visit our website on

www.travelpublishing.co.uk
or ask for our leaflet by phoning
0118-981-7777 or emailing
info@travelpublishing.co.uk

107 HAZEL BANK COUNTRY HOUSE

Rosthwaite, Borrowdale, Keswick, Cumbria
CA12 5XB
☎ 01768 777248 Fax: 01768 777373
e-mail: enquiries@hazelbankhotel.co.uk
⊕ www.hazelbankhotel.co.uk

Four acres of grounds provide a quiet, scenic setting for **Hazel Bank Country House**, an impressive early-Victorian building set against a backdrop of fells, with lush gardens sweeping down to Rosthwaite village. Eight outstanding bedrooms are individually furnished and decorated for style and comfort, with lots of personal touches and commendable attention to detail. All are named after the surrounding fells; some have four-posters and two are located on the ground floor. The rooms are bookable on Dinner, B&B basis, and the restaurant is also open to non-residents for traditional candlelit dinners.

An alternative to the rooms in the house is a superb self-catering cottage for two, offering a bedroom, shower room, all-electric kitchen, drying room, patio and spectacular views of fells, fields and woodland. It has its own access drive

and car parking area. In their ten years here, Glen and Brenda Davies have won many prestigious accolades and awards, including an AA 5-Star Gold Country House rating, an AA rosette for fine cuisine and a Visit Britain 4-Star rating for the cottage. Wainwright described Borrowdale as the loveliest and most precious valley in Lakeland, and Keats and Ruskin also waxed lyrical about the glorious scenery.

108 THE FISH HOTEL

Buttermere, nr Cockermouth,
Cumbria CA13 9XA
☎ 01687 70253 Fax: 01687 70287
⊕ www.fish-hotel.co.uk

In December 2007 the Richardson family celebrate 40 years at the **Fish Hotel**. The hotel combines period charm and character with modern comforts in a glorious setting, a popular base for tourists, walkers, climbers and lovers of the great outdoors.

It lies a short walk from Buttermere and Crummock Water at the foot of Honister Pass. Buttermere is a beautiful lake in a dramatic landscape, with wonderful walks, and superb views of the eastern towers of Fleetwith Pike and the great fell wall made up of High Crag, High Still and Red Pike.

The guest accommodation comprises ten upstairs rooms, all with en suite facilities, direct-dial phone, radio, hairdryer and hot drinks tray. The day starts with a

generous cooked breakfast, and packed lunches can be provided to take on a day's walking, climbing, fishing or exploring the local sights and places of interest. Six real ales, including Jennings Bitter, Haystacks and Catbells, come from local breweries, and bar food ranging from sandwiches to full meals, is served in the hotel bar lunchtime and evening.

109 WHINLATTER FOREST PARK

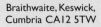

Braithwaite, Keswick,
Cumbria CA12 5TW
☎ 017687 78469
e-mail: whinlatter@forestry.gsi.gov.uk
🌐 www.forestry.gov.uk/northwestengland

Whinlatter Forest Park is an ideal venue for all sorts of outdoor activities. There are walking and orienteering routes, and the more energetic can walk through the forest and out onto the surrounding fells. Or bring your bicycle and cycle on the traffic free forest roads - provided you don't mind the hills! The forest also provides excellent opportunities for photography, sketching and painting, botany, or bird watching. Of particular interest to birdwatchers are the Bassenthwaite Ospreys, which have nested on Bassenthwaite Lake since 2001. The award-winning Lake District Osprey Project provides viewing facilities for these magnificent birds at Whinlatter on the giant screens with up close and personal images of the nest. Nearby, Dodd Wood view point offers fantastic panoramic views of the birds natural environment where you may be lucky enough to see them catching fish on the lake, during the breeding season, April to the end of August.

At Whinlatter children are also catered for too, the gigantic walk in badger sett , the Rabbit Run and Fox Trot trails and the adventure playground will keep them entertained for ages. Supporting your visit to Whinlatter, the Visitor Centre includes an attractive gift shop and Siskins cafe.

Opening hours: 10am - 5pm daily in summer and 10am - 4pm daily in winter. Closed Christmas and New Year, re-opening 9th January 2006.

110 MIDDLE RUDDINGS COUNTRY INN & RESTAURANT

Braithwaite, nr Keswick,
Cumbria CA12 5RY
☎ 017687 78436
e-mail: middleruddings@btconnect.com
🌐 www.middle-ruddings.co.uk

Middle Ruddings Country Inn & Restaurant is a high-quality establishment set in its own grounds close to the main A66, a short walk from Bassenthwaite and a short drive from Keswick. After running a successful Bed & Breakfast guest house, Liz and Andy McMaster became owners here in September 2005. In their 100-year-old home they offer the very best in accommodation, food and drink. The 13 en suite guest bedrooms include two family rooms, and bookings can be made on a B&B or Dinner, B&B basis.

Three rotating ales from Cumbrian breweries are on tap in the bar, and in the 65-cover dining room patrons can enjoy delicious food cooked by Liz and the team and served from 12 to 2 and from 6 to 9. The printed menu and the

daily specials provide a mouthwatering choice that puts the emphasis on prime local produce: typical dishes could include potted shrimps from Silloth; fillet of Scottish salmon with a red pesto layer, wrapped in locally produced pancetta; roast haunch of venison; Keskadale beef burger; steak & Cumbrian ale pie; and asparagus, garlic & wild mushroom risotto. Room should be left for a scrumptious dessert such as chocolate fudge or bread & butter pudding.

111 BRAITHWAITE FARM & BARN HOUSE

Braithwaite, Keswick, Cumbria CA12 5RY
☎ 017687 78411
e-mail: jenny@braithwaitefarm.co.uk
🌐 www.braithwaitefarm.co.uk
www.barnhouseholidays.co.uk

Set on a working sheep and dairy farm in magnificent countryside, **Braithwaite** offers superb Bed & Breakfast accommodation in two comfortable en suite guest rooms. Situated behind the village green, it's a tranquil, civilised place that's made for relaxing and unwinding. The rooms are handsomely decorated and furnished, and an excellent breakfast gets the day off to a perfect start. Packed lunches are also available by arrangement. Children are welcome, but Braithwaite Farm cannot cater for pets.

The combination of outstanding hospitality, great comfort and super breakfasts brings many guests back to enjoy more of the same, and owners Jenny and Stephen Clark also have a charming self-catering cottage (**Barn House**) for up to six guests next to the village pub. The little village of Braithwaite lies close to Whinlatter Pass and the Forest Park, where visitors can spend the day in a variety of activities – or just admiring the glorious views. Another unique attraction in the vicinity is the Lake District Osprey Project set up to protect the nesting birds.

112 LAKELAND COTTAGE HOLIDAYS

Melbecks, Bassenthwaite, Keswick, Cumbria CA12 4QX
☎ 017687 76065 Fax: 017687 76869
e-mail: info@lakelandcottages.co.uk
🌐 www.lakelandcottages.co.uk

The portfolio of **Lakeland Holiday Cottages** covers a wide range of holiday accommodation, including properties of many years' standing and a variety that are newly enrolled. What they have in common is that all are chosen by the firm's owners Jo and David Burton, who are dedicated to ensuring customer satisfaction with and enjoyment of the self-catering properties. They are all also inspected and independently graded by the English Tourism Council and have been awarded a 'Quality Star' rating.

The owners' first-hand knowledge of all the properties means that they can advise on the suitability for each client regarding numbers of guests, location, facilities and individual attractions. They are in charge of about 60 properties sleeping from 2 to 8 or 9, all combining period charm with up-to-date comfort and amenities. The area covered by Lakeland Holiday Cottages covers Borrowdale, Newlands, Penruddock, Threlkeld, Keswick, Bassenthwaite and Cockermouth. All the properties are displayed on the comprehensive website and bookings can be made online.

211

113 THE OLD SAWMILL TEA ROOM

Mirehouse, nr Keswick,
Cumbria CA12 4QE
☎ 017687 74317
🌐 www.theoldsawmill.co.uk

Claire Easton owns and runs a very popular and very successful tea room situated at Mirehouse, on the A591 close to Bassenthwaite Lake. Claire's home cooking makes the **Old Sawmill Tea Room** a magnet for locals, walkers, cyclists and tourists in the know, and the aroma of the baking and cooking is enough to tempt first-timers inside the little stone building to sample the array of delicious dishes.

Claire offers an excellent choice of snacks both sweet and savoury, from scones, teacakes, muffins and cakes to filled brown rolls, soups, baked potatoes and salads. Cumberland sausage and venison burgers are made with Cumbrian-sourced meat, and all the cakes, pastries and pickles are made on the premises. Among the many favourites are the Old Sawmill Special – a ½-pound Cumberland sausage in a warm roll with apple sauce or mustard, a salad garnish and green bean pickle; and to round things off in style, seasonal fruit pies and sticky gingerbread. Drinks include fruit juices, sparkling elderflower, nettle and ginger, and ethically sourced teas and coffees from Farrers of Kendal. The Old Sawmill is open daily from 10 to 5. Cash or cheque only.

114 PONDEROSA GUEST HOUSE

Uldale, Wigton, Cumbria CA7 1HA
☎ 016973 71805
🌐 www.ponderosakeswick.co.uk

Ponderosa Guest House enjoys a tranquil setting among the fells and valleys of the northern part of the Lake District National Park. The handsome house sits in its own grounds on a working sheep and dairy farm and provides a perfect retreat from the hustle and bustle of city life. Uldale has been Margaret Wilson's home for over 40 years; she has been welcoming Bed & Breakfast guests for 25 years, first in the farmhouse and then 15 years ago Ponderosa was built and was worked in with the farmhouse. She moved into Ponderosa 3 years ago and ceased to use the farmhouse. The self-catering has been running since 1998.

Two en suite B&B rooms in the main house are open all year; children over 12 are welcome, but the house cannot accept dogs. A hearty English breakfast starts the day, and guests can enjoy a traditional home-cooked dinner if pre-arranged with Margaret. The self-catering accommodation, for up to five guests, is in an adjacent cottage equipped with all the mod cons. Both the B&B and the self-catering facilities are perfect for touring or walking holidays, and an ideal stopover between England and Scotland.

115 THE SWALEDALE WATCH

Whelpo, Caldbeck, Cumbria CA7 8HQ
☎ 016974 78409
e-mail: nan.savage@talk21.com
🌐 www.swaledale-watch.co.uk

Arnold and Nan Savage have been welcoming Bed & Breakfast guests to the **Swaledale Watch** for 25 years. Their family home is at the heart of a working sheep farm set within the Lake District National Park and surrounded by glorious unspoilt countryside. Guest accommodation is shared between the main house and the nearby annex, a stylishly converted cowshed. The five nicely appointed bedrooms include a family room; four have en suite facilities, the other its own private bathroom.

The tariff includes a generous cooked breakfast, and the owners can recommend a number of local pubs and restaurants. Guests are free to wander around the 300-care farm, and the lambing is an annual highlight;

the owners also breed and keep miniature ponies. Nan and Arnold are happy to tell guests all about the nearby walks, one of which leads to the village of Caldbeck by way of The Howk, a limestone gorge with a beautiful waterfall. And when the weather is unkind, there are books, games and puzzles to while away the time in the cosy lounges.

116 THE MAGIC BEAN 🍴

Poet's Walk, Penrith, Cumbria CA11 7HJ
☎ 01768 867474

In a pedestrian area in the centre of Penrith, the **Magic Bean** is a super place for a snack or a meal. Karen Ingham delights her customers with some excellent home cooking, served during the day Monday to Saturday and also on Saturday evenings. The daytime menu, supplemented by a specials board, brings a good variety of hot and cold dishes (lasagne, tuna melt, Chinese-style duck), while the Saturday evening

choice offers British and Mediterranean-style dishes such as seared scallops with black pudding, braised lamb shank and tartlet of Parma ham and sun-blushed tomatoes with pesto-dressed salad leaves. Everything is made on the premises, including some wonderful breads.

117 LONSDALES BAR

12 Little Dockray, Penrith,
Cumbria CA11 7HL
☎ 01768 867496
e-mail:
theresalanc@lonsdales576.orangehome.co.uk

Theresa and David Lancaster run one of the most popular meeting and eating places in Penrith, centrally situated in a pedestrian area of town. **Lonsdales Bar** is very much a family business, with Theresa and David ably assisted by Janice ain the kitchen and Heather in the bar. Starting life as a cottage and later a hairdressers and an ice cream shop, Lonsdales is now a favourite place to meet for a drink (including a good choice of keg ales and lagers) or a meal.

Food is served daily from 11 to 2.30 and in the early evening

up to 8.30. Dishes on the wide-ranging bar menu include sandwiches, salads, burgers, jacket potatoes, omelettes, steaks, sticky chicken, pasta, curries and 'Back to the 70s' basket meals. The 3-course Sunday lunch features a choice of

three roasts and several other meat, fish and vegetarian main courses.

118 THE CORNER HOUSE

36 Victoria Road, Penrith,
Cumbria CA11 8HR
☎ 01768 863566
e-mail: doreen@cornerhousepenrith.co.uk
🌐 www.cornerhousepenrith.co.uk

A couple of minutes' walk from the centre of Penrith and a five-minute drive from Junction 40 of the M6, The **Corner House** is a guest house that's ideally placed for touring the area. Handsome both outside and within, the late-19th century house has been providing outstanding hospitality for 24 years, and the number of repeat visitors, and their comments in the book, are testimony to the pleasure of a stay here.

Owner Doreen Robinson has three upstairs letting rooms open all year round – one twin room and two double rooms with King size zip and link beds which will convert to singles if required. All have shower rooms en suite. Handsome is also a word that applies to the breakfasts that provide guests with an excellent start

to the day. Packed lunches are also available. Penrith is a great place to stroll round and discover

attractions ranging from the 14th century castle to the exciting Rheged Discovery Centre. Cash and cheque only.

Eamont Bridge, nr Penrith,
Cumbria CA10 2BX
☎ 01768 862081

Martyn and Samantha Swaby are the young, enthusiastic owners of the **Beehive**, which stands just off the main A6 a couple of miles south of Penrith. Open all day, every day, the 18th century inn is a popular spot to break a journey, and there's always a convivial buzz in the bar,

where two real ales are on tap to quench thirsts. The food, served from noon to 9, ranges from sandwiches, jacket potatoes and salad bowls to haddock & chips, chicken tikka masala and superb locally reared beef in steaks, steak pie, cottage pie, burgers and lasagne.

HIDDEN PLACES GUIDES

Explore Britain and Ireland with *Hidden Places* guides - a fascinating series of national and local travel guides.

Packed with easy to read information on hundreds of places of interest as well as places to stay, eat and drink.

Available from both high street and internet booksellers

For more information on the full range of *Hidden Places* guides and other titles published by Travel Publishing visit our website on

www.travelpublishing.co.uk
or ask for our leaflet by phoning
0118-981-7777 or emailing
info@travelpublishing.co.uk

Brougham, nr Penrith,
Cumbria CA10 2AR
☎ 01768 891114
e-mail: enquiries@hornbyhall.co.uk
🌐 www.hornbyhall.co.uk

On a working farm in a quiet rural setting three miles from Penrith, **Hornby Hall** offers the very best in gracious country house accommodation. The Grade II listed property dates from 1550, when it was built of local red sandstone by Edward Birbeck, and today's guests will find a perfect

combination of original features, antique furnishings and up-to-date amenities. The accommodation consists of five main en suite bedrooms and two delightful singles reached up a spiral staircase in the tower. All the rooms face south, overlooking the lovely garden. The chief day rooms are a dining room in the 16th century hall, with a sandstone floor and large open fireplace, and a very pleasant sitting room.

A cooked-to-order breakfast starts the day, packed lunches

are available, and a traditional three-course evening meal (book in advance) features lamb and game from the farm and fruit and vegetables from their own gardens. Fishing is available on a two-mile stretch of the River Eamont between mid-March and the end of September, and the hall can be booked for fishing or shooting parties or for entertaining guests in the wonderful private house ambience. The imposing remains of Brougham Castle, the craft shops and workshops in Brougham hall and the lovely old Parish Curch of St Ninian are all nearby.

121 THE SUN INN

Newton Reigny, nr Penrith,
Cumbria CA11 0AP
☎ 01768 867055
e-mail: suninn-newtonreigny@tiscali.co.uk
🌐 www.thesuninn-newtonreigny.co.uk

The pretty village of Newton Reigny, a couple of miles west of Penrith, is home to the marvellous **Sun Inn**, a popular, traditional free house dating from the 17th century. Tenants Adrian and Carolyne Stevenson-Jones took over here in January 2007, moving from a public house in Glasson Dock.

Adrian is a chef with 15 years' experience, and the food that he and Carolyne prepare is much appreciated both by the regular local customers and by visitors to the area. Food times are 12 to 2.30 every day and 6 to 8.30 Monday to Saturday (Sunday from 5.30 to 8). Local produce features strongly on the menus, and among the specialities are pies, steaks and lamb Henry (braised with red wine and a redcurrant jus).

The bar is open lunchtime and evening and all day Saturday, Sunday and Bank Holidays, and three real ales – Thwaites Original and Bombardier and a changing guest – head the long list of drinks. A garden at the back of the inn runs down to a picturesque stream, providing a very

pleasant spot in the summer months. The Sun is not only a delightful place for a drink and a meal, it's also the perfect base to relax, unwind and discover all the attractions of the region.

The accommodation comprises four good-sized upstairs rooms, three of them with en suite facilities and one of them a family room with its own private bathroom. Children are very welcome, and the inn can cater for private functions and parties – even a dance floor is available.

The scenery hereabouts is truly beautiful, and the inn itself is as pretty as a picture in the summer, when the award-winning gardens and hanging baskets are in full bloom. Penrith is close by and the Lake District National Park is on the doorstep. Ullswater is six miles away, and other places to visit include Aira Force Waterfall, Whinlatter Forest Park, Dove Cottage, Eden Ostrich World and Trotters World of Animals. This is also excellent walking country, and golf, riding, pony trekking and fishing are all available nearby.

122 BRATHEN

The Thorpe, Greystoke, Penrith,
Cumbria CA11 0TJ
☎ 01768 483595
e-mail: stay@brathen.co.uk
⊕ www.brathen.co.uk

In the picturesque village of Greystoke, a
short drive northwest of Penrith, **Brathen**
dispenses hospitality, comfort and character
in a choice of B&B and self-catering
accommodation. Owners Christine and
Michael Mole have six B&B rooms, three of
them en
suite, in a
mixture of
sizes, and a
multi-choice
breakfast
provides
ample energy
for a day's
sightseeing.

The adjacent self-catering cottage, with its
own entrance, sleeps up to six guests in
comfort: bedrooms and shower on the
ground floor, kitchen and living area above.

123 DALEMAIN HISTORIC HOUSE & GARDENS

Penrith, Cumbria CA11 0HB
☎ 017684 86450 Fax: 017684 86223
e-mail: admin@dalemain.com

Eleven generations of the same family have lived at
Dalemain over the last 300 years, so, as the guide
will tell you, this is a much loved family home.
Dalemain began life as a pele tower in the 12th
century, with additions in the 14th and 16th centuries. Finally, the impressive Georgian east front
was completed in 1744, some 65 years after Sir Edward Hasell's purchase of the property. The
home is now in the hands of the Hasell-McCosh family.

Guided tours are offered in the mornings, by timed ticket, but in the afternoons visitors can
walk around at their own speed. The Georgian entrance hall, Chinese room and dining room have
plenty of family portraits, ceramics and period furniture. 16 sheets of hand-painted wallpaper came
in tea clippers from China in 1757 for the Chinese room.

A change of centuries takes you through the servant's passage into the Norman pele tower
where there's a display of uniforms,
photographs and medals devoted to the
Westmorland and Cumberland Yeomanry.
Upstairs the fretwork room has a 16th century
plaster ceiling, oak panelling and part of a 17th
century diary written by Lady Anne Clifford.

Then enjoy the delightful 5 acre plantsman's
garden set against the picturesque splendour of
the Lakeland Fells and parkland. Walk around
the richly planted herbaceous borders, the rose
walk with nearly 200 old fashioned roses and
take in the views on the glorious woodland walk
above Dacre beck.

124 THE TROUTBECK INN & HOLIDAY COTTAGES

Troutbeck, Penrith, Cumbria CA11 0SJ
☎ 017684 83635 Fax: 017684 83639
e-mail: info@troutbeckinn.co.uk
🌐 www.thetroutbeckinn.co.uk

The Ward family have a very warm welcome for all who visit **Troutbeck Inn**. This is their first venture into this type of business, but with their chef Matt Preece they have made it one of the best places to seek out, whether it's for a drink, a meal or the

chance to enjoy a relaxing break in delightful surroundings.

Built as an inn in the late-18th century, it later became a hotel for railway travellers and a watering hole for farmers from the auction room next door. It's now a warm, comfortable base for walkers, cyclists and tourists as well as a much-loved local. Black Sheep, Cumberland Ale and Copper Dragon are on tap to quench thirsts in the bar, or guests can enjoy a glass of wine or a nice drop of malt whisky by the fire while making new friends or planning the day's activities. Matt is passionate about his food,

relying on prime produce from local growers and farmers for his raw materials. His menus combine tried-and-trusted favourites such as battered haddock or steak & mushroom pie with seafood beignets (prawns, squid, cockles and mussels), roasted ham shanks, game casserole and wild mushroom risotto. Room should definitely be kept for a super dessert – maybe lumpy bumpy toffee pie. Lunchtime also proposes lighter options such as fishcakes, omelettes and chilli beef taco shells, and the inn has a top-notch children's menu.

Guests staying at the inn have a choice of accommodation. Six lofty, spacious, tastefully furnished rooms for B&B are in the main building, all with en suite facilities, TV and hot drinks tray. Three beautifully appointed **Holiday Cottages** are located in converted stables in the courtyard behind the inn. Blencathra and Saddleback each have two bedrooms, while Little Mell fell is a romantic nest for two. All have a fully equipped kitchen, dining area and comfortable living area with TV and DVD player.

218

125 THE ROYAL HOTEL AT DOCKRAY

Dockray, Matterdale, nr Penrith,
Cumbria CA11 0JY
☎ 01768 482356 Fax: 01768 482033
e-mail: info@the-royal-dockray.co.uk
🌐 www.the-royal-dockray.co.uk

The **Royal Hotel at Dockray**, which started life as a coaching inn more than 500 years ago, nestles peacefully among the picturesque eastern fells on the A5091 a mile and a half from Ullswater. It's run by Tyrone Castles and his wife Michelle, who offer excellent hospitality, Cask Marque ales, super food and comfortable accommodation. Cumberland Ale, Black Sheep Bitter and guest ales, some from small local breweries, are on tap to quench thirsts, and the hosts and their chefs put local produce to fine use in a selection of dishes served every lunchtime and evening.

The printed menu is supplemented by daily specials such as lamb steak in a honey and mint cream sauce, venison pie and salmon steak with lemon parsley butter. The guest accommodation comprises ten very well appointed en suite bedrooms, and ten more, including two equipped for disabled guests, are due to come on stream in the autumn of 2007. The Royal has a pleasant beer garden and ample off-road parking. The inn was originally called the Cross Keys, and changed its name to commemorate visits by Mary Queen of Scots on her journeys between Scotland and England. It is still allowed to display the Scottish Royal Coat of Arms.

127 THE WHITE LION INN

Patterdale, nr Penrith,
Cumbria CA11 0NW
☎ 017684 82214

The **White Lion Inn** has a tradition of hospitality that dates back more than two centuries. It enjoys a magnificent setting in Patterdale, situated on the popular Coast to Coast walking route and close to the foot of Ullswater. Visitors are assured of the warmest of welcomes from owner Rita Dawes and licensee-managers Alastair and Mandy Howard-Carter.

The bar is open throughout the day, seven days a week, for the service of drinks (two real ales always available) and the printed menu, supplemented by summer specials, tempts with a wide range of home-cooked dishes served from noon to 9. Typical dishes

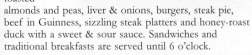

include fish & chips, grilled trout with parsley butter, toasted almonds and peas, liver & onions, burgers, steak pie, beef in Guinness, sizzling steak platters and honey-roast duck with a sweet & sour sauce. Sandwiches and traditional breakfasts are served until 6 o'clock.

Seven guest bedrooms – five en suite, the others with private bathrooms – provide a quiet, comfortable base for a relaxing break or a walking, climbing or touring holiday. Dogs are welcome.

Greystones, Glenridding, nr Penrith,
Cumbria CA11 0PA
☎ 01768 482392 Fax: 01768 482122
e-mail: info@greystonescoffeehouse.com
⊕ www.greystonescoffeehouse.com
www.glenridding.com

Greystones – Coffee House, Art Gallery & Self-Catering – is located in Glenridding, at the southern edge of Ullswater and the foot of Helvellyn. Julian and Nicola Sharman own and run this three-in-one business, the coffee house and gallery standing alongside the stream that tumbles through the centre of the village and the nearby Ullswater House.

The fully licensed coffee house serves a varied range of splendid home baking, along with jacket potatoes and hot and cold snacks and meals to cater for all appetites; the carrot cake is just one of the scrumptious goodies on offer. In the same building, the well-lit gallery space is a showcase for pictures and sculptures, supporting both local talent and visiting/guest artists (Tel: 01768 638159).

Ullswater House provides ideal self-catering holiday accommodation for groups of 2 to 10 guests. On the first floor are a double bedroom and two triples, while above are an open-plan lounge/diner and kitchen, a utility/drying room, a bathroom with shower over the bath and a separate shower cubicle. Well decorated and furnished throughout, the house is the perfect base for discovering the hidden treasures of the Ullswater Valley and the beauty of the Lake District National Park.

128 DEEPDALE HALL

Patterdale, nr Penrith, Cumbria CA11 0NR
☎ 017684 82369
e-mail: brown@deepdalehall.freeserve.co.uk
🌐 www.deepdalehall.co.uk

Deepdale Hall enjoys a superb location on a 160-acre sheep farm in the scenic Deepdale Valley. Owned and run by Chris Brown, son Jimmy and daughter in law Robyn, their family have been providing guest accommodation here since 1954. It is a homely, civilised base for unwinding and relaxing, walking or touring this lovely part of the world. In the 17th century main house, an unusual wooden

spiral staircase leads to the B&B rooms – a family-size room en suite and a double with private bathroom. The adjoiningByre, newly converted from the cattle quarters, provides a comfortable self-catering base for up to four guests. Both properties have been awarded 4 Stars by Visit Britian.

129 WETHERIGGS COUNTRY POTTERY

Clifton Dykes, Penrith, Cumbria CA10 2DH
☎ 01768 892733
e-mail: pottery@wetheriggs.co.uk
🌐 www.wetheriggs-pottery.co.uk

A wealth of history awaits you at **Wetheriggs Country Pottery** – from 1855 to the present day. Wetheriggs has been a working pottery since 1855 and has survived the challenges of the Industrial Revolution, two world wars and times of extreme change and economic turmoil. It is now the only steam powered Country Pottery in the British Isles and, in 1973, was awarded the status of 'Scheduled Industrial Monument ' by English Heritage to preserve this precious place for future generations.

The amenities are excellent and are improved each year. In the Museum you can discover the long family history and

traditions of Wetheriggs, from its beginnings as a brick and tile works right up to the 21st Century. See the early slipware designs, dinnerware and kitchenware from the 1800's and early 1900's and original tools and photographs. Also, see the famous Beehive Kiln, 'Josephine' the Steam Engine plus the steam-powered Blunger and Pugmill.

Guided Tours are available between Easter and October (please ask for details at the Pottery or telephone for details).

130 THE MARDALE INN AT ST PATRICK'S WELL

Bampton, Cumbria CA10 2RQ
☎ 01931 713244 Fax: 01931 713000
e-mail: info@mardaleinn.co.uk
🌐 www.mardaleinn.co.uk

Country roads lead from the A6 at Shap to the **Mardale Inn at St Patricks Well**, a cosy Lake District inn dating from the early 18th century and recently completely refurbished by the new owners. Tucked away in the pleasant little village of Bampton in the Lake District National Park, it's a great base for a walking or touring holiday as well as a warm, welcoming free house open all day, every day for drinks and food.

Up to four real ales are on tap to quench fresh-air thirsts, with Coniston Bluebird the regular brew and recognition by CAMRA. Full service provides a good choice of food, with a lighter daytime menu and the full evening menu served from 6 – booking is recommended to be sure of a table at the weekend.

Guest accommodation consists of four superbly appointed bedrooms – two doubles en suite, a double with private facilities and an en suite family room. The inn is an excellent stopping point on Wainwright's Coast to Coast Walk, and has books and maps of the area for sale. The site was visited by St Patrick, who found a well and blessed it; it was re-discovered during the refurbishment and will become a feature.

The inn is close to Haweswater, one of the few places where golden eagles can be spotted – along with buzzards, woodpeckers, sparrowhawks and peregrine falcons. The most easterly of the 'Lakes', Haweswater is actually a reservoir, created in the 1930s to supply water to Manchester. The inn takes its name from the village of Mardale that was flooded, along with several dairy farms, to create the reservoir. In sustained spells of very dry weather the remains of the village can be seen.

131 THE HERMITAGE

Shap, nr Penrith, Cumbria CA10 3LX
☎ 01931 716671
e-mail:
jeanjackson_hermitage@btopenworld.com
🌐 www.shapcumbria.co.uk

Set in well-kept gardens and grounds in the historic village of Shap, the **Hermitage** is an ideal base for discovering the many scenic and historic sights of the region. Jean Jackson has run this splendid place for 40 years, and she and her son provide their guests – many of whom are repeat visitors – with the very best in hospitality, comfort and service throughout the year.

The four guest bedrooms – three twins and a double – are decorated and furnished to the highest standard. Three are en suite, while the fourth shares the house facilities. The day begins with a superb breakfast, and a home-cooked evening meal is available by arrangement. The ambience is always warm and welcoming, with a traditional charm enhanced by features such as the large open hearth and a beautiful stained-glass window depicting Richard the Lionheart, purchased more then 40 years ago from nearby Lowther Castle. That castle is now just a shell, but its grounds include the much-visited Lakeland Bird of Prey centre, one of the numerous attractions within easy reach of The Hermitage.

132 THE NEW VILLAGE TEA ROOMS

Orton, nr Tebay, Cumbria CA10 3RH
☎ 01539 624886

The **New Village Tea Rooms** are a major asset to the village of Orton, one of the prettiest in the region. Owner Christine Evans, here for 15 years, and her loyal right-hand lady Lynne run one of the very best tea rooms in the whole country; it's a multiple winner of the Tea Guild's Award of Excellence, which means that everything is prepared to the highest possible standard.

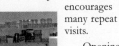

Christine uses many old family recipes for her cakes and pastries, and all these, along with everything else on the menu, can be enjoyed in the charming 18th century cottage or to take away. Soups such as lentil & bacon or carrot & lemon, main dishes like chilli or ham, leek and cheese bake, and wonderful puddings and crumbles provide a meal to remember, an experience which encourages many repeat visits.

Opening hours are 10 to 5 (sometimes later) between April and October and 10.30 to 4.30 November to March. The tea rooms can be booked by arrangement for evening parties. The most memorable approach to Orton is the scenic route across the moors on the B6260 Tebay-Appleby road.

134 THE CROSS KEYS INN

Tebay, nr Penrith, Cumbria CA10 3UY
☎ 01539 624240 Fax: 01539 629922
e-mail: crosskeystebay@btconnect.com
⊕ www.crosskeystebay.com

The **Cross Keys Inn** is a long, low, 500-year-old building located on the A685 and a short drive from J38 of the M6. When the business partnership took over they brought many years experience in the trade, and they have quickly enhanced its appeal as a much-loved local, a place for a convivial drink or a meal and a good base for a break or a holiday.

This splendid free house has retained a good deal of old-world charm, and the bar is the perfect spot for enjoying a glass or two of real ale – Black Sheep Best Bitter and London Pride are the residents; it's also a great place for a chat or a game of one of the pub classics – darts, pool or cribbage – and all-comers are invited to put on their thinking caps for the Sunday evening quiz.

The bar is open all day, every day, and proper homemade food is served either here or in the restaurant that overlooks the

garden and the open countryside beyond. The menu provides a good choice for all appetites and tastes, and among the favourites the steak & ale pie and the Sunday roasts (book) are always in demand. Sandwiches and filled jacket potatoes are satisfying lighter options.

The inn's accommodation, available all year round, comprises nine bedrooms – three standards, three with en suite facilities and three de luxe rooms in the converted barn; six rooms are on the ground floor, and all rooms are equipped with television, radio,

tea/coffee tray and hairdryer. There's plenty to interest the visitor in the vicinity of the inn, and Kendal, Appleby, Kirkby Stephen and Penrith are all within an easy drive. The Cross Keys plays a part in the tale of Mary Baynes, the Witch of Tebay. Her black cat chanced to stray into the inn's garden, where it met its end in the jaws of the landlord's dog. Mary died in 1811 at the age of 91 but the story goes that she still haunts the grounds looking for her cat.

224

133 THE OLD SCHOOL

Tebay, Cumbria CA10 3TP
☎ 015396 24286
e-mail: theoldschool@fsmail.net
🌐 www.accommodationinlakedistrict.com

Joanne and Steve Dunkinson guarantee the warmest of welcomes for visitors to the **Old School**, which is located a short drive from J38 of the M6. The mid-19th century building, a school until the 1960s, has eight well-appointed en suite bedrooms for Bed & Breakfast guests, one of them boasting a luxurious

bathroom complete with Jacuzzi. A full English breakfast starts the day, and packed lunches are available on request. The Old School has ample parking and secure storage for cycles and motorbikes.

135 THE PENDRAGON

Market Square, Kirkby Stephen,
Cumbria CA17 4QT
☎ 017683 71731

The **Pendragon** is a popular café/tea room and restaurant standing on the A685, across the road from the Market Square in Kirkby Stephen at the head of the Beautiful Eden Valley. Robert and Linda Slater and their daughter Sonia have built up a fine reputation among local residents for the quality of the cooking, and they are always pleased to provide refreshment for visitors to this pleasant old market town. It's a café/tea room by day with a menu of familiar snacks and dishes ranging from sandwiches and toasties to baked potatoes, burgers, fish & chips, breakfasts, chilli con carne, broccoli & cheese bake, meat or vegetable lasagne and traditional Sunday roasts.

In the restaurant, Saturday and Sunday evenings bring a wide-ranging menu catering for all tastes, with typical

choices running from soup, pâté and garlicky, herby salmon goujons with a sweet chilli dip to the fish of the day,

stuffed chicken breast with a cranberry & port sauce, lamb chops with minted mash and vegetable tagliatelle. The Café is open from 9.30 to 4ish, the restaurant from 7. Both are closed Wednesdays in winter and Thursdays all year round. Cash only.

136 WESTVIEW & OAKLEA

Ravenstonedale, Kirkby Stephen,
Cumbria CA17 4NG
☎ 015396 23415
e-mail: enquiries@westview-cumbria.co.uk
⊕ www.westview-cumbria.co.uk

Westview & Oaklea provide luxurious Bed &
Breakfast and self-catering accommodation in an
idyllic setting in the pretty village of
Ravenstonedale. William and Jane Ellis insist on the
highest standards, guaranteeing a very pleasant,
comfortable stay for all

their guests. Westview, overlooking the villager green, has two
double rooms and a twin, all with en suite facilities, TV and
hospitality tray. To the rear are a parking area and a large
garden with a summer house for the use of guests, who can
walk straight out onto the Howgill Fells. Rooms are let on a
B&B basis, with the option of an evening meal by prior
arrangement.

Oaklea is a stone-faced bungalow built in the traditional
style of the region with the

advantage of modern comfort and amenities. It has a double-
bedded room and a twin-bedded room, a large lounge with
dining area and spacious, fully fitted kitchen, a bathroom with
separate shower, utility room with deep-freeze, washing machine
and dryer, a large garden and ample parking. This is great
walking country, golf and tennis are available nearby, there are
two pubs and two churches within a few minutes' walk, and
Westview and Oaklea are ideal bases for touring the Lakes, the
Eden Valley and the Yorkshire Dales.

137 STOUPHILL GATE

Ravenstonedale, Cumbria CA17 4NN
☎ 015396 23653
e-mail: martin@wainhouse.f9.co.uk
⊕ www.accommodationkirkbystephen.co.uk

Gillian and Martin Wainhouse ensure a warm and
friendly welcome and a memorable stay for all their
guests at **Stouphill Gate**. In a glorious setting with
spectacular views, they offer a choice of Bed &
Breakfast and self-catering accommodation in a
traditional Cumbrian farmhouse that takes its name from
nearby Stoup Hill.

The two B&B rooms provide the perfect getaway to
relax and unwind or an ideal base for discovering the many
scenic and historic delights of the area. They share a quiet
residents' lounge, and guests start the day with a hearty
Aga-cooked breakfast. Packed lunches can be supplied by
arrangement. Both rooms have very comfortable beds, en
suite showers, TV, radio-alarm and tea/coffee facilities. One
of the rooms is on
the ground floor and
is suitable for

families or guests with mobility difficulties. The first-floor
room is accessed by an external staircase and enjoys great
views from its lofty position. Both rooms can be let with
the adjacent holiday cottage to accommodate larger groups.
The cottage offers charm, character and everything needed
for a relaxed self-catering holiday for up to five guests.
There is a separate laundry room for use by all guests.

Winton, Cumbria CA17 4HS
☎ 01768 371451
🌐 www.thebayhorseinnwinton.co.uk

Visitors to the **Bay Horse Inn** can look forward to the warmest of Lakeland welcomes from host Matthew (Matt) Gott and his staff. This traditional coaching inn stands on the green in the picturesque village of Winton in the heart of the Eden Valley, just off the A685 and a mile and a half north of Kirkby Stephen. Matt greets newcomers like old friends, and his inn is looking in immaculate order after recent refurbishment.

Two bars, the lounge with old oak beams, brasses and a wood-burning stove and the public with a flagstone floor and open fire, are perfect spots for making or meeting friends over a glass or two of real ale – up to five brews are usually available. Matt is a super chef as well as a super host, and patrons can enjoy his home cooking from 12 to 2 and from 6 to 9, and all day Sunday (the inn is closed on Mondays except for bank Holidays). He offers a menu that offers something for everyone, combining both traditional and contemporary dishes: steak & Hawkshead Bitter pie; fish platter; pan-fried tuna steak; chicken breast stuffed with garlic topped with cheese and chive butter; mushroom stroganoff.

Guests staying overnight have the choice of two very comfortable bedrooms – the Blue Room overlooking the village green and the Gold Room looking towards the Howgill Fells. Both have en suite facilities, television and hot beverage tray, and the day starts with a full Cumbrian or lighter continental breakfast. With its picturesque setting and outstanding hospitality, the Bay Horse is a popular choice for any special occasion, from birthdays to weddings and funerals. The village is the start of a number of walks, including the Nine Standards and Wild Boar fell.

4 High Wiend, Appleby-in-Westmorland,
Cumbria CA16 6RD
☎ 01768 351493
e-mail: jesveinsson@hotmail.com

The **Golden Ball** is a cosy, friendly pub open all day for drinks and great bar food, and also providing a relaxed, convenient base for touring the region. Licensees Andy and Jean took over the premises in October 2006 and have quickly put their stamp on the place, making many improvements, creating a warm, welcoming ambience and winning new friends all the time.

Located in the heart of Appleby and featuring the Good Beer Guide, it is open all day, every day for food and drink. Marstons Burton Bitter, Cumberland Ale and two guest real ales head the list of drinks to be enjoyed in the two bar areas or out in the newly created secluded and sheltered garden, which is heated and illuminated at night. Jean is the queen of the kitchen, producing a fine variety of country-style bar food served from noon to 8 in the evening. The board lists the day's specials, which might include excellent soups (cream cheese & mushroom, tomato & rocket) and classics such as

toad in the hole, cauliflower cheese, cottage pie, scampi & chips, beef stew with dumplings and the great favourite chicken & leek pie. Children are very welcome, and all-comers are invited to rack their brains at the Wednesday night quiz.

Appleby, the old county town of Westmorland, is well worth taking time to explore, with walks along the River Eden, the views from the ruins of the Norman castle and the magnificent family tombs and the historic organ in St Lawrence's Church among the attractions. The Golden Ball has five upstairs rooms open all year round for Bed & Breakfast guests.

139 THE LEMON GROVE ¶

5 Bridge Street, Appleby-in-Westmorland, Cumbria CA16 6QH
☎ 01768 354119

Owner Lindsey Dixon has a warm, personal welcome for every visitor to her delightful little café/sandwich bar near the market square in Appleby. The **Lemon Grove** is open from 9.30 to 4.30 Monday to Saturday for a fine selection of dishes all prepared and cooked on the premises using local produce as far as possible.

The printed menu and weekly changing specials board tempt with generously filled hot and cold baguettes, the day's soup and quiche, hearty meat pies and, from the board, cheddar chicken served with rice, garlic bread and a jacket potato. The 16 seats at the Lemon Grove soon fill up with local workers, shoppers and visitors to Appleby, a delightful town on a loop of the River Eden.

141 THE NEW INN ¶

Hoff, nr Appleby-in-Westmorland, Cumbria CA16 6TA
☎ 01768 351317
e-mail: Mitchell-derek@btconnect.com

Real ale expert Derek and talented cook Sue make a great team at the **New Inn**, which stands on the B6260 Tebay road running south from Appleby. A minimum of five real ales is always available in the bar, and the locals can't get enough of her daily specials, typified by Cumberland and Westmorland sausages, fish cakes, and

her signature Bloody Big Battered Cod and chicken & leek pudding. The pub is closed until 7.30 on Monday, otherwise open all day; food is served lunchtime and evening Wednesday to Sunday. Live bands perform jazz, rock, blues and folk music on Friday evening.

142 THE SANDFORD ARMS ¶ ⊨

Sandford, nr Appleby-in-Westmorland, Cumbria CA16 6NR
☎ 01768 351121
e-mail: andfordarms@hotmail.com
⊕ www.sandfordarms.co.uk

Eighteenth-century farm buildings are now a pleasant and popular residential inn lounge, tap room and restaurant. The **Sandford Arms** enjoys a picturesque location a mile or so off the A66 in a charming village by the River Eden. Hosts Stephen and Nicola Porter welcome visitors into a traditional ambience of beams and exposed stonework, with Black Sheep ales and good, wholesome food served every session (except Tuesday lunchtime) and all day on

Sunday. The Sandford Arms also has very comfortable letting rooms with en suite facilities, TV, telephone, beverage tray and stunning views, and also has four rods on the River Eden, renowned for its brown trout.

143 THE HAYBERGILL CENTRE

Hayber Lane, Warcop,
nr Appleby-in-Westmorland,
Cumbria CA16 6NP
☎ 01768 341970
e-mail: enquiries@haybergill.co.uk
⊕ www.haybergill.co.uk

The **Haybergill Centre**, located on the B6259 five miles south of Appleby, was created by Mick and Maggie Hickey and opened in July 1999. It is a brilliantly conceived, fully accessible residential venue for groups from 12 to a maximum of 30 on training courses and conferences, retreats or holidays.

It provides exclusive use of a purpose-built, environmentally friendly timber building, and the versatile space and flexible working style offer freedom and choice for each group, thus encouraging peace, inspiration, excitement and creativity. Some of the training courses are organised by the owners, others by the groups themselves, and the outstanding amenities have attracted a number of universities, colleges and top companies.

The setting is very much part of the attraction, and the three acres of wooded grounds include areas for an open fire, barbecue and small group activities. Red squirrels, badgers, woodpeckers, buzzards and pheasants are among the wildlife that can be spotted on a stroll through the grounds, and the Centre's owners can organise walks, nature rambles, cycle rides, birdwatching, horse-riding, fishing and golf.

The accommodation and amenities include seven rooms with en suite showers and toilet, and three dormer rooms with shared facilities, a spacious lounge/training room, dining room and sauna. Most of the main bedrooms open out onto a covered veranda that commands views down the wood-lined lawns. Most bookings are on a fully catered basis, and all meals are created to meet individual dietary requirements using mainly local produce; the food has won widespread praise, and the Centre has even produced its own cookbook.

Brampton, nr Appleby-in-Westmorland,
Cumbria CA16 6JS
☎ 017683 51231

The **New Inn** stands in the village of Brampton, off the main A66 a few miles north of Appleby. Dating from 1730, the inn has a delightfully old-world interior, with flagstone floors, beamed ceilings, real fires and old artefacts adoring the walls. Leaseholders Stuart Rendall and brothers Gary and Robert Pallas brought many years' relevant experience when they took over here and are maintaining the tradition of hospitality in fine style.

Locals and visitors in growing numbers are enjoying the relaxed, friendly ambience and the quality of the food and drink on offer. The bar is open all day, every day of the week, and among the favourite tipples are the real ales from the local Tirril Brewery, including Old Faithful and Red Barn.

The hosts are talented and experienced chefs and offer an excellent variety of menus to be enjoyed between noon and 9 o'clock (until 6 on Sunday). Local raw materials are used widely in classic British dishes that typically include Cumberland sausages, braised lamb shank, black pudding in a pastry case with a cracked black pepper sauce, beer-battered cod, fillet and sirloin steaks and minced beef with dumplings. The fish specials are always in demand, and the centrepiece of Sunday lunch is roast topside of Eden Farm beef, with other roasts, grills and steak & Guinness pie among other main course choices. Food is big business here, and booking is strongly recommended at the weekend.

The New Inn has a pleasant beer garden and plenty of off-road parking, and the leaseholders hope to add another string to their bow by bringing Bed & Breakfast accommodation on stream. And when they do, the inn will be a splendid base for touring the lovely Irthing Valley and the surrounding sights, including the historic town of Carlisle and Hadrian's Wall.

146 MILBURN GRANGE HOLIDAYS

Milburn Grange, Knock,
nr Appleby-in-Westmorland,
Cumbria CA16 6DR

☎ 01768 361867

e-mail: holidays@milburngrange.co.uk
🌐 www.milburngrange.co.uk

Milburn Grange Holidays are based in cosy self-catering cottages in the unspoilt Eden Valley, directly below the Pennines in a designated Area of Outstanding Natural Beauty. Owners Russell and Debbie Clark have seven superb cottages available all year round, the largest sleeping up to 6 or 7 guests, standing in three acres of picturesque gardens surrounded by miles of beautiful countryside affording glorious views.

The largest cottages, Fell and Helm, have three bedrooms, with room for a Z-bed for a seventh person; Brambles, Holly and Stable have two bedrooms; Hayloft has a bedroom, as does the Studio Apartment on the first floor, at the top of the external staircase. All the accommodation is centrally heated, with fully fitted kitchens, comfortable sitting areas and access to clothes washing and drying facilities, either in the cottage or in the communal utility room.

The cottages are the perfect base for walking or cycling holidays, touring the area or just relaxing in the relaxed rural setting. Walking could be a gentle stroll by the river or a vigorous hike on the Fells; for cyclists, the Pennine and Cumbria cycleways pass the gate; fishing is available on the Eden or on local lakes; Appleby is a ten-minute drive away, and it's only five minutes more to the M6 (J40).

145 MIDTOWN FARM

Midtown Farm, Dufton, nr Appleby,
Cumbria CA16 6DB
☎ 017683 51296
e-mail: liamandsue@btinternet.com
⊕ www.midtownfarm.co.uk

Sue and Liam O'Halloran offer superb self-catering accommodation in the picturesque village of Dufton, just off the A66, 3 miles from Appleby. Midtown Farmhouse is a spacious grade II listed traditional Westmorland longhouse. It has been recently restored to provide luxurious

accommodation whilst retaining traditional features such as the huge stone fireplace and many original beams. The large lounge and kitchen plus three bathrooms provide ample and well equipped accommodation for six guests, in one double ensuite, one double and one twin.

Behind the farmhouse stands a converted barn, providing bright and spacious living for four, with lovely views onto the Pennines. A second barn, to be ready for 2008, will sleep up to eight. There is off street parking and

private access to each property.

Dufton, on the Pennine Way in the beautiful Eden Valley, is located in an area that offers both gentle and strenuous walks and cycling from the doorstep, whilst being rich in historic and scenic attractions. The Lakes, Yorkshire Dales and Hadrians Wall are all a short drive away, or you can just relax in the garden or walk to the pub!

147 SLAKES FARM

Milburn, nr Appleby-in-Westmorland,
Cumbria CA16 6DP
☎ 01768 361385
e-mail: oakleaves@slakesfarm.co.uk
⊕ www.slakesfarm.co.uk

Christine and Bernard Braithwaite own and run **Slakes Farm**, where they offer top-class Bed & Breakfast accommodation in quiet open countryside between Milburn and Knock. In their 18th century farmhouse at the heart of a 40-acre working beef and sheep farm they have two superb guest rooms – a double and a twin, both en suite. The tariff includes an excellent breakfast, and evening meals are available by arrangement; home baking is a speciality.

The lounge/dining room, with a cosy coal fire, has

a television, books and brochures, and is an ideal spot for planning the day's activities. The beautiful Eden Valley provides great

walking, and among the local attractions are the superb gardens at the National Trust's Acorn Bank. Appleby is 6 miles away, and it's 10 miles to Penrith. The farm, which lies just a few minutes' drive from the A66, is open from Easter to October.

148 THE KINGS ARMS HOTEL

Temple Sowerby, nr Penrith,
Cumbria CA10 1SB
☎ 01768 361211

Visitors exploring the delights of the lovely Eden Valley will find a friendly, civilised base at the **Kings Arms Hotel**, whether it's for a drink, a meal or a comfortable place for a break. The new family owners have carried out a major programme of refurbishment, striving and succeeding in enhancing even further the appeal of this splendid place.

The 300-year-old former coaching inn is open all day in summer, and lunchtime and evening in winter, and the old-world bar is a warm, welcoming spot to enjoy a chat and a glass or two of real ale – the choice changes constantly. Bar and restaurant menus provide plenty of choice for hungry customers, with many dishes based on fresh local produce.

Ten guest bedrooms – doubles, twins and triples – seven of them with en suite facilities, can be booked on a room only or B&B basis, and are available all year round. The hotel has fishing rights on the River Eden, and offers fishing holiday packages. Temple Sowerby prides itself on the title 'Queen of Westmorland Villages', an accolade justified by the lovely setting in the Eden Valley. This is great walking country, offering everything from a gentle stroll to the National Trust's Acorn Bank with its unique collection of herbs to the hike up Cross Fell, the highest point in the Pennines.

History also abounds hereabouts: the A66 was formerly a major Roman road, marked by a milestone that can be seen just outside the village; evidence of a Stone Age settlement has also been found. Temple Sowerby is currently next to the busy main road, but by early 2008 a by-pass will provide a quieter setting.

Culgaith, nr Penrith,
Cumbria CA10 1QW
☎ 01768 88223
e-mail: info@blackswanculgaith.co.uk
⊕ www.blackswanculgaith.co.uk

Set in the heart of the Eden Valley the picturesque village of Culgaith lies between the ancient market towns of Appleby & Penrith. **The Black Swan** is a stunning 17th Century Cumbrian Inn, which is equally popular with regulars from the surrounding towns & villages as with the many tourists and holiday makers who visit the Eden Valley throughout the year.

With its original oak beams, cosy open fires in winter and peaceful gardens in summer the Black Swan could not be more accommodating. Real Ales are a major selling point at this traditional inn, Theakstons Best Bitter is the regular ale on offer with a guest ale changing 3-4 times a week hosting a range of locally made ales such as a variety from Tirril Brewery. The main trade mark for this marvellous inn is the fresh local Cumbrian produce used in their dishes. Food is a large part of the business here and the menus truly reflect

how much thought and care is put into it by the owner and head chef Richard Fenn. The menu changes each month, therefore Richard & his wife Joanne are able to provide you with an ever-

changing variety of dishes when the produce is at its very best. The Cheese Board has a wide selection of locally made cheese and all of the Pork, Beef, Lamb and Chicken come from local Cumbrian farmers within a 15 mile radius. They use as many local suppliers as possible to bring dishes such as Home Cured Salmon with Lemon & Dill Crème Fraiche and Wholemeal Bread, Fresh Asparagus wrapped in Air Dried Ham or Confit of Duck Leg coated in Sea Salt and Thyme with a Tomato Salad & Balsamic. This is just for starters! The main courses range from Homemade Pie of the Day to Rack of Cumbrian Lamb with Sweet Potato Mash or Roasted Monkfish Tail to Gressingham Duck Breast on a Fondant Potato with a Rhubarb Puree and a Port Reduction. The Black Swan has a fabulous reputation for homemade desserts; the choice ranges from Crème Brulee, Treacle Tart & Vanilla Panna Cotta with Basil Scented Fruits.

Seven stunning newly refurbished en-suite bedrooms are also on offer with flat screen digital TV's and tea & coffee facilities which make a very comfortable base for visiting the Eden Valley, Lake District, Yorkshire Dales & the historic City of Carlisle. This friendly inn also has fishing rights on a 4.5 mile stretch of the River Eden, famous for trout and salmon fishing and is available to all guests on request. It is also close to many local attractions and activities such as boating, cycling & golf. The renowned Settle to Carlisle Railway also passes the village.

151 THE HIGHLAND DROVE INN

Great Salkeld, nr Penrith,
Cumbria CA11 9NA

☎ 01768 898349 Fax: 01768 898708

e-mail: highlanddroveinn@btinternet.com

🌐 www.highland-drove.co.uk

Great Salkeld is a pleasant village with picturesque 18th century cottages and farmhouses in red sandstone and an impressive church. The church attracts many visitors, but for those looking for top hospitality the **Highland Drove Inn** is a place of pilgrimage.

Hosts Donald Newton and his son Paul, here since 1998, are continuing a tradition that started more than 200 years ago. John Smith's Cask and Theakstons Best Bitter head the list of drinks served in the cosy bar, and guests can also enjoy a pre- or post-dinner drink in a pleasant seating area next to the new downstairs restaurant. Chefs use local produce to great effect in the separate bar and restaurant menus, which mix much-loved favourites with some imaginative variations. Among the former are haddock & chips, ploughman's platters, burgers, steaks and steak & ale pie, while typifying the latter are the house special salad of black pudding, toasted pecan nuts, preserved apricots and a red wine dressing;

seared duck breast with a duck hash brown and a cherry & redcurrant sauce; and Nile perch on stir-fried vegetables with mussels and a creamy curry sauce. Desserts such as roasted pineapple with a sweet white wine sabayon and coconut and Malibu ice cream keep the enjoyment level sky high right to the end. Food is served every session except Sunday and Monday lunches.

The Highland Drove is also an ideal base from which to explore the many attractions of the region, and the five pleasantly appointed bedrooms are available all year round.

Langwathby Station, nr Penrith,
Cumbria CA10 1NB
☎ 01768 881902
e-mail: geeedgar@aol.com
🌐 www.briefencounterlangwathby.co.uk

Gordon and Elsie Edgar own and run **Brief Encounter**, located in a station building on the north platform on the Settle-Carlisle line. Beautifully restored to preserve all the elegance of a bygone age, it's an atmospheric setting in which to enjoy morning coffee, a light lunch, traditional Sunday lunch or afternoon tea, with evening meals available by prior booking.

As much of the produce as possible is sourced locally to create a wide variety of mouthwatering dishes that bring in customers from near and far. Steak & ale pie made with Newcastle Brown Ale is just one of the superb dishes that have earned Brief Encounter several awards, including a

Certificate of Excellence from the Romany Society – presented by Terry Waite. This outstanding café-restaurant is closed in January and February, also Mondays in November and December. Cash and cheque only.

152 CROSSFIELD COTTAGES

Staffield, Kirkoswald, nr Penrith,
Cumbria CA10 1EU
☎ 01768 898711
e-mail: info@crossfieldcottages.co.uk
🌐 www.crossfieldcottages.co.uk

Crossfield is a handsome red sandstone farmstead hidden in its own valley by the River Coglin, a tributary of the Eden. Resident owners Sue and Richard Bottom invite guests to share in the beauty and the tranquility of the surroundings in their exceptional self-catering accommodation. Barley Mow is a first-floor barn conversion sleeping up to 5, while Fisherman's

Walk comprises four purpose-built one-bedroom studio apartments. All are equipped with everything needed for a relaxing stay, and guests have exclusive use of a well-stocked fishing lake. Pets are welcome.

HIDDEN PLACES GUIDES

Explore Britain and Ireland with *Hidden Places* guides - a fascinating series of national and local travel guides.

Packed with easy to read information on hundreds of places of interest as well as places to stay, eat and drink.

Available from both high street and internet booksellers

For more information on the full range of *Hidden Places* guides and other titles published by Travel Publishing visit our website on

www.travelpublishing.co.uk
or ask for our leaflet by phoning
0118-981-7777 or emailing
info@travelpublishing.co.uk

153 HOWSCALES COTTAGES

Howscales, Kirkoswald, nr Penrith, Cumbria
CA10 1JG
☎ 01768 898666 Fax: 01768 898710
e-mail: liz@howscales.co.uk
🌐 www.howscales.co.uk

Howscales Cottages provide superb self-catering accommodation set in award-winning gardens nestling in the beautiful, tranquil countryside of the Eden Valley. Former outbuildings of Liz Webster's 17th century red sandstone farmhouse have been sympathetically converted to offer a choice of five very comfortable, characterful units with one or two bedrooms. Granary (the old grain store) and barn conversions

Geltsdale and Ravendale each occupy two floors, with bedroom/s and bathroom on the ground floor and kitchen and living areas above; while Hazelrigg and Inglewood are all on one floor. Hazelrigg, is the best equipped for disables guests,

with a Category 2 Rating from the National Accessibility Scheme. All are centrally heated and fully carpeted, with well-fitted kitchens and comfortably furnished sitting areas with TV and radio. Liz has thoughtfully provided information packs on local walks, places of interest and eating places. Walks from the cottages can be as gentle or energetic as appropriate, and the Coast2Coast Cycle route is just a mile away. There are opportunities nearby for golf, fishing and pony trekking, and several castles, historic houses, gardens and museums are within an easy drive.

238

Melmerby, nr Penrith,
Cumbria CA10 1HE
☎ 01768 881811
e-mail: info@village-bakery.com
e-mail: restaurant@village-bakery.com
🌐 www.villagebakery.com

The **Village Bakery** comes very near the top of the must-visit places in the Lake District, and the people of Melmerby and the surrounding area are lucky to have such a gem on the doorstep. At the top of the tree among organic bakers, it stands by the green in the centre of the village on the wonderfully scenic A686 Alston road and just 15 minutes from J40 of the M6.

The Village Bakery was established in 1976 in a converted stone barn with the aim from the beginning of producing food that not only tastes good but contributes to positive health. The artisan organic breads, cakes and biscuits include many that are suitable for people with special dietary needs. Organic means provided by farmers and growers who use natural methods; avoid chemical fertilisers and persistent pesticides; give animals the space and conditions they require for well-being and contentment; conserve biodiversity and care for wildlife; and avoid genetically modified organisms. Most of the bakery's suppliers are local,

licensed under strict organic regulations. Breakfast, including juices, cereals, toast, croissants, free-range eggs, home-cured bacon, sausages and ham and oak-smoked kippers, is served from 8.30 (9.30 on Sunday) until 11.30. From then until 4.30 come snacks and light meals (bruschetta with interesting toppings like houmus and roast vegetables and desserts (lemon tart, fruit pies, bread & butter pudding, pear & ginger pudding). Main meals served from 12 to 3 could include penne pasta, smoked salmon platter and steak & kidney with gratin potatoes. And, of course, there's a day-long array of outstanding cakes and pastries to enjoy in the restaurant or to take away from the bakeshop, which also sells a selection of hampers and gifts.

To accompany the superb food is a wide variety of teas, coffees, juices and organic beers, cider and wine. The Village Bakery operates a full mail order service and supplies many specialist food shops, delis, health stores and supermarkets. The Bakery's founder Andrew Whitley runs breadmaking courses on the premises, and the Gallery at the Bakery hosts regularly changing exhibitions between February and November.

Ousby, nr Penrith, Cumbria CA10 1QA
☎ 01768 881374

The **Fox Inn** is at the social heart of the village of Ousby, reached off the A686 Penrith-Alston road after the turn-off between Langwathby and Melmerby. Dating from 1790, this splendid free house is owned and run by Sid and Katy Hughes, who provide a special brand of hospitality that makes it a popular spot both with the locals and with visitors from further afield. Old Faithful, from the local Tirril Brewery, is among the favourite drinks served in the cheerful bar, which is open from 6 o'clock Monday to Saturday evenings, and at lunchtime and from 7 on Sunday.

Katy satisfies hearty appetites with a selection of tempting, traditional dishes from the printed menu and the frequently changing specials board. At the back of the inn is a privately owned static caravan park with up to 40 vans on display, for sale and offering an excellent combination of quality and value for money.

To the front, across the road, is a caravan and camping park open all year, with space for 20 caravans, electric hook-ups and a toilet block. It's an excellent place to bring a caravan, as there are many interesting places to visit within a short drive: the National Trust's Acorn Bank at temple Sowerby, the Ostrich Farm at Langwathby, the prehistoric site of Long Meg and her Daughters, the 12th century Church of St Cuthbert at Edenhall, and the numerous attractions in Penrith, where Sid and Katy own the Country Coffee Shop in Princes Road; they also run an outside catering service.

240

156 HARBUT LAW

Alston, Cunbria CA9 3BD
☎ 01434 381950
e-mail: thomas@younger.fsnet.co.uk
⊕ www.cumbria-cottages.co.uk

Harbut Law is a large Victorian country house with warm, spacious rooms and views of the picturesque countryside from its position off the A689 Alston-Brampton road. Thomas and Susan Younger are the welcoming hosts, and their guests have the choice of Bed & Breakfast accommodation available from Easter to the end of October or self-catering accommodation which is open all year.

Two en suite B&B guest rooms are in the main house, while behind the property the owners have created four superb self-catering cottages from old barns and other outbuildings; one cottage sleeps 2, two

cottages sleep 4 and the fourth sleeps 5. Children are welcome

in both options. Golf can be arranged locally, and the central location makes Harbut Law a convenient base for touring not only the Lake District but Northumberland, County Durham and the Scottish Borders. Cash and cheque only.

157 LOWBYER MANOR COUNTRY HOUSE

Hexham Road, Alston, Cumbria CA9 3JX
☎ 01434 381230 Fax: 01434 381425
e-mail: stay@lowbyer.com
⊕ www.lowbyer.com

Lowbyer Manor Country House is a perfect base for a walking, cycling or driving holiday, or a retreat in which to relax and unwind on the fringe of the cobbled town of Alston. When built in the late-18th century, it was part of the estates of Greenwich Hospital for Sailors which were arraigned by King George1 from the Earls of Derwentwater. It later became a girls' school and now it offers a taste of luxurious country house living in nine superbly appointed bedrooms. These range from single to King size, which are the Stuart Room with a beamed ceiling, King size bed and splendid views across the South Tyne River valley, and the Derwentwater Room with a King size four-poster bed and a view of the front garden, where a handsome sequoia grows. Many of the beds have beautiful quilts made by a relative of

the owners Laura and Richard Elston.

Among the many plus points here are beautiful gardens and an outstanding breakfast menu that features Cumberland sausage, black pudding, bacon, tomatoes and mushrooms all supplied in Alston, Claire's Home-made preserves and Nook Farm honey. The preserves and honey can be bought to take home. Nimble-fingered Laura makes cross-stitch items, some of them on sale as home-made cards, and she's also a knitter – some of her scarves are also for sale.

241

158 THE CUMBRIAN PANTRY

Front Street, Alston, Cumbria CA9 3HU
☎ 01434 381406

Alston has claims to being the highest market town in England, and in the **Cumbrian Pantry** it has a quality family-run business that reaches the heights with a range of excellent snacks and meals. Lilian and Colin Parker and their son Jack only took over here in January 2007, but Jack's super home-cooked fare is already bringing back regular patrons from near and far, and the smell of home baking is an irresistible draw for anyone passing by with an appreciation of good simple food, freshly prepared and full of flavour.

Jack's home-baked cakes and pastries and scrumptious desserts are particularly popular, but the hot and cold savoury dishes also have a big fan club. Among the

favourites guaranteed to produce a satisfied smile are steak pie special, homemade lasagne, quiche and cheese scones, freshly made paninis, toasties and sandwiches; and the rolls – bacon, cumberland sausage or egg – fit the bill perfectly when a quick snack is what's wanted. The Cumbrian Pantry is open from 10 to 5; closed on Mondays except Bank Holidays. Cash only.

159 THE CUMBERLAND HOTEL

Townfoot, Alston, Cumbria CA9 3HX
☎ 01434 381875
e-mail: info@alstoncumberlandhotel.co.uk
⊕ www.alstoncumberlandhotel.co.uk

In their mid-Victorian hotel at the foot of the main street, Guy and Helen Harmer provide a warm family welcome to all their patrons. The **Cumberland Hotel** is a place of wide appeal – a convivial spot to meet for a drink, a fine choice for a meal at any time of day and a comfortable base for both leisure and business visitors. In the two licensed bars, four real ales, including Yates Bitter and guest local brews, can be enjoyed over a chat, and when the sun shines the patio is a pleasant alternative; this area overlooks the quoits pitch, used by the players in the summer local league.

Guy makes excellent use of the best local produce in his dishes, which are served daily between noon and 9 in the evening. Diners can eat either in the restaurant or in the lounge bar, and booking is recommended to be sure of a table on Saturday evenings and Sunday

lunchtimes. The hotel is a popular venue for birthday parties and other special occasions and a civilised, convenient base for touring the region. The accommodation comprises five well-appointed rooms, all en suite, sleeping up to 14 in total; they can be block-booked for families or groups of friends. Alston is an important centre at a major crossroads, and numerous visitor attractions are within easy reach, including the Gossipgate gallery in town, the Nenthead Mines Heritage Centre, Ashgill Force Waterfall, the Pennine Way and Hartside Pass with views of the fells and Solway Firth.

160 NENTHEAD MINES 🏛

North Pennines Heritage Trust, Nenthead,
nr Alston, Cumbria CA9 3PD
☎ 01434 382726 (winter 01434 382037)
e-mail: mines@npht.com
⊕ www.npht.com/nentheadmines

Nenthead Mines make up the largest lead-mining complex in Britain, taking visitors into authentic, real-life mine workings and providing a unique insight into the lives and working conditions of the men who transformed the landscape of the fells in the region. Guided trips take in Carrs Mine, last commercially worked for lead in1920. In the huge Power of Water interactive area, visitors can open sluice gates to operate water wheels and drive machinery.

A viewing platform allows visitors to gaze down into the vertiginous 328ft Brewery Shaft and wonder at the courage of the men who descended daily into the depths to earn their living. Various restored buildings contain exhibits and interactive displays illustrating the geology, wildlife and social history of the area.

The 200-acre site in a lovely North Pennines setting also includes a café and gift shop, woodland walks, a new nature trail, waterfalls and mountain stream. Nenthead is open from 11.00 to 5 Easter to October and at other times by appointment for groups of 10 or more.

162 NO 10 🍴

10 Eden Mount, Stanwix, Carlisle, Cumbria
CA3 9LY
☎ 01228 524183
e-mail: paulminett@uwclub.net
⊕ www.no10restaurants.co.uk

Paul Minett, a chef for 20 years, and his wife Sarah run one of the best eating places in the Carlisle area, a short drive towards the city centre from J44 of the M6. Very much their own creation, **No 10** is the first restaurant they have owned; it is open 5 days a week (not Tuesday or Sunday) from 7 o'clock in the evening for a superb selection of dishes featuring prime local produce.

One of Paul's specialities, and a dish that's always in demand, is fillet of Eden beef with a creamy mushroom or pepper sauce, but everything on the à la carte and set menus tastes as good as it reads:

typical choices might include sautéed scallops with a lobster broth and broad beans, pan-fried monkfish with a Pernod sauce and spring vegetables, braised Cumbrian lamb shank, asparagus & fennel risotto and ginger & apple sponge with toffee sauce. No 10 is also available with notice for lunchtime parties of 6 or more.

161 TULLIE HOUSE MUSEUM & ART GALLERY

Castle Street, Carlisle, Cumbria CA3 8TB
☎ 01228 618781 Fax: 01228 810249
🌐 www.tulliehouse.co.uk

Tullie House Museum and Art Gallery is Carlisle's premier visitor attraction, with an excellent museum, changing exhibitions in the galleries, a gift shop, restaurant and beautiful gardens, each offering the very best quality possible.

Set in beautiful gardens, Old Tullie House houses an impressive collection of important Pre-Raphaelite art, with many of the classical features of 17th century architecture still remaining, such as the beautiful Jacobean staircase.

From fine art to interactive fun, there's something for everyone, as the newer buildings in the Tullie House grounds are home to many exciting interactive games and features for children of all ages. Come and see the world famous cursing stone for yourself, and take a trip to the underground millennium gallery where the whispering wall can tell you tales from Cumbria from many years ago.

Freshwater Life is a major exhibition that dives into the world of the special wildlife and habitats of the rivers and lakes of Cumbria.

The Millennium Gallery is transformed to follow the River Eden from it's source to the sea, exploring the changing wildlife along the way such as Otters, Salmon and even rare fish of the Lake District like the Charr and Vendance.

Kids will love learning while they play, whilst adults will enjoy exciting experiences such as 'The Border Reivers'. Take a walk down our roman replica street, or climb our life size section of Hadrian's wall! Tullie House takes you on an exciting travel through time, from the present day, right back to the early Romans.

Plenty of Time should be allowed for a visit, don't leave without visiting the must-see areas on the Top Ten Trail. With changing exhibitions in the Special Exhibitions Gallery and travelling exhibitions in the Art Gallery, there's always something new and exciting to see.

The gift shop stocks a wide range of beautiful handcrafted gifts and souvenirs, while our award wining Garden Restaurant is perfect for lunch, afternoon tea, or coffee. The kitchen uses the freshest local produce to create a variety of dishes, from hearty soups and main meals to jacket potatoes, salads and sandwiches. Not forgetting the tasty range of freshly baked cakes and scones.

The 15th Century Guildhall Museum is located in the heart of the city. Take a break from shopping and step back in time in one of the oldest buildings in the city centre. Displays and exhibitions include Guild rooms, civic history, law and order, markets and shops, industrial heritage, a Tudor town scene and town treasures. Includes a new Childrens Tudor play area where kids can discover what Tudor life was like by dressing up and trading as a Tudor Merchant.

Ramped access lifts to all main areas, automatic doors, adapted toilets, parking for adapted vehicles help to make Tullie House user friendly and accessible.

163 THE ROSE & CROWN

Low Hesket, Carlisle, Cumbria CA4 0HG
☎ 016974 73346

The **Rose & Crown** is a renowned venue for food and drink alongside the A6 south of Carlisle. Built as cottages in the early 18th century, it later became an alehouse and is now a popular pub with friendly hosts in Linda and Keith. Open every evening and Saturday and Sunday lunchtimes, the pub keeps three real ales in excellent condition, and professional chefs prepare classics like Cumberland sausage,

steaks and lamb Henry alongside less familiar dishes such as trout tempura, seafood lasagne and vegetarian (quorn) chilli. A transport theme runs through the public areas, including the recently created dining room inspired by the famous Royal Scot train.

165 THE HARBOUR BAR & PORTHOLE RESTAURANT AT THE HOPE & ANCHOR

Port Carlisle, nr Carlisle,
Cumbria CA7 5BU
☎ 016973 51460 Fax: 016973 52602

Licensees Bryan and Jo have long experience running leisure centres, golf clubs and other social outlets, and in April 2006 they transferred that experience and all the associated skills to the **Harbour Bar & Porthole Restaurant at the Hope & Anchor** in an attractive setting overlooking the Solway Firth. Jo has been a chef for more than 30 years, and patrons, both regular customers and visitors from outside the region, can take their pick from the printed menu and the daily changing specials board.

The choice ranges from lunchtime sandwiches, ploughman's platters and snacks to classics such as garlic king prawns, moules marinière, Cumberland sausages, steak & ale pie, lasagne, chilli con carne and home-baked ham, with some more exotic options like duck breast marinated in soy sauce and ginger. Families are always very welcome, and many of

the main courses can be ordered in smaller portions for children. Diners can eat in the 30-cover restaurant, in the bar or outside on the patio.

Up to three real ales, usually Cumbrian brews, are available to accompany a meal or to quench thirsts, along with a choice of wines. Opening times are summer all day every day; winter from 5 on Monday, 12 to 3 and from 5 Tuesday, Wednesday and Thursday, and all day Friday, Saturday and Sunday.

164 THE CROWN INN RESTAURANT

Broadfield, Southwaite, Carlisle,
Cumbria CA4 0PT
☎ 016974 73467
e-mail: crowninnrestaurant@i12.com
🌐 www.crowninnrestaurant.co.uk

Two miles from Southwaite, near Southwaite Services on the M6, the **Crown Inn** is an excellent free house with a superb menu of exciting dishes. Nick and Marie Pinnell came here in 2003 and have established the inn – built as a drovers' inn in 1820 – as one of the very top eating places in the region, highly rated, widely recommended and almost always busy with contented diners.

Nick's experience and talent shine through his dishes, which take their inspiration from the world's cuisines and pose a pleasant problem for diners – what to order when everything is so tempting. The printed menu, with 'Chef recommends' changing fortnightly, is supplemented by a dinner menu and grill section, and fresh local produce is prominent throughout. Steaks and black pudding (made in Stornoway) are among the specialities, but there really is something for everyone: sizzling Cajun king prawns; hoi sin chicken salad with a pumpkin seed oil dressing; pan-fried Holme Hill pheasant with a cranberry

and port reduction; baked sea bass with olive oil, garlic and chillies; prime Lakeland sirloin and fillet; rump steak from the Castle of Mey royal estate. A typical Sunday lunch menu offers a centrepiece of roast lamb and beef, chicken breast, a fish dish and a vegetarian dish, with a choice of half a dozen starters and sweets.

Diners can enjoy a glass of real ale from Thwaites Brewery or something from a wide-ranging wine list. The Crown is closed on Tuesdays, otherwise open from 7 to 9 (9.30 Friday and Saturday) and from 12 to 2 on Saturday and Sunday. This is a deservedly very popular place, so booking is recommended especially at weekends to make sure of getting a table.

166 THE KINGS ARMS

Bowness-on-Solway, Wigton,
Cumbria CA7 5AF
☎ 016973 51426
🌐 www.kingsarmsbowness.co.uk

The **Kings Arms** is situated in the heart of Bowness-on-Solway, at the western end of Hadrian's Wall, within the Solway Marshes and close to the sea. This splendid inn is family owned and run by David and Margaret Wiseman, daughter Janice Milne and son-in-law David. The interior has been superbly refurbished, and the bar, open every session in summer (most in winter) and all day Saturday and Sunday, is a very comfortable, civilised spot for enjoying a drink and meeting the regulars. Margaret is a terrific cook, and her dishes are in demand every evening except Wednesday. Everything she cooks is fresh and tasty, and her repertoire covers fish, meat, game and vegetarian options, with a hard-to-resist apple pie among her desserts.

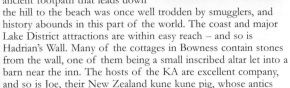

The Kings Arms is also a great place for a family holiday, and the three guest bedrooms are open throughout the year. The

ancient footpath that leads down the hill to the beach was once well trodden by smugglers, and history abounds in this part of the world. The coast and major Lake District attractions are within easy reach – and so is Hadrian's Wall. Many of the cottages in Bowness contain stones from the wall, one of them being a small inscribed altar let into a barn near the inn. The hosts of the KA are excellent company, and so is Joe, their New Zealand kune kune pig, whose antics put a smile on the face of every visitor to the inn.

168 THE SYCAMORE TREE CAFÉ

40-42 Bridge Street, Longtown,
nr Carlisle, Cumbria CA6 5UD
☎ 01228 791919

Local residents, visitors to the region and motorists driving along the A7 are pleased to drop in at the **Sycamore Tree Café** for breakfast, morning coffee, lunch or afternoon tea. After running a successful business producing meat pies, John and Sharon took over here in February 2006, and success has come soon thanks to the quality of what they offer and the excellent hospitality.

The menu caters for all appetites and all tastes, including vegetarians and those with special dietary needs such as coeliacs. The special all-day breakfast is always popular, along with dishes based on Lakeland meats,

including the traditional roasts that are added to the menu for Sunday lunch (served from 12 to 4, and booking is recommended). Children are always very welcome at the Sycamore, which is open from 9 to 5 every day except Wednesday. It stands in the centre of Longtown, the most northerly town on the west side of England, on the River Esk, beyond Hadrian's Wall and close to Gretna green and the Solway Firth.

167 THE HIGHLAND LADDIE INN ¶

Water Street, Glasson, Carlisle,
Cumbria CA7 5DT
☎ 01697 351839
e-mail: info@highlandladdieinn.co.uk
🌐 www.highlandladdieinn.co.uk

Mark and Karen Messenger run a cosy, traditional 200-year-old inn in a superb setting opposite Hadrian's Wall. The **Highland Laddie Inn** is a real magnet for walkers, with several marked walks nearby and the length of the wall to explore, but it also attracts local residents and tourists in cars looking for a pleasant spot to take a break from their sightseeing.

The well-stocked bar keeps a wide range of beers (CAMRA approved), lagers, wines, spirits and soft drinks, and the bar is a very congenial spot for enjoying a drink and socialising. The bar is open all day, seven days a week, and food is served every day except Tuesday, lunchtime from noon to 2.45 and in the evening from 6.30 to 9. Walkers are renowned for their healthy appetites, and they rave about the generous portions and the quality of the food prepared by Karen with the valued assistance of Auntie Jean. The printed menu and the daily changing specials board tempt with a wide variety of English and Continental dishes, but for many of the regulars the steak & ale pie, the Sunday roasts and the sticky toffee pudding fit the bill perfectly.

The Highland Laddie Inn is good enough reason to visit this tranquil part of the world, but there are many others. The coastline from Carlisle right round to Millom is home to numerous diverse wildlife habitats, and close to the inn are Finglandrigg Wood National Nature Reserve and Campfield Farm RSPB, where visitors can see barnacle and pink-footed geese. The pub is also close to the eastern end of Hadrian's Wall, and a few hours' walking and sightseeing is likely to generate a serious thirst – and that's where the Highland Laddie comes in!

169 MARCH BANK HOTEL & THE SPORTSMAN'S RESTAURANT

Scotch Dyke, north of Longtown (A7),
Cumbria CA6 5XP
☎ 01228 791325 Fax: 01228 791216
🌐 www.marchbankhotel.co.uk

Three miles north of Longtown on the main A7, **March Bank Hotel & The Sportsman's Restaurant** occupies a Victorian villa set in four acres of mature gardens close to the River Esk. It's owned and personally run by the Moore family, who ensure a warm welcome and excellent service in both hotel and restaurant. The wide-ranging lunch and dinner menus highlight prime local produce such as Lakeland game, Esk salmon and trout and raspberries from across the border. For resident guests the hotel has six attractive en suite bedrooms, one with a four-poster. A generous breakfast starts the day, and packed lunches are available.

170 LIDDEL PARK

Catlowdy, Penton, Carlisle,
Cumbria CA6 5QW
☎ 01228 577440
e-mail: holiday@liddelpark.co.uk
🌐 www.liddelpark.co.uk

Liddel Park offers excellent self-catering accommodation for all the family in a secluded setting in woodland, close to the Scottish border and a ten-minute drive from Longtown. Refurbished two-bedroom cottages Pine, Cypress and Fir are set around a quiet courtyard; all have an open-plan kitchen and dining/living area, TV, DVD and radio with CD player; they share a patio area with seating and a barbecue. This is great walking country, and three local rivers provide fine salmon and trout fishing.

172 THE SPORTSMAN INN

Laversdale, nr Carlisle, Cumbria CA6 4PJ
☎ 01228 573255

The **Sportsman Inn** stands in the picturesque village of Laversdale, standing off the A6071 or A689, northeast of Carlisle and west of Brampton. Local couple Tracy and Kevin Irving, who took over at this late-18th century inn (formerly called the Dog & Gun) in 2006, have really given the old place a new lease of life with their outgoing personalities and the friendly ambience they have created. Locals, walkers and tourists come here to enjoy the best in food and drink, and the proximity of Carlisle Airport also makes it an excellent spot for travellers to pause for refreshment.

Tracy cooks using local produce for a menu that ranges from sandwiches and jacket potatoes to classic pub fare such as Cumberland sausage, scampi, pasta, cod & chips, steak pie with a rich ale gravy and rump, sirloin and gammon steaks. Booking is advisable on

Saturday and Sunday, particularly for the 1, 2 or 3-course Sunday lunch. The inn is open from 5 Monday to Friday and all day from 12 Saturday, Sunday and Bank Holidays. Food times are 6 to 8.30 Monday to Thursday, 6 to 9 on Friday, 12 to 2 and 5 to 9 on Saturday and from 12 to 9 on Sunday. The Sportsman has a large beer garden and plenty of off-road parking.

171 CROSBY LODGE COUNTRY HOUSE HOTEL & RESTAURANT

High Crosby, Crosby-on-Eden, nr Carlisle,
Cumbria CA6 4QZ
☎ 01228 573618 Fax: 01228 573428
e-mail: enquiries@crosbylodge.co.uk
🌐 www.crosbylodge.co.uk

'Crosby Lodge…..delightfully situated a short distance from the River Eden, in a fine sporting country, has an extensive lawn in front and commands a fine view of the Vale of Eden and distant mountains'. That's how a notice in a newspaper of 1831 described **Crosby Lodge**, and the description still reflects the setting of what is now one of the region's outstanding country house hotels.

The crenellated towers give the building the appearance of a fortified manor, but it was actually built in the first decade of the 19th century as a stately residence for a gentleman named David Kennedy, later to become a Deputy Lieutenant of Cumberland. The building, now Grade II listed, was acquired in 1970 by the Sedgwick family, who opened it as a hotel in the following year after major and always sympathetic refurbishment.

Personal attention and the highest standards of comfort, service and hospitality have kept Crosby Lodge at the top of the tree ever since, providing calm, peace and pampering far away from the bustle of everyday life. The guest accommodation, which can be booked on a Bed & Breakfast or Dinner, Bed & Breakfast basis, comprises nine beautifully appointed en suite bedrooms, each of them individually designed and furnished with the impeccable style and taste that are a hall mark of this superb place.

The food at Crosby Lodge is as outstanding as the accommodation, served lunchtime and evening in the elegant restaurant or the guest lounge. The table d'hote and à la carte menus make excellent use of prime fresh ingredients in classic British and Continental dishes ranging from battered haddock & chips to Madeira-sauced veal medallions, roast rack of lamb and kidneys with brandy and cream, sumptuous desserts from the trolley. The fine food is complemented by an equally distinguished wine list compiled by Phillipa Sedgwick Wines, who have a wine warehouse in the courtyard.

This most gracious of country mansions, located off the A689 and a short drive from J44 of the M6, is the perfect base for discovering the many attractions of Carlisle and the surrounding area, extending to Hadrian's Wall, the Scottish Borders and the Lake District……or for just relaxing, unwinding, revelling in the aura of peace and strolling in the gardens and enjoying the outstanding hospitality extended by the Sedgwick family and their dedicated staff. It is also the ideal venue for weddings – it holds a licence for civil ceremonies – and other celebrations, business entertaining and conferences.

174 THE BELTED WILL INN

Hallbankgate, Brampton,
Cunbria CA8 2NJ
☎ 016977 46236 Fax: 016977 46900
⊕ www.beltedwill.co.uk

The **Belted Will Inn** is a truly delightful old hostelry run in fine style by Stephen and Alyson Starkey. It is located at Hallbankgate on the A689 Brampton-Alston road at the foot of the North Pennine Fells, on the edge of a designated Area of Outstanding Natural Beauty.

It's equally appealing as a place to pop into for a drink, somewhere to enjoy a leisurely meal cooked by talented chef Stephen, and a very comfortable, civilised base for tourists. The range and quality of the real ales have earned the inn the Solway branch of CAMRA's pub of the season winter 2006/7. Lovers of good food can enjoy Stephen's cooking lunchtime and evening Monday to Friday and all day Saturday and Sunday, and booking is recommended evenings and weekends, especially in the summer high season. The menus combine snacks and light meals (sandwiches, baguettes, salads, jacket potatoes) with classics such as steaks, Cumberland sausage, lasagne, curries and chilli con carne with daily

specials typified by mango & brie pastry parcels, chicken korma, rack of BBQ ribs and red pepper stuffed with onions, rice, mushrooms and farmhouse cheddar. The dining area is available for private parties and functions for up to 30 guests.

This is a very attractive corner of the county, and the inn's five comfortable guest bedrooms provide a particularly appealing base for discovering all the local sights. Recently refurbished to a very high standard, they comprise two doubles, two twins and a family room, all with en suite facilities, TV and tea/ coffee tray. The area caters for walkers, cyclists, anglers and golfers, and tourist sites

within easy reach include Hadrian's Wall (free transport can be arranged), Birdoswald Roman Fort, Lanercost Priory, Talkin Tarn Country Park and the Geltsdale RSPB Reserve. The inn is named after Lord William Howard (1563-1640), who lived at nearby Naworth Castle. His exploits against the marauding Scots were celebrated in Sir Walter Scott's *The Lay of the Last Minstrel*, in which he refers to Howard having a sword

'hung in a broad and studded belt:
hence, in rude phrase, the Borderers still
Call'd noble Howard, 'Belted Will'.

173 LONG BYRES AT TALKIN HEAD

Talkin Head, Brampton,
Cumbria CA8 1CT
☎ 016977 3435
e-mail: stay@longbyres.co.uk

Long Byres at Talkin Head offers superb self-catering accommodation in a picturesque, isolated location on a hill farm in the North Pennines Area of Outstanding Natural Beauty, 10 miles east of Carlisle and 3 miles south of Brampton. Owner Mrs Harriet Sykes has overseen the conversion of old farm buildings into seven self-contained cottages with 1, 2 or 3 bedrooms. They feature quarry-tiled floors, exposed beams and pine panelling, and fittings include a gas cooker, toaster, fridge, teletext TV and shared laundry facilities.

The two largest cottages, with three bedrooms and two bathrooms, have recently been completely refurbished to an impressively high standard. All are available throughout the year, and central heating and double glazing keeps things cosy and peaceful at all times. Guests can

meet the cows and ponies that live on the farm, and while strolling around they might spot red squirrels, badgers, hares and foxes. This is great walking and nearby attractions include golf, riding, the RSPB Reserve at Geltsdale and the many activities for all the family at Talkin Tarn.

175 BIRDOSWALD ROMAN FORT

Gilsland, Carlisle, Cumbria CA8 7DD
☎ 016977 47602
🌐 www.english-heritage.org.uk

Birdoswald stands high above a meander in the River Irthing, in one of the most picturesque settings on Hadrian's Wall. A Roman fort, turret and milecastle can all be seen on this excellent stretch of the Wall.

With probably the best preserved defences of any Wall fort, this was an important base for some 1,000 Roman soldiers, succeeding an earlier fort of turf and timber. The section of Wall to the east, also of stone replacing turf, is the longest continuous stretch visible today.

Archaeological discoveries over the past 150 years have revealed a great deal about Roman military life at Birdoswald. Three of the four main gateways of the fort have been unearthed, as have the outside walls, two granary buildings, workshops and a unique drill hall.

People continued to live at Birdoswald after the Roman withdrawal. In the 5th century a large timber hall was built over the collapsed Roman granaries, perhaps for a local British chieftain. Later, a medieval tower house was raised here, replaced in the 16th century by a fortified 'bastile' farmhouse designed to protect its inhabitants from the notorious 'Border Reivers'. Later still in more peaceful times, a farmhouse stood there.

The Birdoswald Visitor Centre provides a good introduction to Hadrian's Wall, and tells the intriguing story of Birdoswald and the people who have lived there over the past 2,000 years. There is a cosy tearoom at the site if you need refreshments, and a wellstocked shop for souvenirs.

252

Tourist Information Centres

ALSTON MOOR

Town Hall
Front Street
Alston
Cumbria CA9 3RF
e-mail: alston.tic@eden.gov.uk
Tel: 01434 382244

AMBLESIDE

Central Buildings
Market Cross
Ambleside
Cumbria LA22 9BS
e-mail: amblesidetic@southlakeland.gov.uk
Tel: 015394 32582

APPLEBY-IN-WESTMORLAND

Moot Hall
Boroughgate
Appleby-in-Westmorland
Cumbria CA16 6XE
e-mail: tic@applebytown.org.uk
Tel: 017683 51177

BARROW-IN-FURNESS

Forum 28
Duke Street
Barrow-in-Furness
Cumbria LA14 1HU
e-mail: touristinfo@barrowbc.gov.uk
Tel: 01229 894784

BOWNESS

Glebe Road
Bowness-on-Windermere
Cumbria LA23 3HJ
e-mail: bownesstic@lake-district.gov.uk
Tel: 015394 42895

BRAMPTON

Moot Hall
Market Place
Brampton
Cumbria CA8 1RW
e-mail: ElisabethB@CarlisleCity.gov.uk
Tel: 016977 3433

BROUGHTON-IN-FURNESS

Town Hall
The Square
Broughton-in-Furness
Cumbria LA20 6JF
e-mail: email@broughton-tic.fsnet.co.uk
Tel: 01229 716115

CARLISLE

Old Town Hall
Greenmarket
Carlisle
Cumbria CA3 8JE
e-mail: tourism@carlisle-city.gov.uk
Tel: 01228 625600

COCKERMOUTH

Town Hall
Market Street
Cockermouth
Cumbria CA13 9NP
e-mail: email@cockermouth-tic.fsnet.co.uk
Tel: 01900 822634

CONISTON

Ruskin Avenue
Coniston
Cumbria LA21 8EH
e-mail: Conistontic@lake-district.gov.uk
Tel: 015394 41533

EGREMONT

12 Main Street
Egremont
Cumbria CA22 2DW
e-mail: email@egremont-tic.fsnet.co.uk
Tel: 01946 820693

GRANGE-OVER-SANDS

Victoria Hall
Main Street
Grange-over-Sands
Cumbria LA11 6DP
e-mail: grangetic@southlakeland.gov.uk
Tel: 015395 34026

KENDAL

Town Hall
Highgate
Kendal
Cumbria LA9 4DL
e-mail: kendaltic@southlakeland.gov.uk
Tel: 01539 725758

KESWICK

Moot Hall
Market Square
Keswick
Cumbria CA12 5JR
e-mail: keswicktic@lake-district.gov.uk
Tel: 017687 72645

253

KIRKBY LONSDALE

24 Main Street
Kirkby Lonsdale
Cumbria LA6 2AE
e-mail: kltic@southlakeland.gov.uk
Tel: 015242 71437

KIRKBY STEPHEN

Market Street
Kirkby Stephen
Cumbria CA17 4QN
e-mail: ks.tic@eden.gov.uk
Tel: 017683 71199

MARYPORT

Maryport Town Hall
Senhouse Street Maryport
Cumbria CA15 6BH
e-mail: maryporttic@allerdale.gov.uk
Tel: 01900 812101

MILLOM

Station Building
Station Road
Millom
Cumbria LA18 5AA
e-mail: millomtic@copelandbc.gov.uk
Tel: 01229 774819

PENRITH

Middlegate
Penrith
Cumbria CA11 7PT
e-mail: pen.tic@eden.gov.uk
Tel: 01768 867466

RHEGED

Rheged Tourist Information Centre
Rheged
Penrith
Cumbria CA11 0DQ
e-mail: tic@rheged.com
Tel: 01768 860034

SEDBERGH

72 Main Street
Sedbergh
Cumbria LA10 5AD
e-mail: tic@sedbergh.org.uk
Tel: 015396 20125

SILLOTH-ON-SOLWAY

Solway coast Discovery Centre
Liddell Street
Silloth-on-Solway
Cumbria CA7 5DD
e-mail: sillothtic@allerdale.gov.uk
Tel: 016973 31944

SOUTHWAITE

M6 Service Area Southwaite
Carlisle
Cumbria CA4 ONS
e-mail: southwaitetic@visitscotland.com
Tel: 016974 73445

ULLSWATER

Main Car Park
Glenridding
Penrith
Cumbria CA11 0PD
e-mail: ullswatertic@lake-district.gov.uk
Tel: 017684 82414

ULVERSTON

Coronation Hall
County Square
Ulverston
Cumbria LA12 7LZ
e-mail: ulverstontic@southlakeland.gov.uk
Tel: 01229 587120

WHITEHAVEN

Market Hall
Market Place
Whitehaven
Cumbria CA28 7JG
e-mail: tic@copelandbc.gov.uk
Tel: 01946 852939

WINDERMERE

Victoria Street
Windermere
Cumbria LA23 1AD
e-mail: windermeretic@southlakeland.gov.uk
Tel: 015394 46499

WORKINGTON

21 Finkle Street
Workington
Cumbria CA14 2BE
e-mail: workingtontic@allerdale.gov.uk
Tel: 01900 606699

Towns, Villages and Places of Interest

TRAVEL PUBLISHING ORDER FORM

To order any of our publications just fill in the payment details below and complete the order form. For orders of less than 4 copies please add £1.00 per book for postage and packing. Orders over 4 copies are P & P free.

Name:

Address:

Tel no:

Please Complete Either:

I enclose a cheque for £ _____ made payable to Travel Publishing Ltd

Or:

Card No: Expiry Date:

Signature:

Please either send, telephone, fax or e-mail your order to:

Travel Publishing Ltd, 7a Apollo House, Calleva Park, Aldermaston, Berkshire RG7 8TN

Tel: 0118 981 7777   Fax: 0118 940 8428   e-mail: info@travelpublishing.co.uk

	Price	Quantity		Price	Quantity
HIDDEN PLACES REGIONAL TITLES			**COUNTRY PUBS AND INNS**		
Cornwall	£8.99	....	Cornwall	£5.99	....
Devon	£8.99	....	Devon	£7.99	....
Dorset, Hants & Isle of Wight	£8.99	....	Sussex	£5.99	....
East Anglia	£8.99	....	Wales	£8.99	....
Lake District & Cumbria	£8.99	....	Yorkshire	£7.99	....
Northumberland & Durham	£8.99	....			
Peak District and Derbyshire	£8.99	....	**COUNTRY LIVING RURAL GUIDES**		
Yorkshire	£8.99	....	East Anglia	£10.99	....
			Heart of England	£10.99	....
HIDDEN PLACES NATIONAL TITLES			Ireland	£11.99	....
England	£11.99	....	North East	£10.99	....
Ireland	£11.99	....	North West	£10.99	....
Scotland	£11.99	....	Scotland	£11.99	....
Wales	£11.99	....	South of England	£10.99	....
			South East of England	£10.99	....
HIDDEN INNS TITLES			Wales	£11.99	....
East Anglia	£7.99	....	West Country	£10.99	....
Heart of England	£7.99	....			
South	£7.99	....			
South East	£7.99	....	**TOTAL QUANTITY:**		
West Country	£7.99	....	**POST & PACKING:**		
OTHER TITLES					
Off the Motorway	£11.99	....	**TOTAL VALUE:**		

VISIT THE TRAVEL PUBLISHING WEBSITE

Looking for:

- *Places to Visit?*
- *Places to Stay?*
- *Places to Eat & Drink?*
- *Places to Shop?*

Then why not visit the Travel Publishing website...

- Informative pages on places to visit, stay, eat, drink and shop throughout the British Isles.

- Detailed information on Travel Publishing's wide range of national and regional travel guides.

www.travelpublishing.co.uk

HIDDEN PLACES GUIDES

Explore Britain and Ireland with *Hidden Places* guides - a fascinating series of national and local travel guides.

Packed with easy to read information on hundreds of places of interest as well as places to stay, eat and drink.

Available from both high street and internet booksellers

For more information on the full range of *Hidden Places* guides and other titles published by Travel Publishing visit our website on

www.travelpublishing.co.uk
or ask for our leaflet by phoning **0118-981-7777** or emailing **info@travelpublishing.co.uk**

READER REACTION FORM

The *Travel Publishing* research team would like to receive reader's comments on any visitor attractions or places reviewed in the book and also recommendations for suitable entries to be included in the next edition. This will help ensure that the *Country Living series of Guides* continues to provide its readers with useful information on the more interesting, unusual or unique features of each attraction or place ensuring that their visit to the local area is an enjoyable and stimulating experience. To provide your comments or recommendations would you please complete the forms below and overleaf as indicated and send to:

The Research Department, Travel Publishing Ltd,
7a Apollo House, Calleva Park, Aldermaston, Reading, RG7 8TN.

Your Name:

Your Address:

Your Telephone Number:

Please tick as appropriate:

Comments ☐   Recommendation ☐

Name of Establishment:

Address:

Telephone Number:

Name of Contact:

READER REACTION FORM

COMMENT OR REASON FOR RECOMMENDATION:

....

....

....

....

....

....

....

....

....

....

....

....

....

....

....

....

....

....

....

....

READER REACTION FORM

The *Travel Publishing* research team would like to receive reader's comments on any visitor attractions or places reviewed in the book and also recommendations for suitable entries to be included in the next edition. This will help ensure that the *Country Living series of Guides* continues to provide its readers with useful information on the more interesting, unusual or unique features of each attraction or place ensuring that their visit to the local area is an enjoyable and stimulating experience. To provide your comments or recommendations would you please complete the forms below and overleaf as indicated and send to:

**The Research Department, Travel Publishing Ltd,
7a Apollo House, Calleva Park, Aldermaston, Reading, RG7 8TN.**

Your Name:

Your Address:

Your Telephone Number:

Please tick as appropriate:

Comments ☐   Recommendation ☐

Name of Establishment:

Address:

Telephone Number:

Name of Contact:

READER REACTION FORM

COMMENT OR REASON FOR RECOMMENDATION:

....

....

....

....

....

....

....

....

....

....

....

....

....

....

....

....

....

....

....

....

....

Index of Advertisers

265

FOOD AND DRINK

PLACES OF INTEREST